"How Long This Road"

Race, Religion, and the Legacy of C. Eric Lincoln

Edited by

Alton B. Pollard, III and Love Henry Whelchel, Jr.

First published in 2003 by PALGRAVE MACMILLAN™
175 Fifth Avenue, New York, N.Y. 10010 and
Houndmills, Basingstoke, Hampshire, England RG21 6XS.
Companies and representatives throughout the world.

PALGRAVE MACMILLAN is the global academic imprint of the Palgrave Macmillan division of St. Martin's Press, LLC and of Palgrave Macmillan Ltd. Macmillan® is a registered trademark in the United States, United Kingdom and other countries. Palgrave is a registered trademark in the European Union and other countries.

ISBN hardback 1–4039-6272–3
ISBN paperback 1–4039-6273–1

Library of Congress Cataloging-in-Publication Data

How long this road : race, religion, and the legacy of C. Eric Lincoln / edited by Alton B. Pollard, III and Love Henry Whelchel, Jr.
        p. cm.
    Includes bibiliographical references and index.
    ISBN 1–4039-6272–3 —ISBN 1–4039-6273–1 (pbk.)
        1. African Americans—Religion—Congresses.   I. Pollard, Alton B. (Alton Brooks), 1956-   II. Whelchel, L. H. (Love Henry)

BR563.N4H68 2003
277.3'082'08996073—dc21   2003048680

Frontispiece photo, the poem "This Road Since Freedom" by C. Eric Lincoln, and the essay "Human Values and Inhuman Systems" by C. Eric Lincoln used by permission of the C. Eric Lincoln Estate, Durham, NC.

A catalogue record for this book is available from the British Library.

First Palgrave Macmillan edition: November 2003
10 9 8 7 6 5 4 3 2 1

Printed in the United States of America.

Contents

I. The Legacy of C. Eric Lincoln

II. The Social Analysis of Religion

III. The Religious Community Bears Witness

IV. Lift Every Voice

Series Editors' Preface

"How Long This Road" inaugurates the black religion/womanist thought/social justice series at Palgrave Macmillan. We are proud to have such a fine book that exemplifies a creative, interdisciplinary approach to the study of African American religious thought and life. Appropriately so, the series begins with a comprehensive and diverse look at the work of C. Eric Lincoln, who is considered the dean of black religious studies in the contemporary era. Dr. Lincoln is noted for his social scientific investigation of black religion. In addition, he was a novelist, a poet, and a prolific essayist. Lincoln's productivity covered a wide range of topics from the first definitive treatment of the Nation of Islam (1961), the first two major edited works on multiple approaches to the black religious experience (1968 and 1974), a cogent analysis of the Civil Rights movement (1968), a pictorial history of the Negro in America (with Langston Hughes and Milton Meltzer), a critical interrogation of E. Franklin Frazier's classical text on the Negro Church (1974), a profile of Martin Luther King, Jr., a revisiting of Gunnar Myrdal's American Dilemma (1984), a decade-long study of the black church (1990), to his evocative book of poetry (1990). Lincoln, moreover, nurtured and groomed several generations of scholars who would later become a who's who of authorities on all aspects of black religious thought from the 1960s into the twenty-first century. And Lincoln was the editor of, to our knowledge, the first black religious series in the history of the United States.

The scholarship of Lincoln and the vast array of analyses in *"How Long This Road"* indicate the direction of the black religion/womanist thought/social justice series. The series will publish both authored and edited manuscripts that have depth, breadth, and theoretical edge and will address both academic and nonspecialist audiences. It will produce works engaging any dimension of black religion or womanist thought as they pertain to social justice. Womanist thought is a new approach in the study of African American women's perspectives. The series will include a variety of African American religious expressions. By this we mean traditions such as Protestant and Catholic Christianity, Islam, Judaism, Humanism, African diasporic practices, religion and gender, religion and black gays/lesbians, ecological justice issues, African American religiosity and its relation to African religions, new black religious movements (for example, Daddy Grace, Father Divine, or the Nation of Islam), or religious dimensions in African American "secular" experiences (such as the spiritual aspects of aesthetic efforts like the Harlem Renaissance and literary giants such as James Baldwin, or the religious fervor of the Black Consciousness movement, or the religion of compassion in black women's club movement).

Dwight N. Hopkins, University of Chicago Divinity School
Linda E. Thomas, Lutheran School of Theology at Chicago
May 2003

This Road Since Freedom

C. Eric Lincoln

America
My native land
How long this road since freedom
How scourged with peril is the path
How bitter is the aftermath
of our sojourn in Edom?
America
My native land
Here on your promises I stand.

O Land
Land of the free
Home of the brave
Will ever there be
for the son of a slave
a place in your scheme:
the American Dream?

O Land
Land I have loved so much
Land I have served so long
When did I fail you
Where did I falter
What is my crime
but my belief
in America?

America
You were my teacher.
In the statement of your law
I heard of justice.
In the dogma of your faith

I learned of mercy.
Enshrined in every public place
I meet your precepts face to face:
Democracy
Equality
Morality and
Love.

America
You commanded me
and
I surrendered up
the ancient ways,
the ways I knew
before this land
became your land,
before
you gave your law
to be my law,
before
you made your God
to be my God.
The ancient ways,
the laws I kept,
the Gods I knew
are gone.
How can I know
those ways again?
What am I if
I am not American?

Three hundred-fifty years and more
Three thousand miles from the Afric
shore.

A new law
American
A new language
American
A new God
American

American
American
American!

American
But my face is black
What is **black**
What is **white**
What is **man**
What does it mean to be
American?

> God made Man
> Out of one clay
> One love
> One will
> One breath
> One plan
> God made Man
> No man above another
> But man to man a brother.

America
In God we trust.
If God is worthy, God is just.
Did God fail in His creative task;
does black some Godly error mask?
If not, then how could God's decree
Be somehow different for me?

> God is the father
> Man is the son
> Men make distinctions
> God makes none.

God made man
What kind of a man
am I?
What kind of a world
is this?
What kind of God

is God?

God is good
The author of mercy
God is just
And righteous altogether.

Where is God?
I wonder if
God saw me
strung high upon a tree
strung high
away up there
embarrassing the summer air
strung high
among the shimmering white magnolias,
the pale white sickening-sweet magnolias?
I wonder if
God saw me suspended there
Somewhere
above God's earth
Somewhere
below God's heaven
Hanging
in the middle of the world,
waiting
for the buzzards overhead
gathered
for a final act of mercy:
to flay my quivering flesh,
to claw my skin away?

Black skin
Black skin
What does it do
to White men
that robs them of their reason?
Is black some kind of treason
that interrupts
the American Dream
and triggers the hateful

American scream:
Nigger
Nigger
Nigger
Black Nigger?

Buzzards
Merciful buzzards
Black like me.

I wonder if
God sent the buzzards out
to pick my bones
and leave them hanging there,
dancing on the air,
bleaching in the sun?

How white they were
How white they were
Your bones among the white magnolias
Sweet-scented white magnolias
Above the silent water
The turgid silent water
The ever-silent witness
That tells no tales whatever
How peaceful were the people
How gentle and how tranquil
How silent like the water
When all your flesh was gone
When your black flesh was gone
And all your bones were white.

I wonder if
God saw me burning at the stake
or heard my skin pop open in the flame?
God, did you hear me call the Savior's name
and offer Him my tortured soul to take?

God
did you see my swollen lips

stretched tight and dry
and cracking in the heat
and did you hear the silent prayer
my bloated tongue could not repeat?

There was no sound, I know;
no sound could come.
My prayer, O Lord, was stifled in the flame
each time I tried to say the Savior's name.

No sound could come:
I could not say the words
I heard you say
on Calvary.
No words could come.
The odor of my roasting flesh
filled up my throat.
I retched:
My prayer was vomitus
and agony.

> Forgive them
> For they know not
> What they do.
> What they would do to me
> They do to you.

I wonder if
God saw my shame
when those
who set my pyre
out-raced the flame
to strip my body bare.
The women and the children standing there
looked at my nakedness and cursed my name.
Forgive me!
O forgive me for my shame!
I could not hide myself:
My roasted hands
were pinioned with a chain.

And then they brought a Barlow knife
to rob me of my tree of life
God
Did you see my shame
God
Did you see my tears
when
they hacked my nature off for souvenirs?

> God-a-Mighty
> What a trigger
> On that son-of-a-bitchin' nigger!
> God-damn-looka-there!

Freedom
When will you come at last?
Fearsome has been the past,
bitter the aftertaste,
tragic the human waste.
God grant there yet may be
true freedom for the free.
Justice on every hand
throughout this troubled land.

> True freedom for the free
> Freedom for you and me.

So long this road since freedom,
so dismal has been the way.
Strange flesh in the flames at night,
strange fruit on the trees by day.
Traveling this road alone
so many thousands gone.

> 1882, a hundred-thirteen
> So many thousands gone.

O Land
Of white white cotton
With the ax and the plow and the hoe
I felled your forests

I raised your corn
I made your cotton grow.

1884, two hundred-eleven
So many thousands gone.

Your little ones
sucked at a black black breast.
Your young ones
wept on a black black chest.
Black black hands
Laid your old ones to rest,
O Land of Cotton and Corn.

1892, two hundred-thirty
So many thousands gone.

O Land
of golden empire
bound together with ribbons of steel,
I bridged your rivers
I laid your track
I fired your iron wheel.

1900, a hundred-fifteen
So many thousands gone
1901, a hundred-thirty
So many thousands gone!

O Land
when the world's resentments
did threaten your golden store
I bore your colors
I faced the foe
I guarded your sacred shore.
On every star
and every stripe
and on the field of blue
of the flag that waves so gallantly
my blood was shed for you.

1919, eighty-three
So many thousands gone.
1933, twenty-eight
So many thousands gone
1964, three to go
So many thousands gone.

Thank God
this bitter cup
shall pass.
And those who died for freedom
shall at last
be rescued from
the nameless thousands gone
when justice shall have come
into its own.
Yes, write their epitaphs
on parchment scroll
lest America forget
the awesome toll
we paid for liberty
long after we were free.

So long
This road since freedom
This road the martyrs trod
This perilous road from Edom,
we walk this road with God.
So many thousands gone
We do not walk alone.

We do not walk alone
God walks beside His own.

America
Of freedom sing
On freedom's road
Let freedom ring
On every hand
Across this land
Let freedom ring

By God's decree
Let freedom ring
For you and me
So long this road since freedom
Let freedom ring!

—1968

Foreword

William Bobby McClain

The essays and chapters in this book grow out of the C. Eric Lincoln Lectures established to honor the late Professor Charles Eric Lincoln, a United Methodist minister born in Athens, Alabama—just about 75 miles north of my hometown of Gadsden, Alabama. Lincoln, at his death, was William Rand Kenan, Jr., Professor of Sociology of Religion and Social Philosophy Emeritus at Duke University, Durham, North Carolina. I am still so very happy to have chaired the committee that established the lectureship. I am even happier that we did so while he lived and could share in them with us for many years.

C. Eric and I often shared our pride about being born in Appalachia in the Lookout Mountain range of North Alabama. C. Eric's home church was Village View Methodist Church in Athens, and his pastor in his early boyhood was the Reverend Lindsay Garfield Fields, a quiet, dignified, saintly, and cultured deep ebony man who had a tremendous influence on C. Eric and his decision to enter the ministry and the field of religion and, later on, on me as my pastor a couple of decades later. He was the connecting link between C. Eric and me as I entered Clark College in Atlanta, Georgia, to major in religion under Mr. Lincoln. Eric was later to go to Boston University to earn his Ph.D., but at the time he was a professor of religion and philosophy at Clark, the assistant dean of men, and "Mr. Lincoln," although his religion and philosophy majors called him simply "Prof."

The same Rev. L. G. Fields was a member of the board of trustees of Clark College, a fact of which C. Eric and I were justly proud. And our one-time pastor took a great deal of pride in saying that he had brought us together—and, yes, we were to remain together the rest of Eric's life. It was sheer joy for me to dedicate my first major book in 1984, *Black People in the Methodist Church: Whither Thou Goest?* to these two great black men from the North Alabama mountains. In the dedication I said: "*. . . Both of these men have insisted on excellence in themselves and others, and given so much to so many—most of the time without mentioning what they gave.*"[1]

I began as his student, and then his teaching assistant at Clark College. We shared the final year of his doctoral studies as fellow graduate students. In fact, the first month or so of my seminary days I lived with him in the graduate student quarters at Boston University at Warren Hall, where both Malcolm X and Alex Haley came to visit as C. Eric put the final touches on his dissertation, "The Black Muslims." We became colleagues in the ministry and then colleagues in teaching and writing in the field of religion, and fishing buddies and friends. I still have to stop myself from picking up the telephone to call him and say "C. Eric, Mac [as he always called me] here," as our telephone conversations always began.

When a group of C. Eric's former students at Clark College got together at my suggestion to talk about establishing the first major lectureship at a predominantly black university and college named for a major African American scholar, the excitement was high. I was elected chair and mandated to contact C. Eric's former Clark students across the country to ask them to contribute toward endowing the lectureship. I remember so well compiling the list; it was not just students who had majored in religion and philosophy and had become pastors of churches and professors of religion but also those who had become scientists, musicians, librarians, teachers in schools and colleges and universities— and some presidents and deans—business people, doctors, lawyers, and various other endeavors. After all, the one we were naming the lectureship after was a "scholar for all seasons." His influence and mentoring were not limited to religion and philosophy, or even to the social sciences, but covered the academic spectrum and the spectrum of learning and human efforts. Doctors and lawyers, teachers and preachers, scientists and artists and actors quickly responded to my call to contribute big bucks to honor Dr. Lincoln with this lectureship. Not only did they contribute, but they came and they still keep coming and giving to support and endow this lectureship. I remember what was said by Dr. Horace C. Laster, a heart surgeon at Howard University Hospital and then associate dean of the Howard University Medical School in Washington, D.C. Horace's words were "Bobby, let me know if you need some more."

Well, we did need more and still need more to fully endow this lectureship. Proceeds from the sale of this wonderful book of essays and lectures will go toward that endowment, and we will still need some more. But thank God we finally have this book of some of the C. Eric Lincoln Lectures, including the very first one delivered by "the man, himself," as always, a brilliant analysis of the human situation. I was there, as I have been for every subsequent lecture so far.

This book is appropriate because it honors the man and his broad spectrum of interests: religion, race, ethics, literature, human rights, the arts, science, social philosophy, the university, business and economic enterprises, the Black Church, civil rights, culture, poetry, sociology, classical philosophy, education, and the whole lyceum. Those topics and more are here as these lectures have been presented by some of the sharpest and most able minds in this nation. Each year, we have spread the net wide to find the appropriate persons and the relevant topic. Dr. L. Henry Whelchel, my old roommate and classmate from Boston University (who was also a fellow student with Dr. Lincoln at Boston University), and the very fine Department of Religion and Philosophy, which he chairs at Clark Atlanta University, are to be thanked and commended for their diligence and excellence in consistently outdoing themselves year after precious year.

This book, whose coeditor is Dr. Alton B. Pollard, III, of Emory University, another of Dr. Lincoln's prized students, represents vintage C. Eric Lincoln. It was in the making before he died and the project received his blessings. He surely smiles now from afar as he observes the sheer excellence and preeminent quality of this volume. It is my hope that scores of thousands will purchase it. Not only purchase it but actively engage the ideas and propositions and principles set forth in the contents of this book. It even lends itself to book clubs and discussion groups in sororities and fraternities, and works well as a study book for classrooms and churches, retreats, and action-reflection groups. The scholar will find here sufficient ideas and thought to start the wheels of the mind turning and to interest the analytic part of the brain engaged to respond and to react. I hope it will be reviewed by those who are discerning of ideas and relevant issues in the society and the church. Indeed, this volume represents the man, *"a scholar for all seasons."*

Notes

1. William B. McClain, *Black People in the Methodist Church: Whither Thou Goest?* (Nashville: Abingdon Press, 1984), p. xi.

To Lucy Cook Lincoln

Acknowledgments

Without the support of former students, colleagues, friends, and family of Dr. Lincoln's, we would not have been able to sustain the longevity and sterling quality of this intellectual enterprise. Also, I would be remiss not to express gratitude to the scholarly community at Clark Atlanta University, including the current religion and philosophy faculty and staff: Ms. Gwendolyn Donaway, Dr. David Cann, Dr. Philip Dunston, Dr. Ralph Ellis, Dr. Herbert Marbury, Dr. Janet Melnyk, Dr. Thomas M. Scott, and Dr. Norman Fischer. Finally, I owe an endless debt of gratitude to Larma and my four young adult children, April, Kenyatta, Noel, Love III, and my son-in-law, Terrence, who are more precious to me than all the money in the world.

—*Love Henry Whelchel, Jr.*

To Ms. Ayanna Abi-Kyles and the Program of Black Church Studies staff, Ms. Renee Burwell and the Candler Faculty Support Suite, and colleagues Dr. Teresa Fry Brown, Dr. Luther Smith, and Dr. Dianne Stewart, with thanks for your able minds and kindred spirits. To my colleagues at the Candler School of Theology, who equally inspire and tire with their surpassing work ethic, and to Dean Russ Richey for helping to make this work possible. I am especially grateful to my family, whose love and support enables and endures: my parents, Alton B. Pollard, Jr., and Lena L. Pollard, and my siblings, Donna M. Garcia and Kevin D. Pollard and their families. Finally, the faith, hope, and love that my wife Jessica, son Brooks, and daughter Asha share with me on a daily basis sustains me on the journey. Nyame nhyira'w!

—*Alton B. Pollard, III*

Introduction

The C. Eric Lincoln Lecture Series, held annually at Clark Atlanta University, began in the fall of 1983. Conceived by former students of C. Eric Lincoln and graduates of the former Clark College, the Lincoln Lectures bear the distinction of being the longest-running series to honor a living black scholar.[1] Fittingly, the title for this work derives from the first stanza of Lincoln's epic meditation on lynching, whose haunting lyrics were recited at the inaugural lecture: "How Long This Road Since Freedom." This edited volume represents 20 years of critical intellectual reflection in the spirit of C. Eric, whose unsurpassed commitment to issues of race, religion, and equality in the United States affectionately earned him the title of "Dean of Black Religious Scholars" from several generations of students, religious leaders, and colleagues alike. Originally conceived through a series of conversations between myself, Henry Whelchel, and Eric—and further developed by the coeditors over lunch meetings at Atlanta's delectable soul food landmark Paschal's—the project grew beyond the original idea of a festschrift or commemorative compilation to something eminently more worthy of Eric, a collection of probing social analyses reflecting the height and depth and breadth of Lincoln's own scholarly commitments. In this anthology, we hope to further the discourse on race, religion, and social justice in the pursuit of an America that has not yet come to pass but one day most certainly will.

This book should thus be read within the matrix of contemporary race relations in the United States and the social study of African American religious patterns and dynamics. Its broader aim is to add to the scholarly literature on the power, meaning, and value of the sacred in African American culture, affirming the full partnership and agency of black folk in the social and historical context of the United States even as Americans of African descent continue to contend against being unequally situated participants in the nation's economic, political, educational, and legal life. The title, *"How Long This Road,"* reflects the historic and continuing legacy of race and racism and, more, a people's hope-filled and incessant struggle against hegemonic oppression, wherever it is to be found, in institutional spaces as well as in the interstices of social and personal life.

The questions and issues facing Americans of African descent today are vast. They include unresolved issues of intraracial and interracial identity, explored through distinctions based on material possessions, educational attainment, social class ascension, color consciousness, gendered patterns, generational perspectives, dual heritages, and endogenous relations with immigrants from Africa, the Caribbean, and South America over the last quarter of a century. They also reach a more recognizable consensus on the indifference of the state apparatus to deliver equitable health care, housing, education, employment, and other quality-of-life indices, and encourage a commensurate critical awareness of coalescing and interlocking degradations based on race, gender, sexuality, ecology, and ethnicity. No single monograph can satisfactorily address such a multiplicity of crises and concerns, nor does this scholarly text purport to cover all of said issues. Nonetheless, the essays assembled here from a variety of disciplines and perspectives have at least one factor in common: They address notions of race, identity formation, and racial justice and inequality as elements that are in multitudinous ways influenced by and, in turn, influencing the larger societal and religious landscape.

In 1954, the same year that C. Eric Lincoln began his career as a professor at Clark College (now Clark Atlanta University), the social dynamics of the nation were undergoing substantive change. Brown vs. the Topeka Kansas Board of Education was heralded, at least by black Americans, as the beginning of the end of de jure segregation and repression in the land. However, the legal and political victories that were at long last beginning to appear in Montgomery, Little Rock, New Orleans, Baton Rouge, Tallahassee, and elsewhere were seldom accompanied by any kind of commensurate moral or ethical commitment on the part of the nation. This was no less true in the realm of academic scholarship and critical debate: Only on the rarest of occasions was the rightness of white racial supremacy, and hierarchies of oppression in general, questioned. A major scholarly exception to considerations of the function of race, color, and religion as operative dimensions of social inequality and injustice was the work of Lincoln.

Half a century later, the general public and scholars alike acknowledge the oppressive existence of multiple axes of social inequality; however, far too little consideration is still given to understanding the critical causal connections between them. Lincoln's principle scholarly concern with the racial factor in the social and religious life of the United States expands in these pages to include such crucial and correlative factors as gender, the African Diaspora, and social class. Taken together, the essayists gathered here represent a qualitative departure from standard studies of African American religion and life, disclosing through their work the interdependent and multivalent nature of the scholar-activist project. Their results underscore the fact that the manifold consequences of what Lincoln deemed "the continuing American dilemma" of racial inequality—religious, cultural, social, political, and economic in scope—cannot truthfully be interpreted through a monocausal lens. Subjects as seemingly disparate as womanist studies, social ethics, history, and education are connected by the multifarious ways in which racial identity and difference consciously and unconsciously impact gender and sexual dynamics in the church; black wealth, well-being, and life chances; the changing face of national identity, and the conceptualization of a communal destiny.

The emphasis in this volume is largely but not entirely focused on scholarship in religious studies and the social sciences. The contributors are sociologists, lawyers, theologians, educators, historians, pastors, and preachers. The methodologies, themes, and issues addressed—racial justice, womanist resistance, social theory, philosophy, and literature—are even more varied and insightful still. The broadly interdisciplinary nature of the essays, each in their own way building upon and moving beyond the hopes and concerns of C. Eric Lincoln, should prove of considerable use for persons with an interest in sociology, religion, race, gender, and ethnic relations.

The Social Analysis of African American Religion and Life: A Brief Overview

The question of social analysis and its relation to the African American religious experience has been problematic for as long as social research has existed in the United States. More than a century ago the pioneering social scientist and advocate W. E. B. DuBois wrote a now all but largely forgotten essay called "The Atlanta Conferences."[2] From such a nonde-script title one might easily arrive at the assumption that DuBois was merely reporting for the record on some conference proceedings. In point of fact, his intent was considerably more involved. DuBois hoped to advance the fledgling new science of sociology through a series of extensive studies of African American life, including the Black Church, with Atlanta University as his base. But as one of the founding figures in the nascent social sciences, his deeper commitment was to using sound social analysis to improve the social condition of black people. Implicit in his scholarship was a belief in the worth of a pragmatic, empirically based form of social research, which, if properly practiced and pursued, would be foundational to societal change. Like other scholars during the late nineteenth and early twentieth century, the collection and analysis of social data was, for DuBois, equal parts moral-ethical and empirical, an undertaking in which scientific methods, data, and inter-pretations, but also religious motivations and beliefs, should have an eminent bearing on public policy.

DuBois was not the only exceptional researcher of his time. Ida B. Wells-Barnett and Anna Julia Cooper wrote and worked tirelessly to articulate the utter humanity and equality of African Americans. What especially distinguished their work from their male and white contem-poraries was a profound commitment to gender and racial justice in the social scientific investigation of United States culture and life. Both Wells-Barnett's *A Red Record* (1895) and Cooper's *A Voice from the South* (1892) were seminal insurgent studies advocating gender equal-ity and racial justice in the United States of a century ago. Not surprisingly, racism, sexism, and elitism in the social sciences would largely void any relationship between them and white members of the guild, female or male. Yet and still Wells-Barnett, Cooper, DuBois, and a small cadre of black scholar-activists took the social fact of racial and gendered antagonism seriously enough to create a genuinely alternative form of conflict and confrontation analysis that was not in the end simply beholden to white sociology's theoretical frameworks.

Some matters are slow to change. From the pioneering work of DuBois, Wells-Barnett, and Cooper until the writings of Lincoln, the role of the African American socio-religious researcher remained, with rare exception, essentially the same. From 1900 to 1960 only a handful of major empirical investigations of black religion were conducted, all by African American male scholars: DuBois's *The Negro Church* (1903), Carter G. Woodson's *The History of the Negro Church* (1921), Benjamin E. Mays and Joseph Nicholson's *The Negro's Church* (1933),

Arthur Huff Fauset's *Black Gods of the Metropolis* (1944), and the posthumous work by E. Franklin Frazier, *The Negro Church in America* (1964).[3] Moreover, what acceptable literature on the Black Church and black religion existed was hard to locate outside the "Negro holdings" of a few black college libraries. The broader academic community, theological education not excepted, appeared to be innocent of the suspicion that anyone could want to study the black experience, or that there could be any educational value derived from so doing. By every indication little had changed on the race relations front as the first half of the twentieth century drew to a close.

By 1965, black religion could scarcely be ignored by the general public or the academic community in the United States. The leadership of the Rev. Dr. Martin Luther King, Jr., Septima Clark, Ella Baker, the Student Non-Violent Coordinating Committee, the Southern Christian Leadership Conference, Fannie Lou Hamer, Fred Shuttlesworth, Bernice Reagon, James Lawson, Diane Nash, and others in the Civil Rights movement made visible a dimension of the black sacred tradition that belied earlier otherworldly caricatures and stereotypes. So, too, did the empowering and consciousness-raising militancy of the Nation of Islam, Malcolm X, Muhammad Ali, Angela Davis, the Black Panther Party for Self-Defense, the men of Attica Prison, the black arts community, the Black Power movement, black labor unions, and black liberation theology. Not coincidentally, the Death of God movement emerged in white theological circles as one response to the turbulent times. But an even more direct and consequential byproduct of this profoundly sacred and black-led struggle for the transformation of a nation—both in its civil rights and black consciousness phases—was the emergence of black studies, with black religious studies as a subdiscipline of inquiry. Over the years religious historians, ethicists, and theologians have generated a substantial body of scholarly materials. Leading the way in terms of social analysis was Lincoln's celebrated study of the Nation of Islam, *The Black Muslims in America,* published in 1961 and followed by such writings as *The Black Experience in Religion* (1973), an excursus into the diversity of African American religion—the Black Church, Black sectarian groups, and Caribbean and African religions—and his *Black Church Since Frazier* (1974).

Over the next three decades, Lincoln's probing examination of the social and religious context of the United States continued in such analytical works as *Race, Religion, and the Continuing American Dilemma* (1984), the monumental *Black Church in the African American Experience* (with coauthor Lawrence Mamiya in 1990), and the

semi-autobiographical *Coming Through the Fire* (1996). His complementary accomplishments in music, literature, and poetry, equal parts
aesthetic and analytical, are evidenced in his wide-ranging collection of
verse, *This Road Since Freedom* (1990). Throughout, his writings
powerfully challenge and critique white racism and privilege where the
church, the academy, and the nation are concerned. Even more em-
phatically, he explores and expresses the creative genius that is the
Black Church and the African American experience.

Other researchers of this generation deserve prominent mention—
the writings of George Kelsey, Gayraud Wilmore, Charles Long, Vincent Harding, James Cone, Joseph R. Washington, and J. Deotis
Roberts, succeeded by those of Peter Paris, Katie Cannon, Jacquelyn
Grant, Delores Williams, James Washington, Cheryl Townsend Gilkes,
and Cornel West, among others—come immediately and appreciatively
to mind. Like Lincoln, they have encouraged religiously grounded
social change through their incisive scholarship. For these and other
scholars black religion was not then, and is not now, an uninteresting or
insular phenomenon associated with political pacification, fatalism,
and otherworldliness, but an ever-potential source for social change.
Nevertheless, even the most generous review of the literature reveals
that much of the contemporary scholarship in religion by social scientists retains a strikingly familiar detachment and indifference where
issues of race and social justice are concerned. What is even worse, the
situation in other disciplines has not necessarily changed for the better
either.[4] The invisibility or marginality of African Americans—a concept famously explored by DuBois in his classic book *The Souls of Black
Folk*—and the paucity of liberative data pertaining to people of color in
general remains a matter of deep and abiding concern.[5]

The generations of religious researchers now succeeding Lincoln are
characteristically interdisciplinary in perspective and preparation; they
are theologian, historian, ethicist, phenomenologist, biblical interpreter, psychologist, political scientist, economist, sociologist, aesthete,
and preacher, depending on what is called for by the context. Most by
definition are scholars whose approach to the promise and peril of
African American religion and life is multiple, comparative, and more
theoretically innovative than in the past. With varying degrees of
investment in more nuanced approaches, their writings reflect the
struggle to restructure understandings of black oppression, survival,
resistance, and liberation by refracting race through the multiple lenses
of religion, region, gender, class, sexuality, and other categories of
analysis. The majority of the writers in this volume represent this

transition beyond the social conflict models representative of the civil rights era to multidimensional analyses of African American social and religious life. They include socio-religious researchers Delores C. Carpenter, Jualynne E. Dodson, Cheryl Townsend Gilkes, Lawrence H. Mamiya, Alton B. Pollard, III, and Mary R. Sawyer; religious historians Love Henry Whelchel, Jr., and Lillian Ashcraft-Eason; and religious philosophers Ralph Ellis and Jon Michael Spencer. Minister Ava Muhammad, from the Nation of Islam, and Baptist and A.M.E. ministers Gardner C. Taylor and Floyd H. Flake are present day exemplars of the moral and prophetic wisdom emanating from the black religious community. Intellectual stalwarts James H. Cone, Charles H. Long, John Hope Franklin, Asa G. Hilliard, and John R. Silber present additional analytical perspectives. On the whole and in practice, all are participants in the effort to create a new social vision for a new American nation. What is far less clear is whether the scholarly and ecclesial communities today are any better prepared to embrace new empirical and interpretive perspectives in their ranks, for the advancement of knowledge and in the name of justice.

The Contributions

Part I: The Legacy of C. Eric Lincoln

Collectively, the essays in this volume place African American socio-religious analysis in revealing cultural, historical, and cross-cultural perspective. C. Eric Lincoln's article opens the first section with a classic reformulation of the American Dilemma identified by the Swedish social scientist Gunnar Myrdal half a century earlier. Lincoln writes here: "the human values we hold as individuals are routinely eviscerated by the inhuman systems we create to negate them in our consuming passion to distinguish and separate humans from other humans." This moral-ethical conflict between "human values" and "inhuman systems" is, according to the author, particularly acute in the circumstance of race and religion in the United States. The chief symbol and primary irrational precipitate of the nation's spiritual and cultural malaise is white prejudice and racial xenophobia. The national condition is forlorn; we continue to sacrifice on the altar of white supremacy succeeding generations who struggle to be free. Lincoln's opening essay lends insight into the agency of a people, the obstinacy of a nation, and the escalating cost of chronic denial.

In the estimation of Charles H. Long, it is the depth of Lincoln's thought conjoined with his aesthetic sensibilities that accounts for his especially insightful approach to the study of religion and race in American society. Long elaborates by stating that the distinctiveness of Lincoln's writings rests not only in his consistent empiricism as a social scientist but in his critical empathy for religion. Poetic wisdom and intellectual work are lauded as complementary components of Lincoln's scholarly studies and literary pursuits. But far and away the most important factor to consider in understanding the power and meaning of Lincoln's work, Long says, is the inward measure of a life well lived. Lincoln's is an enduring testimony to the power of a social vision that springs from worlds within to effect change in the world without.

The intellectual legacy of Lincoln was one in which race and religion were recognized as deeply flawed constructs, especially in their institutional manifestations. Mary R. Sawyer's chapter excavates some of the history of racial discrimination and oppression during the life of Lincoln, providing a philosophical and social foundation for understanding the American Dilemma. Sawyer indicates how Lincoln's life and thought, in personal and scholarly ways, reflected the ambivalences and ambiguities of a conflict-laden America. Throughout, the American Dilemma is used to underscore the myriad of ways in which Lincoln struggled with his country and the Christian faith on the one hand, while seeking to provide liberating visions for his community of origins and the beloved community, on the other. Racial discrimination and civic and religious faith are at the paradoxical heart of the American republic. The intellectual sojourn that Sawyer so movingly describes is in fundamental respects a public dialogue between Lincoln the problematic native son and prophetic intellectual, and an internal one between Lincoln and his own deep and abiding sense of hope.

The influence that exceptional professors have on their students remains a largely understudied and unappreciated phenomenon. The contours and complexities of this relationship are deftly and eloquently explored in Jon Michael Spencer's lyric analysis of creative pedagogy. Referring to Lincoln as a professor of "heroic" distinction, Spencer goes on to delineate those qualities he discerns to be requisite for inspiring learning and self-awakening in others. In fine, Spencer's chapter is about teaching as both the practice and gift of freedom. His is an inspiring and challenging call for more professors to raise their threshold of teaching and for more students to demand it. Lincoln's own life and learning have been so instructive, Spencer informs us, precisely because he effectively elicited and evoked in others the ability to access their own "internalized intuitive professor."

The ideas of Jualynne E. Dodson provide an important critical complement to those found elsewhere in this section. Like Long and Sawyer, Dodson is committed to constructive reflection on the writings of Lincoln, but in a decidedly interpretive, post-structuralist vein. Dodson is unequivocal in terms of the need to bring new social and theoretical interpretations to bear on the African American religious experience. Undervalued in Lincoln's studies, she contends, are indications of black cultural distinctiveness and international engagement. Clearly a product of his time, Lincoln's work also overlooks the indispensable role and agency of women in the church. As the most enduring institution in the African American community, the Black Church exhibits certain dynamics, processes, and patterns of gender, race, and class that in turn interact with other forces and variables in the community and society at large. In Dodson's trenchant critique are heard echoes of the ancestors—Cooper, Wells-Barnett, and DuBois. Joined in sociological convergence with Lincoln, her work at the same time represents the continuing methodological and theoretical maturation of a field.

Part II: The Social Analysis of Religion

Working largely from empirical data and quantitative studies, sociologist Lawrence H. Mamiya explores the current relationship between African American and immigrant Muslim groups. Like Lincoln, Mamiya has a longstanding interest in the phenomenon of African American Islam, from the Nation of Islam to Sunni and Sufi Islam, and lesser known forms. With some 40,000 African Americans converting to Islam annually, this study of African American's conversion to Islam and the tensions that arise with larger society is timely. The even more rapid increase in the immigrant Muslim population in the United States indicates not the co-optation of African American Islam but rather shifts in how both populations identify themselves in relation to each other and the larger society. Mamiya's findings note the historic cultural and ethnic differences in American Islam but probe even more so the steady and increasing turn toward *Ummah* or community among Muslims. Mamiya's essay further reflects the growing mood of religious and political mobilization among African American Muslims and confirms extant possibilities for reviving a black legacy of organized social renewal and change.

My contribution, "W. E. B. DuBois and the Struggle for African America's Soul," revisits the history of the struggle for racial equality and identity in the United States with an eye toward understanding some crucial contemporary challenges facing the African American community. Long considered a given in the African American community, I suggest that the morality of racial solidarity has, with the rising significance of class, increasingly been eclipsed by a solipsist-like view of economic success that with somber regularity portends a surrender of cultural values as well. The ancestral wisdom of W. E. B. DuBois is mined to underscore the ways in which the communities of African descent in America have long floundered and flourished on the shoals of collective worth and responsibility. The black community has on the one hand identified with being African and American, displaying distinct patterns of racial-ethnic consciousness and pride, and at the same time has struggled through enervating bouts of cultural amnesia and ambivalence. Now, as never before, the souls of black folk hang dangerously and perilously in the balance.

The manner in which the politics of racial struggle cut across many social dynamics is presented with no greater clarity than in James H. Cone's theological reading of the life and thought of Martin Luther King, Jr., and Malcolm X. Cone's assessments, based on groundbreaking analysis of the religious message and social commitment of these exemplars, provide stark evidence of the relentless inequalities faced by the African American community. Though Martin is "America's most influential theologian and preacher," and Malcolm this nation's "most trenchant race critic," the centrality of race (and religion) analysis, no less gender and class, lags in the critical struggle for the recognition of the humanity of all persons. The importance of Martin appears limited to the degree that he can be made palatable to the national mind and mood. Malcolm, by contrast, deserves even less consideration where the public is concerned. Once again, the importance of racial analysis founders on the shores of white discomfort and black ambivalence.

Cheryl Townsend Gilkes's chapter on the socio-theology of the Rev. Florence Spearing Randolph is a prime example of a story sometimes acknowledged but seldom known: the profound and enduring legacy of pioneering African American preaching women. Not only does Gilkes highlight Randolph's historical importance as a black female pastor and leader in the black women's club movement of the early twentieth century, but she identifies how through her religious faith she sought to address the social ills of the day with a relevance that is strikingly contemporary. Resident in Randolph's sermons are the seeds of modern black liberation theology and womanist theology, as well as an enabling and empowering pneumatology. As Gilkes's research shows, the courage and conviction of early daughters of thunder like Randolph would help pave the way for future generations of women to follow the call of God. African American women have always been pivotal sources of religious knowledge and purveyors of spiritual power in the black community. Only the means to more publicly and prominently employ their spiritual gifts has been missing.

Delores C. Carpenter's careful and systematic reading of ministerial opportunities and income earnings for African American women and men discloses the manner in which the politics of gender injustice and discrimination continue to play out in Black Church leadership in the early twenty-first century. Carpenter's findings, based on analysis of ministry opportunities for black female and male Master of Divinity graduates over a 20-year period, provide stark evidence of continued vocational and earning inequality for African American women. Her results represent a structural basis for understanding the distinct axes of inequality that separate black women clergy from their black male counterparts. The conjunction of gender and race issues, often and especially related to family life concerns, has necessitated multiple strategies for African American women clergy to succeed. At the same time, neither black women nor men in the ministry receive compensation comparable to other professional groups, or even to their white clergy counterparts. With the advance of African American women in graduate theological institutions across the country, the underadvancement of African American women in congregational leadership and life demands womanist resistance, black male advocacy, ecclesiastical transformation, and a communal practice of freedom.

Part III: Witnesses from the Religious Community

As religious leaders in the African American community, Gardner C. Taylor, Floyd H. Flake, and Ava Muhammad provide insights into the more quotidian aspects of race, religion, and life in the United States, insights rife with spiritual, socio-political, and theoretical implications. Poverty, racial discrimination, gender, community, and a transcending faith were the building blocks for their self-identity and social agency, as evidenced in their contributions to this text.

Gardner C. Taylor, African America's preacher laureate, addresses a recurrent refrain within the African American religious tradition, namely song as a sign of God's intervention in human affairs, and especially in the affairs of the oppressed. Drawing upon the Hebrew Scriptures and the enslavement experience of Africans in the United States, he talks about music as the measure by which we have moved as a people and a nation.

In a related vein, Floyd H. Flake, a former member of the U.S. Congress and a prominent activist-pastor, sets forth a framework for black economic development. The three phases of black liberation described in his chapter are emancipation, enfranchisement, and empowerment. According to Flake, the first two phases have in fact been accomplished; lamentably, the third has barely begun. The present and pressing challenge for African Americans in this land of promise and opportunity is to establish economic self-help and self-sufficiency. Historically, Flake's position is a permutation on the theme explored by Mr. Booker T. Washington and others. His contribution also discusses the internalization of beliefs of racial inferiority and fatigue crucial to the reproduction and maintenance of white racial hegemony.

Minister Ava Muhammad's essay is a compelling contribution to this volume. Presented scant weeks after the September 11, 2001, bombings, Muhammad's fierce and righteous indignation is in the tradition of the African American jeremiad, challenging the politics and parameters of religious, racial, and gendered identity in the United States. Muhammad echoes one of the wider themes of the volume in terms of the need to bring innovations to bear on the new politics and dynamics of difference in the United States of the twenty-first century. In her wide-ranging comparative analysis she further argues that in the case of Americans of African descent and the Muslim faithful, the denial of full democracy is racially and ethnically based. She utilizes this claim to urge increased understanding and cooperation between the two communities, which, while distinct in terms of their historic dilemmas, are similar in their respective demands for justice and equality. Muhammad vigorously illustrates that the United States also suffers from a profound moral and ethical malaise; the time has come for a renaissance of black spiritual as well as intellectual commitment. Her practical, relevant, and oppositional approach to many of the key problems facing America place her on the contentious fringes of society—and somewhere near the center of African America.

The activities of Gardner C. Taylor as a pastor-at-large and community presence, Floyd Flake as a political and economic advocate for the rights of the poor and dispossessed, and Ava Muhammad as a cultural and religious activist and proponent of the formation of race and gendered consciousness all indicate the multiple axes of religious and political mobilization as an outgrowth of manifold forms of social inequality. Through the narratives of these religious figures, readers are afforded a glimpse of how African American religious leadership assumes multiple roles—as preachers, politicians, activists, developers, Muslim and Christian, women and men—in the ongoing black struggle.

Part IV: Lift Every Voice

Except for historical and biblical studies, much of the scholarly work in black religion has yet to acknowledge the intersecting impact of other disciplines and purviews. For instance, African-centered scholarship is with rare exception not noted in the work of black religious scholars. The nature of the academy as an enclave of intellectual elitism and exclusivity that discourages or dismisses black discourse is yet another situation warranting scholarly attention and response. In this section are found essays representing history, education, and African-centered perspectives. Some of the writings are more directly linked to matters of religion than others. In the final analysis, each contribution significantly enhances our understanding of the black religious and intellectual struggle that still awaits us.

Asa G. Hilliard's chapter opens this final section with a look at current debates in light of the past. Hilliard notes that people of African descent were once the teachers of the world, a point lost on many people in the modern context. By elucidating the manner in which African civilizations cultivated life and learning long before the advent of Europe, Hilliard complicates a facile line of demarcation between Africa's encounter with Europe and subsequent African enslavement and discrimination here and elsewhere. The interactions between early African or Kemetic civilizations and other peoples, as well as between the various African communities themselves, provide a departure for a more constructive understanding of early African peoples and of how Africa's descendants both on the continent and throughout the diaspora might similarly perceive and treat themselves. Deeply encoded into the United States and Western belief and practice is the inherent inferiority and insignificance of all things African. Differently stated, the shift from enslavement to freedom in this land—the bestowal of certain inalienable rights, resources, and, sometimes, privileges—was not the first or only moment in the history of African-descended people when the mantle of humanity descended. African-centered theory remains a fairly contentious approach in the world of black religious scholarship.

Still, Hilliard lends considerable power, clarity, and insight to yet one more means by which African Americans seek to establish greater self-affirmation and equity between themselves and larger society.

One of the principle means by which the Euro-American slaveholders sought to break the resistance of their African captives was through the colonizing of their minds. If the power and meaning of African religion and culture could be eliminated among the enslaved in the New World, then their will to resist would be similarly eroded and eradicated. For religious scholar Love Henry Whelchel, Jr. the historical evidence is compelling that the grand design of the enslavers did not finally succeed. Deprived of freedom of body and limb and denied their rightful heritage, Africa's dispossessed nevertheless clung tenaciously to life-saving traditions that were reborn in the African American Christian Church. Whelchel's particular emphasis is on the life-giving sustenance made manifest in the African American Methodist communions, which he describes in these pages as "heart religion." From the social democratizing tendencies of early eighteenth century revivalism to the emergence of black liberation theology and more recently still neo-Pentecostalism, black Methodists are among the African American faithful who seek to remain faithful to a holism that was the hallmark of African religion and culture from the very beginning.

The eminent historian John Hope Franklin enriches our understanding of religious history with his semibiographical chapter on George Washington Williams. Williams, a Baptist minister, legislator, lawyer, diplomat, and editor, among other incarnations, is perhaps best known as the first serious historian to come out of the African American community. His two-volume, one thousand–page work published in 1882, called *A History of the Negro Race in America from 1619 to 1880: Negroes as Slaves, as Soldiers, and as Citizens,* is magisterial in scope and epic in reach. Franklin narrates how he came to share with the world the story of this pioneering historian of Africans in America who, only one generation removed from his death, had already fallen into obscurity. The interrelationship of race, religion, aptitude, and ambition in the biography of Williams can be linked to broader ruminations on the politics of inclusion and the role of the black public intellectual in the United States of the late nineteenth and early twentieth century.

Unquestionably, Boston University Chancellor John R. Silber has made an impact on the academy with his calls for a renewal of interest in and expanded commitment to the public life on the part of higher education. For example, he highlights affirmative action and sustaining the public trust as areas pertinent to the strengthening of democracy. His often controversial points of view are deeply informed by laissez-faire preoccupations with technological advancement and modernization. His discreet efforts to identify the discrimination of African Americans as individuals and not as a group, while well-intended, mirror contemporary and, often, decidedly conservative debates about race. The concept of a disprivileged *group,* however identified and on whatever grounds, is for Silber the antithesis of modernity and, hence, an impediment to prospects for America's future well-being. The implication drawn here is that a broad program of black empowerment and incorporation—a liberating and democratizing response to centuries of systemic white racism, advantage, and privilege—is incompatible with the strategic needs and agenda of the nation and should therefore be abandoned. Silber's ideas are in sharp juxtaposition to many of the ideas presented in this book.

The chapter written by Ralph Ellis and Lillian Ashcraft-Eason occupies the final pages of this volume because it offers an apt summation behind the reason for this work, here named and interpreted as *Sankofa. Sankofa* is a metaphysical word from the Akan language that means "to return and retrieve."[6] As social researchers, we understand it to be our personal, communal, and professional duty to accurately embrace the past in order to ameliorate the present and the future. In reviewing the scholarly commitments of C. Eric Lincoln and the history of the lectureship, Ellis and Ashcraft-Eason conclusively provide a significant and forward-looking glimpse into the future of African American religious research and life.

Hopefully, this book will provide the backdrop for further reflection and inquiry into the social and sacred worlds of African American religious life, not only for scholars but also for students, religious leaders, and laity alike. In this sense, ours is but a modest continuation of the efforts of DuBois, Wells-Barnett, Cooper, C. Eric Lincoln, and that darkly radiant cloud of witnesses whose writings were an instrument of resistance in addressing issues of religion and culture, gender and race, justice and equality, the enfranchisement of our humanity, and more.

Alton B. Pollard, III
Emory University
Candler School of Theology

Notes

1. C. Eric Lincoln died in May 2000. See the epilogue for a brief history of the lectureship.
2. Dan S. Green and Edwin D. Driver, eds., *W.E.B. DuBois on Sociology and the Black Community* (Chicago: University of Chicago Press, 1978), pp. 53–60.
3. Other scholars who gave notable attention to African American religion during this period are St. Clair Drake, George Edmund Haynes, Melville Herskovits, Zora Neale Hurston, Charles S. Johnson, and Kelly Miller.
4. Willie Pearson, Jr., and H. Kenneth Bechtel, eds., *Blacks, Science, and American Education* (New Brunswick: Rutgers University Press, 1989).
5. Alton B. Pollard, III, and Mary R. Sawyer provide a more detailed analysis of African American underrepresentation in the sociological analysis of religion in "Justice and the Social Scientific Study of Religion: Wither Black Religion?" (unpublished paper, 1996).
6. The Akan-speaking peoples are found mostly in southern Ghana and adjacent Côte d'Ivoire. For religious and cultural inferences see Anthony Ephirin-Donker, *African Spirituality: On Becoming Ancestors* (Trenton, NJ: Africa World Press, 1997), p. 11.

I

The Legacy of C. Eric Lincoln

1

Human Values and Inhuman Systems

C. Eric Lincoln

There is a popular adage to the effect that "you are what you eat." Perhaps. But I prefer to believe that you are what your values proclaim you to be. Values constitute the contextual framework out of which our more critical decisions are made and our volitional behavior is determined. The behavioral psychologists would object to this, I am sure, for the rats and pigeons they work with suggest that all behavior is but a patterned response to external stimuli. But most people are not rats, and fewer still are pigeons. And neither rats nor pigeons have values in the first place.

A better way to test the importance of human values is to review, if you will, the very broad spectrum of significant changes that have occurred in our own society since World War II. Advances in technology, medicine, ecology, etc., have been accompanied by new and differing perceptions of what values are worth pursuing. In consequence, it is increasingly difficult for people to retain a strong sense of security or to maintain confidence in their perceptions of what is right, or whether right or wrong makes any difference. Mental depression becomes endemic as more and more people struggle to sort out and make sense of the competing notions and experiences that seem to crowd in upon us. Human values, particularly those that are based on religious understanding, function as stations of security in a world where all else is in flux. And because they are primal and immutable, those values expressing the creativity of God and the dignity of humanity become even more critical to meaning and direction in human life. Some things must change; some things must persist through change, or change itself becomes the only value of significance. How a society deals with change in consistence with those fundamental values that do not change is the measure of its vitality, and the prognosis of its future.

The Cardinal Values

There are at least four values I consider to be fundamental to every civilized society, and from these other values may be derivative. They are: life, dignity, creativity, and responsibility. *Life,* because it is the ground and the condition of all else. Where there is no life, there is no possibility. To have life, to give life, to conserve life is to affirm the creative genius of the Divine, and to participate in the divine scheme at the highest level. I know of no moral sentiment superior to that which values life above all else and finds in that valuation the sanctions by which all behavior is to be ultimately determined.

Where life is not the superlative value, no culture can preserve itself, for the appreciation of life begets life, protects life, nurtures and enhances life. And life in turn writes on the *tabula rasa* of the material world the purpose for which all that is has come into existence.

To be, or not to be, is but part of the question. For not merely to be, but to be with *dignity* is the first condition of being human. Dignity is the inalienable corollary of human life, and the affirmation of life is the confirmation of life with dignity. If, as Plato suggested, the unexamined life is not worth living, it is no less true that the life that is bereft of the elemental symbols of human recognition is a negation of divine purpose and intent, and a mockery of the meaning of humanity.

To be human and to be so considered, that is the meaning of dignity. Dignity means to be able to live and to move among one's fellows clothed with all those symbols, tangible and intangible, which convey to the self and to all others that one's being is a matter of consequence, not a mere spasm in the flux. But dignity implies *creativity,* the organization and projection of those peculiar attributes that constitute the "who-ness" and the "what-ness" of personality into some expression of personal significance. It is the act of bringing something new into existence; the imprimatur of the self upon the backdrop of human history. Creativity is the indisputable evidence of human existence. It is one's personal signature of the joie de vivre every person knows when one recognizes their life as an endowment, a privilege, and an opportunity.

As life is the supreme product of the creative will, so must *creativity* be the unimpaired option of every life. It is said that "a life is a terrible thing to waste." But where the creative potential inherent in human existence is stifled, or permitted to atrophy for want of nurture, human existence is a contradiction in terms, and society is feeding on itself.

Finally, there must be *responsibility,* for responsibility is the minimum condition for parity participation in the social enterprise. When people choose to live in cooperation with each other in pursuit of that spectrum of common values not available to them as individuals, such an arrangement can be viable only to the degree that all parties are capable of responding adequately to the requirements of that mutual undertaking. But responsibility implies the ability to respond, and where this ability has been impaired or distrained from selected individuals or classes, by whatever means and for whatever reasons, those so deprived are robbed of a vital element of human consideration. Their impairment conditions every aspect of their participation in the common ventures of the human enterprise, and they can never be responsible because they will never have the means to be responsible. *If you break a beagle's back, he can't run with the rabbit pack!* And if the ability to run rabbits is the primary criterion by which a beagle's worth is determined, so is the ability to respond in kind the criterion for human valuation. *Responsibility presumes the means to be responsible.* To be human is to be confirmed in the possession of those minimum facilities that make responsible participation possible in the ordinary spectrum of human affairs.

These, then, are the fundamental human values: *life itself* and its inalienable corollaries, *dignity, creativity,* and *responsibility.* For those of us in the Judeo-Christian tradition who perceive humankind in the image of God, these are the critical elements of that perception. But religion aside, every human individual is at a minimum the counterpart of every other human individual, and the brutalization of one implies the susceptibility of all. If being human has any significance whatever, it must by definition include the assurance that the symbols by which humanity is defined and distinguished cannot be arbitrarily ignored or discounted. In short, human life requires and must always be accorded conditions of existence commensurate with its superlative position in relation to all other possible values. In the absence of life, all else is of course academic; but in the absence of life's critical refinements, there can be neither meaning nor measure to mere human existence, for it is through these embellishments that the larger spectrum of values, including those of love, peace, justice, tranquility, and the like find expression and enhancement.

The values of which I speak are all "normative." They are all a part of the moral portfolio of the typical American. They are prominent in our religious creeds, encapsulated in the school day lore of our children, and enshrined in the principles that structure our understanding of America and what it means to be an American. But they are commonly negated in practice through the covert systems of antivalues by means of which we protect the privileges and prerogatives of some through the blatant devaluation of others. It is this disjunction between what we will to believe and what we will to do that constitutes the continuing American dilemma, that persistent condition in values that enervates and qualifies our national life and makes us a nation of cynics.

The Problem of the Color Line

What is the basis of the contradiction that turns America against itself and issues in the compulsive mass negation of the critical values by which we claim to live? It was Atlanta University's own W. E. B. DuBois whose unerring appraisal gave us fair warning nearly three quarters of a century ago. Said Dr. DuBois:

> The problem of the Twentieth Century
> is the problem of the color line. . . .
>
> The Nation has not yet found peace
> from its sins. . . .
>
> The race problem will be solved when. . . .
> Human beings learn to apply in dealings with their
> fellows the simple principles of the
> Golden Rule. . . . [1]

A lot of time has passed, and we still have not found peace from our sins, nor is the evidence that we entertain a serious commitment to the principles of the Golden Rule one of the compelling features of our generation. Prominent among our problems remains the *perennial problem* DuBois complained of when the twentieth century was still in its infancy. That problem persists despite the cosmetics of countless "political solutions" and "unwritten agreements" that promised the people change without changing anything, and despite the tortured strategies of those good Americans whose consciences are always agonized but whose convenience remains rooted firmly in the status quo ante. It is still a problem of the color line, and that problem ramifies in all of our more critical relations, polluting the environment and straining the parameters of credibility in which the democratic ideal is somehow expected to function.

Wherever important human interests happen to lie, there the problem seems to lurk. It is not, as is so often urged by simplistic thinking, merely a matter of economics, for in America the economic condition functions as the first line of determination for most other worthwhile values and opportunities. For example, when race and economics are so conjoined that one implies the other, millions of bona fide Americans find their opportunities of participation in America reduced to nothing palpable at all. They have "rights without lights," which is to say that they have no means whatever of going where they have a *right* to go, or the *will* to go. As far as meaningful participation in America is concerned, they are functionally disqualified. Shut out. A people thus handicapped, reasoned Doctor DuBois, cannot reasonably be asked to compete with those who are free of such impediments. *If you break the beagle's back, how can he run rabbits with the rabbit pack?*

Our strange dilemma is that the human values we hold as individuals are routinely eviscerated by the inhuman systems we create to negate them in our consuming passion to distinguish and separate humans from other humans. It was to such a system, for example, to which former Interior Secretary James Watt unconsciously appealed when he absently alluded to his advisory panel as "a Black . . . a woman, two Jews and a cripple." America was outraged, *of course!* But the outrage was more because Mr. Watt embarrassed us by "going public" with some of our most deeply held private sentiments than because we honestly objected to the substance of his gaffe. We care about the poor, the disadvantaged, the disabled, etc., in the abstract, because there is always the abstract possibility that any of us as individuals could someday encounter poverty or disadvantage. But the fact that we create and defend with such vigor the very systems that produce and perpetuate poverty and disadvantage gives a decidedly hollow ring to our protestations about calling them to public attention.

The deluge of suits against affirmative action filed over the last several years reveals even more about the confused state of American values. Some of the cases argued before the Supreme Court, like Bakke, Weber, and Fullilove, for example, illustrate the ease and the cynicism with which the prior issues of human rights and simple justice get lost in the torturous labyrinth of specious counterclaims, which would effectively nullify even that *minimum* gesture of moral concern that affirmative action is supposed to represent.

Affirmative action was conceived as a remedial approach to accumulated injustice and its long and tragic train of consequences. It is the official, belated recognition that America has a Problem, but the problem with the Problem is that we have approached it so tardily, so tentatively, so testily, and without grace or moral conviction.

The American Dilemma

Americans as a people are not given to admission of failure or of doubt, but it seems that the more loudly we proclaim our perfection the more insistent seems to be our need for corroboration from significant others. Somewhere there must be a moral in all this. Even in the formative years of this republic when an exuberant, unchastened idealism committed us to the notion of a perfect society here in the West, we were so certain, but still we longed to be told just how right we were, and how well we were doing. However, when Alexis de Tocqueville offered his appraisal of American democracy after its first half century of effort, America may have been titillated by the attention of the distinguished French observer, but there is no evidence that his criticisms of our racial practices were taken to heart. A hundred years later, still in search of some external confirmation of our national self-image, we invited Gunnar Myrdal, the Swedish social scientist, to appraise our progress and tell us how far we had come. After an exhaustive study Myrdal offered an assessment we were hardly prepared to receive. He said America had a "dilemma," and the dilemma derived from the conflict between the high-sounding Christian precepts embodied in the American creed and the way Americans really behaved. That dilemma is still with us and it ramifies in every aspect of contemporary American behaviors and ideology. Once again, there is an apparent inability to extrapolate the schedule of values with which we seek to confirm self-identity into behaviors that would give substance to the moral fantasies in which we are wont to indulge.

In the course of his 1978 commencement address at Harvard University, Alexander Solzhenitsyn, the celebrated Russian novelist, addressed the American dilemma in terms even less complimentary than de Tocqueville or Myrdal, although he did not (as they did) speak specifically to the issues of our racial hypocrisy. But Solzhenitsyn did chide America for glorified technological achievements that do not redeem our moral poverty, and he accused us of a preoccupation with the worship of man and his material needs while our sense of responsibility to God and society grows progressively less pronounced. He referred to

America as an "abyss of human decadence," against which we seem to have no defense. We are characterized, he said, by the "misuse of liberty," having prostituted our vaunted freedom for cheap satisfactions. We were warned that courage is in decline and the stage is set for the triumph of mediocrity.

The dilemma pictured by Alexander Solzhenitsyn is essentially the same as the "American dilemma" described by Gunnar Myrdal in the heyday of American power and prestige a half century ago. But the power, the prestige, and the self-assurance have all wavered. There is a pervasive erosion of confidence in American leadership, and perhaps in the American Dream itself. Our national purpose is fragmented and confused, and the symptoms of our cultural malaise are everywhere apparent. We seem incapable of learning from the past or planning effectively for the future. It was not very long ago that racism expressed in differential housing, black unemployment, segregation in education, and in most other practical aspects of our common existence caused our cities to be laid waste and our schools to become battlegrounds. But in spite of the hard lessons of the sixties, we still managed to profess surprise and shock when the seventies threatened a repeat of history— even though the bread lines in the black ghettoes were longer than ever before, even though the Ku Klux Klan was resurgent all over the country, and even though the South was devising ever-new stratagems for maintaining segregation in the public schools.

What is new in racial justice in America is so often what is old: a somber tale that has been too long in the telling; a weary variation on a theme that never seems to find retirement. We cannot avoid the conclusion that few of the changes we hoped for have been truly accomplished, even though the cosmetics of progress are always being paraded before us with cynical reassurance. But true reassurance comes hard, because the most convincing data is read not from charts and graphs but in the faces of the hopeless legions of the battered, the jobless, and the dispossessed who people the back streets of affluent America.

In spite of our persistence in the distortion of our own ideals, God has been gracious (or at least patient), and America has become a mighty power in the world. America counts her bathtubs and television sets in the millions; her war machine is sufficiently intact to deter any aggressor, real or imagined. We have sent human beings to the moon, and the Coca-Cola sign is a signal for light-hearted refreshment in the most remote hamlets of this terrestrial globe. But there are people in America who are dying for want of bread. And there are people in

America whose principle struggle is to retain a last clutch of dignity before some impersonal behemoth of power and progress claims them for its provender.

The American Dilemma in Perspective

The same fetters that bind the captive bind the captor, and the American people are captives to their own myths, woven so cleverly into the fabric of our national experience. When a serious candidate for president of the United States can testify candidly, as did Ronald Reagan in his debate with Jimmy Carter in 1980, that when *he* was growing up, "this country didn't even know it *had* a racial problem," then the candor of selective ignorance has swung full circle to re-emerge as the casuistry of presumptive innocence. If the American people ever come to take seriously the political rhetoric of innocence by ignorance, the erosion of our credibility for world leadership will be in even greater escalation than it is at present. Mr. Reagan's posturing was recognized, of course, for what it was—a classic instance of the way in which our systems of antivalues function to protect us with selective ignorance from the unpleasant realities we do not want to know about. Nevertheless, if we ever get through the mist and the murk of our self-willed naiveté, we will discover that our moral values have long since been corroded, the democratic ideal has been corrupted, and we have allowed ourselves to be transported by dreams that never were to a Shangri-La we know does not exist. Unfortunately, after the dreaming there has to be a waking, and sooner or later reality will confront us with a bill we may be ill prepared to meet.

The Problem as Violence

The threats to our basic schedule of human values come to us in a variety of forms, but whatever the guise, DuBois's assessment of the Problem remains intact. The problem of the color line feeds the American Dilemma, and the dilemma retains our normative values in continuous escrow while we continue to borrow time. Among the most pervasive threats to our normative schedule of human values is violence. Americans like to imagine themselves affronted by the murder of political leaders like the brothers Kennedy, or of spiritual leaders like Martin Luther King, Jr. But there is cynicism and hypocrisy implicit in our willingness to be shocked by such violence, for violence has long been an integral part of our way of life. It began with the effort to exterminate the Indian; it was confirmed as *modus vivendi* in our protracted effort to dehumanize the African. Neither human life nor human dignity is characteristically sacred to us.

The poor, the black, and the faceless have never been free of the shadow of violence, whether under color of law or through tacit consensus. The rivers and bayous of the rural South, like the streets and alleys of the black ghettoes that pockmark urban America, have a long, sad tale to tell about violence and about the forces that converge in the selection of its principal victims. But let America take notice: There is little comfort and less security to be derived from the statistics that make violence a phenomenon of the ghetto. Human sensitivity is narcotized by the implied license for selective aggression, and whenever violence is permitted or urged upon an approved subject, sooner or later the lines become blurred and one subject becomes as much of a potential target as another. It is madness to believe that the forces we have loosed in this society against the black, the poor, the disinherited will retain the power of discrimination. *A dog gone mad knows no master—only the taste of blood!*

Power and Responsibility

The alternative to an organized society, reasoned Thomas Hobbes, is a "state of nature," a dismal and unrewarding existence characterized by unlimited aggression and counteraggression; an existence in which every individual is a law unto her or himself, in which there is no definition of morality, and in which force and fraud are the respected instruments for the realization of self-interest which, in the state of nature, is the sole factor of human motivation. While it is not important that we accept Hobbes's theory as an adequate explanation of society, it is important to recognize that a society in which large numbers of people find life to be "solitary, nasty, mean, brutish and short" cannot be far from a "state of nature," by whatever name. When the power that belongs to all the people is fraudulently and consistently manipulated in the preservation of selective interests, what stake have the distressed and the oppressed in the maintenance of that society? To have all the responsibility of citizens and none of the power needed to fulfill those responsibilities is not a pervasive argument for law and order.

Responsibility without power is slavery. Power without responsibility is tyranny. If the interests of the oppressed are not among those protected by the society, if the power they relinquish is a power that is

used against them capriciously, if solitariness is exchanged for alienation, meanness for poverty, brutishness for perpetual anxiety, what
then is such a society except a sophisticated state of nature? A society in
which life is devoid of dignity, creativity, and responsibility is a
charade, which for its perennial pigeons may not prove worth the candle.

The Power in City Hall

The prime prerequisite of any organized society is power. The corollary
of power is responsibility. The logical consequence of legitimate power
responsibly exercised is peace, order, and a reasonable participation in
the common values of the society. The irresponsible exercise of power is
the invitation to anarchy and the prelude to revolution. The ultimate
expression of power is control, direct or indirect, manifest or covert.
The most sophisticated expression of power is control over decisions
and the decision-making process. Who participates in the *real* decision-
making process in America? That is an issue for Americans to ponder.
And redress.

Life in America is manipulated through the instrumentality of
decisions made or avoided. Men who sit in board rooms remote from
the scene make the decisions that control the life circumstances of
millions they have not seen, will never see, and do not want to see. When
"City Hall" was lily white, the procuration of the black ghetto was a
national scandal.

Each morning all over America the great American tragedy was re-
enacted each time a black man was forced to look at himself in the
mirror as he shaved, and each time a black woman put on the face she
would wear in her efforts to find bread for her family in the kitchens of
the elegant houses far from the decaying flats and tenements of the
racial compound to which she was assigned. What each saw in the
looking glass was a cipher citizen—an American who would have no
serious input in any of the decisions that would determine the quality of
his or her significant experiences for that day, or any day; whose life
chances had already been programmed with sinister predictability by
persons unknown, or even if known, unavailable and unconcerned.

Wherever the life chances of some are consistently manipulated by
others, freedom is in contest and the struggle to redress is inevitable.
Where freedom has been long withheld, people who have never experienced it may not know what it is precisely, but they are nevertheless
sensitive to the absence of some vital quality, an absence that deadens
their lives and eliminates them from meaningful participation in the

significant experiences of the human enterprise. Conversely, those who distrain freedom from others equate it with privilege—privilege to which they alone are entitled. That is why it is possible that America misread Martin Luther King, Jr. Certainly, not many Americans had King's full dream in mind, even though "black and white together" they locked arms and marched through the South with such apparent purpose. But the South was only the *symbol,* not the problem. The problem was attitudinal, not regional. What Dr. King wanted was not merely to reform the South but to make *all* America safe for the kind of democracy that could accept full participation of all her citizens regardless of color. Freedom implies power—*the power to be responsible.* But such power was unthinkable because black responsibility lay well beyond what America envisioned when it endorsed the black struggle to "overcome."

It will be argued that City Hall is no longer lily white; that in fact some of America's largest cities and scores of smaller towns have black mayors and other black elected officials. True. But in 1983, blacks still constitute only about 1 percent of all elected officials. Meanwhile, black income is only 56 percent of whites', *down* 5 percent from its best showing in 1970; and while 74 percent of all black men over 16 were employed in 1960, only 55 percent are employed in 1983. Other indicators of the economic status of blacks are consistent. What they say in sum is that no matter who sits in the mayor's office, the economics of being black are not substantially improved. Not yet. Black mayors win and retain their offices through coalitions with established power, and the significant interests of such power are seldom coordinate with those of the people confined to the ghetto. The black masses, whose circumstances are most desolate and most desperate, will generally remain beyond the effective reach of the most conscientious black mayor, at least for the time being. Obviously, we can improve the tentativeness of the power of black elected officials by electing more of them, and by giving stronger support to and demanding greater responsibility for those we elect, not just for blacks, but for all Americans. Only then will the black unreachable be brought into range and the democratic process have a reasonable chance to mature.

Power and Morality

Today, there is a deep suspicion that the power that informs America is at best morally indifferent, that America as a society has come perilously close to abandoning the notion that justice is possible, or even desirable, and that morality is a factor of consequence in either social relations or individual well being. Our prime commitment seems to be to expedience, and since neither justice nor morality lends itself to mere opportunism, what is "right" seems increasingly to be equated with whatever bobbles up in the ebb and flow of human intercourse. Justice, like the price of pork bellies, becomes a function of the market, and morality is whatever it takes to keep the market active.

Our distorted sense of justice at home often sends us rushing off to settle the world's problems in the style in which we still imagine best exemplifies our national image. But the national image we cherish so much at home and want so desperately to export to the world is unfortunately at serious odds with the way we are often perceived abroad. To much of the world we are "the ugly Americans." The toll we are required to pay for the privilege of being hated is astronomical, and the intent of our efforts to export our American principles and values to remote corners of the globe when our own camp is in such serious disarray invites suspicion and strains our credibility. Here at home, too often the professional brokers to whom we entrust our moral investments do not themselves show the best evidence of serious commitment. In consequence, the moral leadership of our seminal institutions is frequently quite shallow and unconvincing. Government, religion, communications, education, and even the family are all susceptible and suspect. Moral management by consignment or by consensus is restructuring our moral patterning through the casual, almost subliminal substitution of so-called "alternative values" designed to erase the age-old distinctions between up and down, right and wrong, the beautiful and the monstrous.

Today, we are invited to believe that the only real responsibility persons have is to themselves and their own gratifications, and that all moral alternatives are equally valid since they have no meaningful reference beyond the self. Cloaked in the casuistry of our new sophistication, this ancient, convenient nonsense is no less destructive for all its cleverness. And it is no less vulgar for all the notables who endorse it through fear, or by default, or merely because in a moment of weakness they prostitute themselves to the cheap opportunism that the retreat from responsibility always seems to engender. But it *is* confusing, for we live in a time when the issues of personal and social intercourse are exceedingly complex, and the parameters of personal and social responsibility grow more indistinct with each new problem we are called upon to confront. In recent times the enduring problem of racism has been joined by such formidable issues as abortion, euthanasia, biogenetics, nuclear energy, technocracy, and the arms race. Ironically, these are all of a piece. They are all new expressions of our troubled understanding about the value of human life and the inalienable rights that inure to it.

Civilized Decadence

The price of freedom is always the risk that it may be corrupted or taken away by perverse ideologies, which claim shelter under its protection, and the decline of great civilizations is characteristically initiated by internal assaults on their systems of value. If the eternal verities by which society is ordered can be forced into question, if the good, the true, and the beautiful can be challenged openly and without fear, that is democracy. But if democracy is patently and inherently masqueraded as a reasonable "alternative" to that which affirms human life, human dignity, and human responsibility, we need not worry about armies of invasion. The civilization where this can happen is self-committed to dissolution and demise.

We have never come close to realizing the notion of *righteous empire* that excited the Puritan founders of this society, but we seem further from that ideal now than ever before. Our minds are keener, our perceptions are more acute, our information is more prodigious, but our selfish inconsistency disarms our determination to succeed. Somehow we have managed to survive a full generation of domestic tension and turmoil. The feverish fifties, the savage sixties, the sensual seventies are mercifully behind us, but their harvest is still to be winnowed. The schoolhouse door has lost its attraction for political posturing. The cattle prods are sheathed, the snarling attack dogs have been leashed, the church bombers have cached their dynamite, and the storm troopers have put away their dark glasses and scraped the gore from their billy clubs. Surfeited with blood, and reproved by the world for our savagery, we persist in fitfully trying to blot out the reality that haunts us. But reality will not go away, and to recognize reality is to return to responsibility. There is no compromise.

Anxiety is the characteristic mood of our times, and our national sentiment seems to echo that forlorn old blues entreaty that goes:

Hurry, hurry sundown
See what *tomorrow* brings
Please hurry, hurry sundown
Let's see what tomorrow brings. . . .

Tomorrow? However painful it may be, the fact is that before we can have tomorrow, we must first get through today. That, in brief, is the crux of our dilemma. We will never create the bright new world we dream about until we confront the tawdriness of the world we have made with a new kind of determination to tidy the litter of our decadence. We still have time to relearn, if we have the will, that there is evil in the world, and that to compromise with evil in any of its guises is to be destroyed by it. A system of values without consistency and without constraint cannot be trusted with the ordering of any society worthy of the name. And if our commitment is merely to be narcotized rather than to earn the tranquility to which we hold ourselves entitled, then we must be prepared for the delirium and the agony that come inevitably when the fix has lost its magic and the morning after has arrived.

Countless billions of dollars and untold quantums of time and energy have been poured into a continuing patchwork of strategies designed to reserve for some what belongs to all, and millions of lives have been shortchanged or corrupted in the process. Our racial madness has exacted an enormous toll of American potential in the form of poverty, ignorance, race hatred, self-hatred, high mortality, low morality, insecurity, ethical compromise, and selective exclusion from the ordinary pursuit of the common values we all helped to create. We shall never know what genius, black and white, has been sacrificed to the racial Moloch, which designated some of us to be keepers and others to be kept. The possibilities stagger the imagination. What great music was never written? What miracles of medicine remain undiscovered? What strategies for peace and understanding among the nations of the world have never been developed because we have been preoccupied with building the fences and closing the doors that eliminate the kept and enervate the keepers, to the inconvenience of everybody and to the impairment of our common capacity to get on with the dream we once dared to believe in?

The toll of our sickness continues to escalate, for our guilt is scarcely camouflaged in the abuse of power, sex, drugs, and people—and more particularly in self-abuse. The frantic pursuit of momentary escape from the nagging realization that there is a dilemma, an open chasm between what we claim to be and what we are, dominates our private agendas, colors our national character, and subjects us to international blackmail and ridicule. Our principal allies suffer our eager support even as they castigate our pretensions and impatiently await our demise. And, as if to hold up a mirror before our unwilling eyes, those protégé nations we have appointed ourselves to save uniformly reflect our own bent for the repression of *their own* exploited classes in order to sustain the interests of their own privileged elite.

Such are the tragedies we have opted to live with, an enormous price to pay for the doubtful privilege of aborting the human values to which we subscribe with our reason by abandoning them to our passions. Life, dignity, creativity, and responsibility are more than mere maxims to hang on the walls of our pretense at civilization. *They are the conditions of human existence.* They are the values by which societies honor themselves, sustain themselves, and distinguish themselves, or, in failing their observance, commit themselves to ruin and to oblivion.

Notes

This speech was first presented at the C. Eric Lincoln Lectureship Series, Clark Atlanta University, Atlanta, GA, 1983, as the inaugural lecture.

1. W. E. B. DuBois, *The Souls of Black Folk* (Greenwich, CT: Fawcett Publications, 1961), p. 23.

2

C. Eric Lincoln: A Scholar for All Seasons

Charles H. Long

Introduction

It is with pleasure that I write this essay dedicated to my dear friend C. Eric Lincoln. I knew Eric for over 50 years. We first met as graduate students at the University of Chicago and since those graduate student days we were in touch, in friendship, in scholarly ventures, in collaborations and deliberations about our work. It was a rich and rewarding association.

Let me begin, therefore, in a rather personal manner. Eric and I were part of a coterie of University of Chicago Divinity School students who lived in the dormitory of the Chicago Theological Seminary in the early 1950s. This little group included three African Americans, two Euro-Americans, a Japanese American, and an Indian national. The two European Americans had just graduated from Yale University. The three African Americans had come in a rather willy-nilly manner to graduate school. I think one of us had come from Morehouse College, another from an extra academic program in France after World War II, and Eric from Clark College and a few other places. I know that he had spent some time in Chapel Hill, North Carolina, before coming to Chicago. When I say that this coterie was composed of the seven of us I meant that we decided, in that way that friendships are made, to be friends—to form a group.

We were thus already a distinctive social body in that context, but among us Eric was unique. I think now that I would say that his uniqueness derived from the fact that Eric was a *writer*. We all wrote and some of us wrote well, but what we wrote were academic papers.

Eric also wrote academic papers, quite excellent ones, but Eric wrote all the time. He wrote essays, poems, short stories, novellas, and so on. Eric wrote because he was a writer. Now as we all know, being a writer is much more than simply the act of writing. There is an entire epistemology contained in writing, and I will say something more about this later.

Being a writer meant that even Eric's academic papers were different from ours. He had a way of including what one would call a great deal of nonacademic material in his paper, a kind of "street-wise knowledge" that we knew our professors knew nothing about, and he got away with it. I once read a paper he had planned to turn in to our Old Testament professor in which he had taken such creative license that I just knew that he was going to get a very bad grade. He received the best grade possible in the course! That took courage, and I think that even though Eric's was a God-given talent for writing, for him to be a serious writer always took courage.

I mention this incident because in Eric's career as an academic and as a person of letters he was able to integrate the poetic vision with the logic of the intellect. This gave his work a distinctive quality and style. I should like to discuss our friend and colleague under three categories. First of all, C. Eric Lincoln's sociological vision: race, ethnicity, and culture; second, concreteness and community; and finally, imagination and reality.

C. Eric Lincoln's Sociological Vision: Race, Ethnicity, and Culture

Eric Lincoln is a part of a distinguished tradition of African American intellectuals whose major disciplines have been in the human and social sciences. We have only to remember such luminaries as W. E. B. DuBois, E. Franklin Frazier, Carter G. Woodson, Charles S. Johnson, Benjamin E. Mays, St. Clair Drake, and John Hope Franklin. As distinguished as this group may be, Eric is distinctive among them. His distinction lies in the manner in which he took religion with utmost seriousness in his academic and personal life. Of course I don't mean to imply that this great tradition of African American academics paid no attention to religion or to the African American church. There is Mays, who did so as a theologian and educator, and one can never forget the work of Frazier. But in a sense Frazier did not really know how to speak in an affirmative and consistent manner about religion and church among African Americans. Possibly only St. Clair Drake, a sociologist, comes close to Eric's critical empathy regarding this tradition, and even here, there is a difference. I think that difference has to do with the fact that Eric is a writer, and by that I mean that his poetic style allows for a nonmechanistic manner of knowing what is concrete and human.

Eric, as a person of letters and a scholar, is an interpreter of life. There is a bias against the academic as a person of letters, especially in the human and social sciences. Had he been a mathematician or physicist, he could get away with this much better, but to construe human reality from one of the social and human sciences and still possess a poetic vision is anathema! This did not deter him at all. His best literary work is at the same time his best sociological work, and his best sociological work demonstrates the integrity of his poetic vision.

Eric accepts the "given." That in and of itself is a hard thing for an African American to do. He accepted the fact that he is here in the United States and the circumstances that brought that about. He accepted the fact that other persons and groups are also here and that their being here is the result of circumstances not of his own doing. He accepts the fact of human difference; he not simply accepts it but rejoices in it. And he accepts the givenness of human hope and human creativity. It is from this perspective that we must understand his sociological vision. It is not a small, mean, narrow view of the meaning of the human as *Homo socius*. It is a much broader understanding of human beings and their relationships, which, in all of their ambiguity, tragedy, and joy, are part of the ultimate meaning of existence.

In the words of Langston Hughes, Eric loved the "sweet flypaper of life."[1] And in this regard he is very much like W. E. B. DuBois, who is one of the few other African Americans who was both a social scientist and a person of letters. DuBois wrote three autobiographies, works of fiction and fact, and solid historical and sociological monographs; lectured; did extensive editing; and more. But for the most part, the general public remembers his sociological vision as contained in *The Souls of Black Folk*.[2] This poignant treatise, first published in 1903, is still in print, and his development of the notion of "double consciousness" is one of the great tributes to the poetical epistemology. The same might be said of C. Eric Lincoln. It may be that only scholars will remember his scholarly works, but his other works will become the common property of all for they are equally works of the human heart and head.

While highly self-conscious of his identity as an African American and while highly conscious of the history of vicissitudes—the literal and normal war made upon him and his community—Eric did not give in to the narrowness of racialist absoluteness. As far as I know, he was always open and free in his converse and collaboration with all members of the human community. He never simply limited his orientation, scholarly or otherwise, to the hegemony of a racial or national group. This is one way in which he accepted the givenness of his freedom. His work, while concentrating on the African American community and its religion, placed this community within the sameness of the human, a sameness that can be known only in the form of its distinctive differences.

Concreteness and Community

Eric's first scholarly monograph was his work entitled *The Black Muslims in America*.[3] This work was published in 1961. In 1962 another book appeared on the same group, E. U. Essien-Udom's *Black Nationalism: A Search for an Identity in America*. This is a good book and as a historian of religions, I would even say an excellent book, but it is not *the* book on this movement. The reason that C. Eric Lincoln's book is still the defining book is because of Eric's sense of context and interpretation. Yes, Eric is a Christian, and no, he does not like cultural-religious absolutism. Yet Eric was able to gain the confidence of the Nation of Islam such that he had a certain private access not only to what was going on but also to the meaning of the internal dynamics of Islam within the dynamics of American culture. Our friend and scholar Essien-Udom has written a valuable text, but it lacks a certain insight— and, I would say, poetical insight. Essien-Udom in the last analysis is alien to this context and to the American reality. Eric Lincoln is intimate with the Muslims and with America. This is his country and his people.

Eric sees with another eye. Why are these people, who a generation or two ago would be Baptist and African Methodist Episcopal ministers, now Muslims? Who are these young kids who a few years back would have been trying out for baseball and are now the "Fruit of Islam"? In his perception Eric saw difference and sameness; the difference was becoming the same and the same was becoming different. The structures were intact but they had reversed themselves. That reversal had to do with the Muslims, yes, but more than that it had to do with the style and shape of America. And this is where he has been so valuable as a person and a scholar. I don't know any other sociologist of religion who had the eminently good sense to raise the issue of comparison between Mormons, Jews, and Black Muslims—all groups who for

various reasons have wanted to maintain a prideful and outside interpretation of the power and reality of American culture. In that stroke of
insight, best evidenced in his *Race, Religion, and the Continuing
American Dilemma,* Lincoln makes it clear that he has moved to a new
level, an-other ground of meaning of all the major terms in the title of
the book. As a matter of fact, the text implies rather strongly that if such
a move is not made, then America will always be a conundrum and a
dilemma.

In this manner Eric threatens us with his understanding and perception of the American past. His courteous and professional attitude
toward all persons and groups proves that there need not be confusion
about the relationship of manner and tact to poetic wisdom and
intellectual truth. Two fundamental threats are present in his work:
One is in his first book, the other in his last scholarly work and his
novel. Both are threats of social reality, but not black folk or African
American threats per se. To the extent that they are black or African
American threats, they are what they are by virtue of the autonomous
roles that culture and society has imprisoned African Americans in. It is
not color that is the threat; the only threat for the human person or
group is power. At the end of his book on the Black Muslims, Lincoln
tells us how those African Americans became Black Muslims as the only
avenue to an-other power that could be waged against the imprison-
ment of their persons and communities. He is careful to distinguish
between the genuine religious and sincere option of Islam as a mode of
reality in the world and the amalgam, like all visible religions of this
authentic genuine orientation to the cosmos and its soteriological
meaning. The Black Muslims are in the jeremiad or messianic tradition
of *David Walker's Appeal.*[4] Eric saw this when many ordinary intelligent persons as well as the academy looked upon them as aberrant,
cultic, and bizarre, when in point of fact they were as American as
baseball, apple pie, and motherhood. Such is the concrete insight of Eric
Lincoln's sociological imagination.

In so many respects, Eric was a quintessential American. He admired
in his heart of hearts the bodacious claims of the American revolution
and believed that, in point of fact and order, there could be on the face
of the earth a new kind of human being. A human being that could and
would admire, understand, and build a concrete community of meaning, understanding, and affection that was different from what was the
case in Europe, Asia, Africa, and other parts of the world. Anyone who
has read his work with care feels this vision in his words. But with this
vision they must also feel the concretion of his tragic vision.

Why, why, why, given the time and space and the whole range of human foibles, could we not do as a nation what could and should have been done? I know the despair of this question was in him. I have heard him weep and moan and wail, "Yahweh, why are you messing with us?" There was in this man a hard concreteness, a knowing observation, related as much to the Black Muslims as to the Negro baseball teams that he traveled with for years over the dusty roads of the South and Midwest; their cry is the same.

Imagination and Reality

Allow me to take another style and tact at this point. Given the acceptance of the given, the poetical vision of *Homo socius,* and the failure of the American dream for all Americans, whether they realize it or not, what are Eric Lincoln and the sociology of religion all about anyway? In a different style and tone I want to say what I have said before: Eric is about the meaning and interpretation of life, whatever way it comes or goes. The French sociologist Pierre Bourdieu has defined the arena of practice as a *habitus,* a process that transcends the dichotomies of the social world.[5] I like this in relationship to what I want to say about Eric at this point because it allows me to venture a guess about how he holds together and integrates so many disparate aspects of his life and experience.

By *habitus,* Bourdieu refers to embodied and internalized histories, forgotten because they have been internalized, that make up the spontaneous unconsciousness that propels people into action. It is the active presence of a whole past experienced as unconscious that determines most of our action. The *habitus* is a spontaneity without consciousness or will, opposed as much to the mechanical necessity of things without history in mechanistic theories as it is to the reflexive freedom of subjects, it is "without inertia" in rationalistic theories. The dualistic vision that recognizes only the transparent act of consciousness or the externally determined thing has to give way to the real logic of action, which brings together two objectifications of history, objectification in bodies and objectifications in institutions, or, which amounts to the same thing, two states of capital, objectified and incorporated, through which a distance is set up from necessity and its urgencies. I have paraphrased Bourdieu to get us back into the concrete imagination of C. Eric Lincoln.

I wanted to use this more complex explanation rather than simply use the cliché and say that he was a realist. Too often that cliché means that he puts on a sensitivity but, like all the rest of us, deals with the bottom line, but that would be only a ploy. I know Eric too well to acquiesce to this small solution.

Eric was a realist, but not an abstract realist, as if he knew it all, as if there were no variations in human beings or persons, as if there was an invariant human nature. But on the other hand, in any situation Eric would reject the fact that any human being or group does exactly what they say they are doing. In other words, Eric as an interpreter of life was in life and it was from that perspective afforded him in life that he makes an assessment of the probabilities of what life really is and ought to be. He was different from other sociologists and sociologists of religion because he imagined life within life rather than found it necessary to imagine life as a separation and alienation from life as the sine qua non of theory. Here again is where the poetic imagination as sociological vision makes itself known. It is at this point that Eric as academic scholar, sociologist of religion, and person of letters found himself in the hands of a methodological god! I say "methodological god," for anyone who knew him as I did and who was a perceptive interpreter would ask that question. I know him already as a believer and even as a preacher—but that is personal. I wish to talk more about the integrity of his totality in the terms of God and gods.

In one sense his imagination of America was always seen ideally in terms of the meaning of human exchanges. Exchanges that would establish the intimacies and relationships, the valuations and the pro-prieties, the possibilities for differences in peace and not alienations in terror. His was the sociological vision of Marcel Mauss's total presenta-tions, where the basis of economic relations, the valences of the human relations, and thus the kind of quality of the things and gifts exchanged were venerated as modes of human sentiment.[6] This is what Mauss called a system of total presentation, and thus the exchange of goods and services evokes a range of emotions, illusions, ideals, possibilities, etc. This is real human sociology! And this is the basis for a real sociology of religion. The powers and gods appear in *practice* and not in theory; these extra human beings and surpluses of exchange form the interstices of continuities and disjunctions of the nature of human relationships; they are the correlatives of genuine human exchange.

Professor Lincoln's scholarly imagination and critique don't embody this orientation as much as his life stands as a living testimony to it. In the course of his life and career he taught many, encouraged several, edited and abetted the works of others, was friend and counselor; he lived the exchanges as gifts of the human spirit manifested in concrete form.

As a part of this he unselfishly made it his responsibility to let the common folk know about what was going on, not by speaking or writing down to them but through identifying himself with their *habitus* and using his resources of mind and matter to tell them about the issues of the day. His exchange of ideas has been at the same time an exchange of the matter of things.

Herein did his faith in God abide, not as pie in the sky but in the concreteness, and all too often, the hard concreteness of the life of human exchanges; this is where he met God; this is where it hurt, and this was the place of real joy for in the last analysis one never meets God alone for too long. Others have joined Eric in pain and sorrow, in joy and exultation, and in the sharing of the richness of life. For Eric Lincoln, scholar and poet, a person for all seasons, we have indeed been blessed by your presence. May you rest in peace.

Notes

This speech was first presented at the C. Eric Lincoln Lectureship Series, Clark Atlanta University, Atlanta, GA, 1990.

1. Langston Hughes, *The Sweet Flypaper of Life* (New York: Hill and Wang, 1955).
2. W. E. B. DuBois, *The Souls of Black Folk* (Greenwich, CT: Fawcett Publications, 1961).
3. C. Eric Lincoln, *The Black Muslims in America* (Boston: Beacon Press, 1961).
4. David Walker, *David Walker's Appeal: To the Coloured Citizens of the World, but in Particular, and Very Expressly, to Those of the United States of America* (Baltimore, MD: Black Classics Press, 1993).
5. Pierre Bourdieu, *Outline of a Theory of Practice* (Cambridge: Cambridge University Press, 1977).
6. Marcel Mauss, *The Gift: The Form and Reason for Exchange in Archaic Societies* (London: Routledge, 1990).

3

The "American Dilemma" in the Life and Scholarship of C. Eric Lincoln

Mary R. Sawyer

Introduction

I have entitled this essay "The 'American Dilemma' in the Life and Scholarship of C. Eric Lincoln" because an examination of either his life or his scholarship makes it abundantly clear that the one cannot be separated from the other.

C. Eric Lincoln was a historian and a sociologist who brought the tools of these disciplines to bear on his investigation of race and religion in America. While he would not name himself a theologian, he was trained in religious ethics, and these disciplinary perspectives are also evident in his life-long role as commentator on the state of America's soul. But if he drew skillfully on the resources of his academic training, it was his own sense of moral indignation, on the one hand, and concern for humanity, on the other, that infused his life's work with passion and compassion.

Gazing over the landscape of Lincoln's scholarly contributions, it readily becomes apparent that his life's loves were not of a small order. He loved his country—loved America's ideals, loved her promises, loved her people and her possibilities—and he loved the Christian faith—loved its ideals, loved its promises, loved its people (at least some of them) and its possibilities. He cherished them both in spite of the fact that country and faith alike, in their institutional manifestations, had not only failed him but deeply wounded him.

Lincoln was born black in a nation that exalted whiteness, and this fact is of greater significance in determining the content and character of his scholarship than all his degrees and academic experiences put together. He acknowledges the woundedness in autobiographical references in two of his books: *My Face is Black,* published in 1964, and *Coming Through the Fire: Surviving Race and Place in America,* published in 1996. Because the indignities he suffered were not only deeply personal but inherently communal, he spoke not just for himself but for the multitudes of those who had been wounded in the 400 years since the colonizing of these lands. In doing so, he assumed the role that in religious terms we designate as that of a prophet.

Prophets speak not only "on behalf of," but "in admonishment of." Accordingly, in nearly all of his writings we hear the themes of the brokenness of his country and the brokenness of his faith community. But we hear as well his affirmation of a portion of this faith community— namely, the black religious community as expressed in the Black Church.

Lincoln might have exercised the role of prophet within the parameters of the church. He was, after all, an ordained United Methodist minister (a role to which I will return). But clearly his call was to the academic world (of which more will be said later), and so he made a sanctuary of his classroom, pastored to his flock of students, taught from the hallowed grounds of his lectern, and preached from the pulpit of his pen. Like the poet and song writer that he was, he wove cadenced, harmonic variations around his central text: the immorality of race relations in the United States.

Biography Matters

In 1944, when Lincoln was 20 years old—already four years out of high school—a Swedish sociologist named Gunnar Myrdal published an exhaustive study of race in the United States. The study was called *An American Dilemma.*[1] In one of our many conversations about the American Dilemma, Lincoln shared with me that he had once met Myrdal in person. "We had a long discussion," he said, "and we didn't like each other very much. But that's beside the point," Lincoln added. "I'm still very appreciative of his work." What Lincoln was most appreciative of, it has seemed to me, was the very phrase "American Dilemma" as a shorthand for the discrepancy between America's creed and America's conduct where race was concerned. The phrase captured for Lincoln the one issue that most defined his existential being, which in turn defined his scholarly endeavors.

Lincoln's autobiographical presentation in the 1964 book begins: "My face is black. This is the central fact of my existence, the focal point of all meaning so long as I live in America. I cannot transcend my blackness, but this is only a personal inconvenience. The fact that America cannot transcend it—this is the tragedy of America."[2]

Twenty years later, in 1984, Lincoln published a book entitled *Race, Religion, and the Continuing American Dilemma.* It begins with these words: "This book is a distillation of a wide-ranging series of lectures on various aspects of what Gunnar Myrdal aptly identified as the 'American Dilemma' nearly fifty years ago. I have continued to address the dilemma, because it's still there. . . ."[3] It was still there in 1996 when he wrote *Coming Through the Fire: Surviving Race and Place in America,* which opens with these words:

> *Coming through the Fire* began as "Notes on Race" in the series of journals I kept from 1941 until they were destroyed by fire fifty years later. I am not exactly certain of what I intended to do with the thousands of entries made under "Race," but I found the whole matter of racist behavior fascinating and spent many, many hours over the decades detached from my own involuntary participation in the phenomenon, trying to understand its logic and account for its pervasiveness.

Lincoln will perhaps forgive me for suggesting that one does not keep journals on a singular topic for 50 years if one is truly personally "detached." Furthermore, while scholarly discourse was for him a necessary venue for presenting his analyses of the matter of race, it was not a sufficient venue. Ultimately, he turned to fiction and poetry to express more fully his insights about the "logic" of race, publishing both a novel (*The Avenue, Clayton City*), which won the Lillian Smith Award for Southern Literature, and a book of poems, *This Road Since Freedom.*

Perhaps the one insight about race in America that was most meaningful for Lincoln was the realization that it was intimately, intricately tied up with the matter of religion. Just as his earliest lessons about race were learned in his boyhood, so, too, were his earliest lessons about religion. Lincoln knew firsthand the nature of the "American dilemma" long before Myrdal put it into those words.

I, in contrast, did not. I was born in the year 1944. I was born innocent of the causes of America's dilemma, but born nonetheless a white Protestant—a descendant of the population that created the dilemma and a member of the population responsible for its continuance. In my growing-up years in rural Nebraska—in the very heartland of America—I knew nothing of the trials of a black manchild growing up in the racially segregated South. But I heard in my little Presbyterian church the same message that young C. Eric (Charles, as he was then known) had heard 20 years earlier in Village View Methodist Church in Athens, Alabama: All people were equal in the eyes of God.

It was, perhaps, the most radical idea either of us encountered in our respective childhoods, though at the time I scarcely thought it radical. This appreciation came to me only when I learned, upon leaving home in the early 1960s, that other people who named themselves Christian did not live out this central tenet of the faith. Richard Allen must have smiled upon me from heaven. "Blessed child, innocent child, naïve child," I can imagine him saying. "How much you do have to learn." Lincoln, in contrast, was stripped of his innocence while still a youngster.

In writing of his experience of growing up in the church, Lincoln recalled that "the Village View Methodist Church was for a very long time the symbol of God's love and concern for me." But this under-standing only intensified his theological questioning of the world outside the church, which was ruled by contradictions. Troubled by the inconsistencies between "the faith as taught and the faith as expressed," he approached his pastor for an explanation. The pastor's reply was that "religion is a sometime thing. It depends on who has it, as to whether it's *this* or whether it's *that*. But God knows it when he sees it." This was, Lincoln was to recall, "a bitter revelation," and he became "very greatly disturbed" about this "two-level faith."[4]

In the 1960s and seventies, as I also became increasingly disturbed about the faith as taught and the faith as practiced by white Christians, I relied heavily on the teaching, preaching, and writing of Martin Luther King, Jr., Phillip Lawson, and James Cone for interpretations of the faith that conformed to my own understandings. I became interested in the formal study of the Black Church in 1978 while working for the lieutenant governor of California, who was himself black. Somehow, Lincoln's edited book of readings, *The Black Experience in Religion,* came into my hands, and I recall Governor Dymally and myself discussing the various essays in the book as we traveled from campaign stop to campaign stop.

When, upon Dymally's defeat in the re-election bid, I decided to enroll in graduate school, I wrote to a number of universities expressing my interest in studying black religion and black politics. Some of them responded perfunctorily with a form letter; some responded not at all. C. Eric Lincoln responded with a personal letter telling me that he knew of no such program already in place, but that if I wanted to come to Duke University, he would be happy to work with me. I did, and he did.

Although Lincoln is best known for his writings on the "Black Muslims in America," which was the title of his very first—and now classic—book, his preeminent concern, I am persuaded, was Christianity: what people did to it, and with it, and in the name of it. He wrote about Judaism and Islam—he was a devoted advocate for positive interfaith relations—but it was the brokenness within the Christian family and especially within Protestant America that brought forth at one and the same time his most scathing criticism and his most ardent affirmation.

Christianity is, was, and always has been at the crux of the American Dilemma. America was shaped by white Christians who espoused a creed of equality and freedom on the one hand while enacting a code of racial exclusion, diminishment, and terrorism on the other. Given the centrality of white Protestants and white churches in creating and sustaining the dilemma, Lincoln could hardly forswear a critique of the Protestant establishment.

The Protestant Establishment

While references to the white establishment churches may be found throughout Lincoln's writing, his assessment of them is presented most systematically in a chapter of *Race, Religion, and the Continuing American Dilemma* entitled "The Racial Factor in the Shaping of Religion in America." He might have entitled it "The Religious Factor in the Shaping of Race in America." From the practice of segregating free blacks in northern antebellum white churches to the suppression of black churches in the South, from the preaching of a censored version of the gospel emphasizing pacifity and obedience to the invocation of biblical stories to justify slavery in the first place, white Christians compromised their claim to religious authority and authenticity. Throughout the periods of slavery and Jim Crow segregation, Lincoln writes, "The essential factor at work was a racial tribalism which militated against sharing a common experience with Blacks as equals under any circumstances, religious or otherwise. Social distance must not be breeched by the ordinary amenities of common worship."[5]

Nor had there been, in Lincoln's mind, any serious amelioration of this prejudice-based arrangement as late as the 1960s:

Three hundred years later the churches of America would still be in scandalous agitation over the same issue. There would be kneel-ins and lockouts, and black caucuses and demands for reparations, and a variety of other forms of behavior which, in a Christian democracy, must have appeared to be bizarre to the most tolerant of observers.[6]

Lincoln's assessment from the vantage point of the 1980s was that this "agitation" had had minimal impact on white churches.

> The Black Church has learned something of how power is acquired and how it may be expended to best effect, but whether the church in America has the power and the will to deal effectively with the American dilemma remains critical to its spiritual integrity no less than to its social relevance.

While the major white communions have an impressive variety of strategies, boards, commissions, and committees designed to deal with the embarrassments of racism at some level, none of them speaks effectively to the underlying causes that produce the embarrassments. In fact, while some are undoubtedly sincere and well-intentioned, most of the church commissions or agencies devoted to the issues of racism are embarrassments. Or they would be if we were not so effectively vaccinated against the possibility of an onset of Christian conscience. Incredible as it may seem, racism is seen as primarily a problem to be dealt with overseas. But emphasis ranges from the most casual and incidental references, which merely recognize the problem, to in-house bureaucracies charged with doing something nice about it. In either case, such programs usually turn out to be ponderously innocuous. As Lincoln writes:

> Their chief accomplishment is the happy illusion that the problem is being addressed and that the Christians in *their* church can pursue their usual interests without undue concern about what they see in the streets or read in the press. Their dues have been paid. It *is* an illusion, and the great tragedy of our dilemma is the persistent notion that, having made our ritual ablutions, we are entitled to the peace of the blessed.[7]

"The vast majority of black Christians," Lincoln went on to say, "are not impressed by the quality of the efforts of the White Church to be truly relevant in the rollback of centuries of racially induced disability and exclusion." In fact, Lincoln noted, "The diminished expectations that the White Church will ever address itself seriously to racism in America, and the increasing awareness of its own potential for self-help, have both agonized and energized the contemporary Black Church."[8]

And so Lincoln turned his attention to the history and substance of black churches.

Lincoln was determined that the Black Church be given its due, that it be rescued from the disparagement to which it had long been subjected by white and black scholars alike. That emphasis, too, might be seen as a response, in part, to Myrdal's work, for the full title of his study was *An American Dilemma: The Negro Problem and American Democracy*. Lincoln suffered no illusion that there ever was a "Negro" problem; unequivocally it was a Christian problem, and specifically a white Christian problem, for black Christians had never been complicit in constructing systems of slavery or segregation.

Lincoln was respectful of his sociologist predecessors—W. E. B. DuBois and Benjamin Mays and E. Franklin Frazier—who had written about the Negro Church, but he discerned that there was much more to be said on behalf of the Black Church tradition, not only in terms of its centrality in the black community but in terms of its prophetic role as the moral voice of America.

The Prophetic Character of the Black Church

The context for Lincoln's characterization of the Black Church was precisely the historic racism of the United States and of established churches in the United States. "The extraordinary genius of the Christian religion," he asserted, "is exemplified in the fact that it has always managed to survive its distortions."

> The strategy of American Christianity failed in its effort to make black Christians a class of spiritual subordinates. For, in accepting Christianity in America, the Africans were not necessarily accepting American Christianity. The God they addressed and the faith they knew transcended the American experience. If the white man's religion sacrificed its moral and spiritual validity to the Baal of white supremacy, the Black Church was born of the firm conviction that the racial Baal was a no-god.[9]

Conjoined with the distortions of Christianity were the distortions of the nation as it was coming into being. Lincoln's emphasis on this religious-political relationship was typified in this excerpt from a 1981 address:

> Seldom indeed in the annals of human history has a nation been born under such auspicious circumstances, with so many mature and able

statesmen attending her birth. Never before in modern times has a nation been so certain of the sure hand of God on the tiller of its destiny, or committed itself so irrevocably to divine hegemony and precept. And never has any nation found itself in such wretched default of its own avowed principles before the words of our founding document were fairly formed, or the ink was dry on the parchment. And therein lies the genesis of our continuing dilemma, our national sickness.

In the language of the faith we claim to cherish, America has sinned—mightily, consistently, and with conscious deliberation. Our cardinal sin is idolatry—corporate racial idolatry. This is our national disease. And from this malignancy there oozes a corruption which poisons and contaminates everything it touches.[10]

It is statements such as these that prompt one to characterize Lincoln's scholarly career as one long jeremiad.

During the founding years of this nation, the style of preaching termed "jeremiad," in honor of the biblical prophet Jeremiah, was a familiar rhetorical expression in America's public religious tradition. In its generic form, the jeremiad contains several elements: an analysis of a crisis situation, a reminder of the covenant with God, an assessment that some have failed to keep the covenant, a call to repentance and renewed obedience, and a prediction of the consequences should the people fail to restore the covenantal relationship.[11] In the pulpits of messianic black clergy, jeremiads came to have a specific focus, namely, the failure of America to fulfill its "covenantal duty to deal justly with blacks." Wilson Moses uses the term "jeremiad" "to describe the constant warnings issued by blacks to whites, concerning the judgment that was to come for the sin of slavery"[12]—and later, the sin of segregation. The jeremiad was invoked by black leaders to "boldly and unrelentingly lambaste white Americans for violating the national ideals and covenant by their racism."[13]

Lincoln clearly stood in this tradition, though, as I have noted, his pulpit was in the university rather than the church. Lincoln once told a story of his brief foray into serving a local church following his ordination. Every Sunday, he said, he would work mightily to present a good sermon. After a few months of such earnest endeavor, one of the church mothers said to him, as he greeted her following the service: "That was a fine lecture, son. You keep tryin' and one of these days you'll be *preachin'*." That, Lincoln said, was the day he decided his career was to be in academia. But for the rest of his life, he continued to "preach" a jeremiad, for the theme of the American Dilemma is a constant refrain in nearly everything he wrote.

Preaching a jeremiad was not enough, however. Lincoln needed for there to be something more; he needed for there to be an alternative to the deficient white churches that called themselves Christian. He needed for there to be an authentic expression of Christianity in his life and he needed for white America to know this alternative expression existed. Finally, he needed for Black America to know that it existed— existed partially in reality and partially in potential, but existed none- theless. That alternative was the Black Church.

Lincoln believed that the Black Church was a result of the American Dilemma.[14] In his book *Race, Religion, and the Continuing American Dilemma,* he writes,

> If there had been no racism in America, there would be no racial churches. As it is, we have white churches and black churches, white denominations and black denominations; American Christianity and black religion. . . . Black religion is a unique cultural precipitate, born of the peculiar American interpretation of the faith and the Blackamerican response to the anomalous schedule of exigencies that interpretation entails. It is not really possible to talk meaningfully about black religion and the Black Church without reference, implicit or explicit, to white religion and the White Church, for, in the context of American Christian- ity, one implies the other.[15]

But if the Black Church came into being because of the American Dilemma, it was not thereby *of* the American Dilemma. On the contrary, black religion and the Black Church were inherently pro- phetic. "Any religion of blacks in America," Lincoln asserted, " which did not in some fundamental way address the prevailing issues of racialism would be improbable, if not grotesque."[16] Furthermore, "Any possible black religion will be by definition the Blackamerican's answer to *white* religion—a response to the demeaning and exclusivist practices inherent in an institutionalized racism which has traditionally ignored or transcended the moral requirements of the faith."[17]

In short, the Black Church was ontologically—in its very being— prophetic. But black religion and the Black Church were more than a reaction to white Christianity, more than a "black patina on a white happening";[18] rather, they represented creative cultural expressions in their own right. For Lincoln,

> [Black] religion was the organizing principle around which [Black] life was structured. [Their] church was [their] school , [their] forum, [their]

political arena, [their] art gallery, [their] conservatory of music. It was lyceum and gymnasium as well as *sanctum sanctorum*. [Their] religion was [their] fellowship with [humanity], [their] audience with God. It was the peculiar sustaining force which gave [them] the strength to endure when endurance gave no promise, and the courage to be creative in the face of [their] own dehumanization.[19]

The Distinctiveness of Black Religion and the Black Church

Lincoln's work on black religion and the Black Church had two primary objectives: to extricate these phenomena and to explicate them—to make clear what they were *not*, and then to make clearer what they *were*. The extrication had to do with separating black religion and its institutional manifestations from oblivion or from half-truths and no-truths held by white Christians, and some black Christians as well. Writing in 1978, Lincoln commented that,

> It is inconceivable to many Americans that Blacks may think of them-selves as having a distinctive religion based on a corporate experience and a derivative worldview different from, and independent of the traditional concepts of American Protestantism. That the patterns of black *expression* of religious understanding are "different" is widely accepted as factual, but the possibility that the *content* of understanding may be significantly different is troublesome and unpopular with almost all white Christians, and with many Blacks.[20]

But, he pointed out, "There exists today a growing religious movement with strong representation . . . that sees their religious interests and expressions as being 'authentically black'—rejecting most black middle class religious expression as white religion in blackface."[21] He later acknowledged, however, that it was only recently that "scholars of American history, culture, and religion have begun to recognize that black people created their own unique and distinctive forms of culture and worldviews as parallels rather than replications of the culture in which they were involuntary guests."[22]

Lincoln, of course, was himself part and parcel of this "growing religious movement" to explicate black religion and the Black Church; indeed, he had been one of the movement's chief architects. As such, his role was not only to write about these matters himself but to facilitate the research and writing of others.

Lincoln's efforts in this regard resulted in his edited volume *The Black Experience in Religion,* which brought together some 20 articles by other scholars of black religion who were engaged in the archeological endeavor to unearth the black religious tradition. Another of his contributions was the Doubleday/Anchor C. Eric Lincoln Series in Black Religion, which published seven volumes altogether, including James Cone's second book, *A Black Theology of Liberation,* in 1970 and Gayraud Wilmore's *Black Religion and Black Radicalism* in 1972. Lincoln was known especially for mentoring young scholars, encouraging them in their pursuits, and facilitating the publication of their work.

Lincoln's own treatment of the contemporary Black Church followed from his phenomenological understanding of black religiosity, or what he referred to as the "black sacred cosmos"—by which he meant the worldview, or the spirituality, of African Americans that preceded institutional manifestations of religion. The black sacred cosmos of African Americans, he wrote, "is related both to their African heritage, which envisaged the whole universe as sacred, and to their conversion to Christianity during slavery and its aftermath."[23] The "black sacred cosmos" was not restricted to Christianity, however, but infused syncretized religions and quasi-Islamic and quasi-Jewish expressions of black religiosity as well.

At the core of this spiritual orientation or worldview was the principle of freedom. "Throughout black history," Lincoln wrote,

> the term "freedom" has found a deep religious resonance in the lives and hope of African Americans. Depending upon the time and the context, the implications of freedom were derived from the nature of the exigency. [But] from the very beginning of the black experience in America, one critical denotation of freedom has remained constant: freedom has always meant the absence of any restraint which might compromise one's responsibility to God. The notion has persisted that if God calls you to discipleship, God calls you to freedom.[24]

It was this centrality of freedom in the black sacred cosmos that further led Lincoln to assert that the Church of African Americans not only was *ontologically* prophetic and that it ought to be *manifestly* prophetic but that at times, it actually *functioned* prophetically in its utterances and its actions.

There was, after all, in the immediate past, the sterling example of black ministers in the Civil Rights movement of the 1950s and 70s, and most of all, the example of the Rev. Dr. Martin Luther King, Jr., whom

Lincoln regarded as the exemplar *par excellence* of the prophetic voice of the Black Church.[25] Indeed, he credited King with being "one of the leading architects of the developing Black Church. It was Martin Luther King," he wrote, " who made the contemporary Black Church aware of its power to effect change." In acknowledgement of his extraordinary contribution, in 1970 Lincoln edited a volume of essays on King, which he subsequently updated and expanded in 1984.[26]

Lincoln wrote about the institutional manifestations of black Christianity in two different dimensions. First is the Black Church; second are black churches. Sociologically, by "Black Church," Lincoln meant the totality of the body of black Christian believers in America—not only the traditional black denominations, but also "the black Christians in white denominations because the overwhelming majority of these," he pointed out, "are in all-black local congregations, which, except for their sources of administration and oversight, are rarely distinguishable from the autonomous black churches."[27] Existentially, the "Black Church," in his view, was "the most authentic representation of what it means to be black in America, for it is the one institution in which is crystallized the whole range of credits and debits, of genius and emotion, hope and fear, projection and recoil which characterize the random gathering of peoples of West Africa who were fused in the black experience in America."[28] Theologically,

> For the black believer, the Black Church was not only a symbol of God's intention that all . . . should be free, it was also the instrument of God's continuing revelation of that intent. In the Black Church, while God's love was unqualified, God's challenge was also unconditional, for he called every [person] to realize the highest potential of [their] humanity by being a living testament of the divine image in which [they] were cast. Since God . . . was free, and [humanity] was created free in [God's] image, then [humanity's] struggle must ever be to maintain or to recover the freedom with which [humankind] was endowed by [its] Creator. Such is the first principle of Christian responsibility. God is the archetype and the first endorser of any struggle for liberation.[29]

It followed that the Black Church in its essential character was separate from and different than the White Church. The Black Church, he wrote, "added to the White Church polity and ritual its own unique interpretation and style, in consequence of which the peculiar concerns of the black subculture found inevitable expression."[30] Lincoln allowed, however, that this was so to varying degrees at varying times.

In his 1974 book, *The Black Church Since Frazier,* Lincoln made it clear that this Black Church had not been the only institutional manifestation of African American Christianity. On the contrary, there had been that other ubiquitous institution that he named the "Negro Church." "The Black Church, he insisted, was *not* the Negro Church radicalized." The Negro Church, he said, "died in the moral and ethical holocaust of the [contemporary] Black struggle for self-documentation because the call to Christian responsibility is in fact first and foremost a call to human dignity and therefore logically inconsistent with the limitations of Negro-ness."[31]

> The Negro Church is dead because the norms and presuppositions which structured and conditioned it are not the relevant norms and presuppositions to which contemporary Blacks who represent the future of religion in the Black community can give their asseveration and support. The Black Church is or must become the characteristic expression of institutionalized religion for contemporary Blackamericans because it is the perfect counterpart of the Black man's present self-perception and the way he sees God and man, particularly the white man, in a new structuring of relationships from which he emerges freed of the traditional proscriptions that compromised his humanity and limited his hope.[32]

These words have been cited in virtually every serious analysis of the Black Church since the essay's appearance. But the words must be read carefully. "The Negro Church is dead . . . ; the Negro Church no longer exists," Lincoln wrote, and yet he also wrote, "the Negro Church that died lives on in the Black Church born of its loins, flesh of its flesh."[33] Additionally, "The Black Church is *or must become* . . . the *characteristic* expression of institutionalized religion for contemporary Blackamericans"[34] (emphasis added). I emphasize the words "or must become" the "characteristic" expression. The point is, for Lincoln the blackness of the Black Church was not total, or put another way, the Church of Blackamericans was not monolithic. But he recognized that between the early 1950s and the late 1960s, the Black Church had changed significantly and that it had the potential for still further change.

It goes without saying that Lincoln's writing in the 1970s would have been influenced by his earlier work on the Nation of Islam, by the trenchant critiques of racism and Christianity on the part of Malcolm X, and by the Black Power movement of the last half of the 1960s. He was unwilling, however—and perhaps unable—to acquiesce either to

Malcolm's rejection of Christianity as a white man's religion or to the Black Power movement's more secular rhetoric and form (even as it retained elements of the black sacred cosmos). Instead, he was determined to document and develop the blackness of the Christian churches of African Americans.

Lincoln recognized that in order to pursue this mission, more concrete information was needed about black congregations and denominations than currently existed. "What the Black Church needs to now undertake," he said in a 1978 interview, "is a critical, in-depth self-study of each constituent denomination if it is to fully appreciate its strengths and weaknesses, and if realistic plans for relevance at its full potential are to be made and implemented."[35] Enlisting a former student of his, Dr. Lawrence Mamiya, as co-director of this Lilly Endowment–funded project, Lincoln embarked upon the most comprehensive study of the Black Church that has been undertaken to date. The result was the publication in 1990 of *The Black Church in the African American Experience*.

The Black Church in the African American Experience did, in fact, provide a more empirical profile of black churches as multifaceted institutions that perform different functions in different times and places. "Black churches," the authors wrote, "are institutions that are involved in a constant series of dialectical tensions. The dialectic holds polar opposites in tension, constantly shifting between the polarities in historical time. There is no Hegelian synthesis or ultimate resolution of the dialectic."[36]

They then identified six pairs of dialectically related polar opposites, the first of which was the dialectic of "priestly and prophetic functions." Other pairs were "other-worldly versus this-worldly," "universalism and particularism," "communal and privatistic," "charismatic versus bureaucratic," and finally, "resistance versus accommodation."[37] In this model, one characteristic among the 12 is that of being prophetic, though this function is complemented by such polarities as this-worldliness and resistance.

In reporting the findings of this study, Lincoln and Mamiya essentially described what black churches looked like, what they were doing, and how they were doing it. Only implicitly was the report a statement about what black churches could become. But if this particular offering was subtle on this point, the corpus of Lincoln's writings left no doubt as to his vision and his desire for the Black Church. And these were inextricably tied to that enduring problem of the American Dilemma:

It is the black fraction who are the principal victims of our spiritual and cultural schizophrenia, and in consequence, it is black religion and the Black Church upon which the principal onus of dealing with that malady has fallen by default. . . . The same perceptions and emotional responses which hark back to an era that is mercifully behind us find continued expression in attitudes and behaviors which refuse to let what is past be done with. It is against this continuing agony that the mission of the Black Church . . . finds a compelling reason for the projection of its ministry to America.[38]

Not that he believed the Black Church alone would resolve the American Dilemma. "Only the concerted will of the American people can do that," he conceded, "but the Black Church, like the White, has a role and a mission to be seriously involved in that resolution while involvement may still make a difference."[39]

Heeding his own call to involvement, C. Eric Lincoln himself—member of the Black Church and citizen of the nation—ministered to America. Indeed, through his prophetic scholarship, Lincoln exemplified what he had written of the Black Church:

. . . However nefarious the strategies of humankind, the faith will not be rendered destitute and the righteousness of God will not be left without a witness. If the established oracles are silent or unreliable, then lo, a voice cries forth from the wilderness.[40]

C. Eric Lincoln's Relationship to the Black Church

These brief examinations of Lincoln's treatment of black and white churches would be incomplete without a further word about Lincoln's personal religious journey and specifically his relationship to the institutional church.

I have noted that he grew up in Village View Methodist Church in Athens, Alabama. This congregation, needless to say, was a racially segregated, all-black congregation, and as such a part of the Black Church as Lincoln later defined it. But the congregation was affiliated with the predominantly white Methodist Episcopal Church, South, which had split with the northern branch over the issue of slavery in the 1840s. The northern and southern branches were reunited in the 1930s, while Lincoln and his family were active members. The most divisive issue in this process was the refusal on the part of southern Methodists to allow the appointment of black bishops to southern conferences. The dispute was resolved by creating a racially segregated conference within the newly "united" Methodist Church. This segregated conference existed until 1968.

If Lincoln was not aware of these maneuverings as an adolescent, he certainly became aware of them as a student of religion. Yet, he remained a United Methodist for most of his life. He was originally ordained in the Presbyterian Church (which also had split over the issue of slavery and did not reunite until the 1980s), but then was ordained a United Methodist minister. The salient point is that he did not grow up in a traditional black denomination; he was not ordained a Baptist minister, or an African Methodist Episcopal minister, or an African Methodist Episcopal Zion or Christian Methodist Episcopal minister. He retained his United Methodist ordination even throughout the 1980s and 90s, when he regularly attended a local congregation of a traditional black church, for reasons that were rather circuitous and are discussed later.

From 1974 until the late 1980s, Lincoln was intimately involved in working with the historic black churches through the auspices of two major projects, both of which were funded by the Lilly Endowment. The first project involved a process of interdenominational dialogue that culminated in the founding of the Congress of National Black Churches, an ecumenical organization that admitted to membership only the historic black churches, while excluding black congregations in predominantly white denominations. Exceptions were made for individuals, including Lincoln, who had served as consultants in the formative conversations; Lincoln was even designated as the official historian of the congress. The second project, discussed earlier, was the national study of the Black Church in America that was published in 1990 as *The Black Church in the African American Experience.*

At least in part because he was working so closely with black church representatives in both these capacities over this extended period of time, in 1982 Lincoln began attending St. Joseph's AME Church in Durham, North Carolina. He continued to do so until 1998, though, as noted, he never relinquished his United Methodist ties. Indeed, in 1989, one of his hymns, "How Like a Gentle Spirit," was included in the main United Methodist Hymnal. The last stanza of this hymn is revealing of Lincoln's personal theology:

> Through all our fretful claims of sex and race
> The universal love of God shines through,
> For God is love transcending style and place
> And all the idle options we pursue.[41]

When he left St. Joseph's AME, it was to affiliate with a United Methodist congregation—a brand-new church, a racially integrated church. The Rev. Lawrence Johnson, one of two pastors of the congregation (one black and one white), remembers that when the call was issued for members to be a part of this racially and culturally integrated church, Lincoln was among those who attended the first meeting. "He walked in the door," recalls Rev. Johnson, "and declared, 'This is my dream. I would give up my career and all my experiences to be a part of a church like this. This is my dream.'"

Appropriately, the church was named Reconciliation United Methodist Church. During the last two years of his life, Lincoln gave time, energy, and financial support to this effort to embody Christianity as he believed it was intended to be expressed. In doing so, he was living out his own call, issued in the last pages of his last book, for "no-fault reconciliation."

By no-fault reconciliation, Lincoln meant the unequivocal "recognition that we are all of a kind, with the same vulnerabilities, the same possibilities, and the same need for God and each other."[42] He called for the building of a new, multicultural society that would transcend not only the American Dilemma but the world dilemma. He dared to hope, even, for a Church that moved beyond the color line.

> The resolution of our dilemma is in the critical interest of God and country. And it may be that, in the resolute pursuit of a common task of such challenge and magnitude, black religion and white religion will someday rediscover that larger community of interests they knew when the church was neither white nor black but just a simple fellowship of believers.[43]

For C. Eric Lincoln, Reconciliation United Methodist Church was the future for which he had worked and lived and longed: just a simple fellowship of believers—but also a portent of an America in which the dilemma was finally resolved.

Notes

This speech was first presented at the C. Eric Lincoln Forum, Candler School of Theology, Emory University, Atlanta, GA, 2001.

1. Gunnar Myrdal, *An American Dilemma: The Negro Problem and American Democracy* (New York: Harper, 1944).
2. C. Eric Lincoln, *My Face Is Black* (Boston: Beacon Press, 1961), 1.

3. C. Eric Lincoln, *Race, Religion, and the Continuing American Dilemma* (New York: Hill and Wang, 1984), p. vii.

4. C. Eric Lincoln, "The Matter of Race" (unpublished manuscript, 1959, C. Eric Lincoln Collection, the Atlanta University Center Woodruff Library, Atlanta, Georgia, 1959).

5. Lincoln, *Race, Religion,* p. 36.

6. Ibid.

7. Ibid., pp. 117–118.

8. Ibid., p. 118.

9. Ibid., pp. 58–59.

10. C. Eric Lincoln, "Come Back, Martin Luther King," address at Bennett College, Greensboro, North Carolina, January 18, 1981.

11. Richard E. Wentz, *Religion in the New World: The Shaping of Religious Traditions in the United States* (Minneapolis: Fortress Press, 1990), pp. 197–198.

12. Wilson Jeremiah Wilson, *Black Messiahs and Uncle Toms: Social and Literary Manipulations of a Religious Myth* (University Park, PA: Pennsylvania State University Press, 1982), pp. 30–31.

13. David Howard-Pitney, *The Afro-American Jeremiad: Appeals for Justice in America* (Philadelphia: Temple University Press, 1990), p. 15.

14. Lincoln, *Race, Religion,* p. xiv.

15. Ibid., pp. 31, xviii, xix.

16. Ibid.

17. C. Eric Lincoln, "Contemporary Black Religion: In Search of a Sociology," *The Journal of the I.T.C.* 5, no. 2 (spring 1978): 90.

18. From the foreword to the C. Eric Lincoln Series on Black Religion (Garden City, NY: Doubleday & Co.). This same foreword appears in each of the seven volumes in the series.

19. Ibid.

20. Lincoln, "Contemporary Black Religion," p. 92.

21. Ibid.

22. C. Eric Lincoln and Lawrence H. Mamiya, *The Black Church in the African American Experience* (Durham, NC: Duke University Press, 1990), p. 3.

23. Ibid.

24. Ibid., p. 4.

25. Writing in *Race, Religion,* Lincoln had this to say about Martin Luther King, Jr.: "While America faltered, Martin Luther King, Jr., and his followers did more to embellish the name of Western Christianity than has been done since the original Martin Luther tacked his challenge of corruptions on the door of the cathedral at Wittenberg in the sixteenth century. As a matter of fact, the high moral challenge of King's Satyagraha crusade, and his inevitable martyrdom, did more to reestablish credibility and interest in religion than all the conferences and pronouncements the American church has addressed to human dignity in many a day. King was a living example of what the faith claimed to be about; and King was by ironic necessity a product of the Black Church. . . . " p. 241.

26. C. Eric Lincoln, ed., *Martin Luther King, Jr.: A Profile* (New York: Hill and Yang, 1970, 1984). I was honored that Dr. Lincoln chose to include in the

revised edition an essay I had written about Dr. King while a graduate student of Dr. Lincoln's. This decision, however, was not based solely on the merits of my article. An essay by James Cone was also to be included in the new edition. Inasmuch as Lincoln had mentored both Cone and myself, and knowing of the regard I had for Dr. Cone, Lincoln said he thought it would be appropriate for the two of us to appear in the same book and he proceeded to arrange for that to happen.

27. Lincoln, *Race, Religion,* p. 93.
28. Ibid., p. 73.
29. Ibid., p. 63.
30. Ibid., p. 77.
31. C. Eric Lincoln, *The Black Church Since Frazier* (New York: Schocken Books, 1974), p. 106.
32. Ibid., p. 107.
33. Ibid., pp. 105–106.
34. Ibid., p. 107.
35. "A Look at C. Eric Lincoln, Scholar-Enabler Par Excellence," interview in *The National Black Monitor,* a "Family Editorial Supplement" in the *San Francisco/Sacramento Observer* 3, no. 11 (November 1978): pp. 18–23.
36. Lincoln and Mamiya, *The Black Church in the African American Experience,* p. 11.
37. Ibid., pp. 12–15.
38. Lincoln, *Race, Religion,* pp. xviii, 22.
39. Ibid., p. 258.
40. Ibid., p. xxi.
41. C. Eric Lincoln, "How Like a Gentle Spirit," in *The United Methodist Hymnal* (Nashville, TN: The United Methodist Publishing House, 1989).
42. C. Eric Lincoln, *Coming Through the Fire: Surviving Race and Place in America* (Durham, NC: Duke University Press, 1996), p. 157.
43. Lincoln, *Race, Religion,* p. 260.

4

Heroic Professor:

A Pedagogy of Creativity

Jon Michael Spencer

C. Eric Lincoln was a man of heroic proportion inspired by men and women of heroic proportion, including such academic forebears as W. E. B. DuBois, Carter G. Woodson, Charles H. Wesley, E. Franklin Frazier, and Benjamin Mays, and such historical personages as Harriet Tubman, Nat Turner, and Martin Luther King, Jr. Perhaps Lincoln was even inspired by heroic characters of African American folklore and fiction, given the creative way in which he fashioned and told almost mythic stories about the episodes of his upbringing. But of all the historic and fictional figures that could have gone into his own heroic making, it was Martin Luther King, Jr., whom Lincoln most touted as a magnificent intruder upon the historical moment.[1] One might say that it was a Kingian quality that Lincoln sought to nurture in himself and manifest as a scholar and teacher. That Lincoln in fact had this quality about him made him one whose teaching involved the personality he exuded as much as the information he imparted. Indeed, it was Lincoln's personality that gave the information he was teaching a certain charisma, or, shall we say, immediate potential for meaningfulness.

This personality of heroism that Lincoln fashioned for himself came by way of his dynamic creativity, the same that gave rise to his songs, hymns, poetry, fiction, and even his academic scholarship, and it suggests a "heroic model" of teaching, which is the subject of this creative, even Lincolnian, essay.

There are many heroic personages to whom students have been introduced through the form of history, but black people are hurt and need healing not at the level of history's form but at the level of history's substance, its meaning. The form of history, which at best documents the circumstances in which magnanimous figures rose to prophetic heights, seems calculated to wean students from creative heroic imaginings, for what the form of history cannot do is perform. That is, the form of history cannot *act* upon the fact that there are some aspects of life knowable only from the heights of experience and some aspects knowable only from the depths—the depths of life being those that one discovers for oneself, and the heights of life being those that require a worthy guide of heroic stature, one capable of bearing students up to the heights of historical meaning. How is this "bearing up" to be done?

The principal presumption of the heroic model of teaching is that teaching and learning neither begin nor end in the classroom. Students should be taught to pursue learning under their own compulsion, yes; but more importantly, the personality of the professor should draw students to engage beyond classroom, subject matter, semester, school year, and college education—thus establishing a learning relationship that is independent of the four walls and low ceilings of institutions. First and foremost, the personality of the professor should *carry,* like an idea. When the idea comes, it carries. It carries forth. It carries thinking. It carries the body, like rhythm carries. The idea carries forth and it carries back again, in a groove going around and coming back around; and what it carries back is its own ideal. There is a parameter in which ideas take shape, freeform. For every individual "called" to performance, this parameter not only adds a certain locomotion to the inclining of ideas toward thought and performance but gives ideas and thought a certain thoroughgoing character, a certain spiritual shape that beautifies the personality of thought and performance. In such a manner the personality of the professor should carry, go forth with students. The world they encounter should now be seen through the presence of this new personality in their learning lives.

For this "carrying forth" to happen, the professor must understand that each time the classroom is entered, he or she steps into community. Not only does each class comprise *a* community, but each student in a classroom comprises an infinity in carrying within his or her endless resource *the* community that sent him or her off to school. And each student in the collective community of the classroom carries forth into broader communities the transformations that heroic teaching helps set in motion, knowing that improvements in communities take root through improvement of individuals, infinite individuals. Further still, when transformative teaching leads to life-long relationships between professor and student, the impact of teaching potentially carries into the next generation and beyond. Teaching of this nature does not occur *on* the stage of classroom; rather, it occurs *at* the stage where the professor no longer *goes to* class but *brings* class wherever he or she goes, the stage where the professor no longer *goes to* perform but *brings* performance because he or she is performance. The groove is now ongoing, the line is blurred between the inside and outside of class.

This model of teaching underscores the presumption basic to the heroic model that academic space has no singular hold on teaching and learning. In fact, the only traits solely attributable to academic space tend to be negative ones: intellectual narrowness holding inmates to artificial barriers of disciplines; the relishing of certainty, symmetry, and precision over spontaneity, originality, and potentiality; the putting of knowledge into the mind of students rather than extracting it experientially from within each "heart" so that the knowing becomes more deeply meaningful; the viewing of knowledge as an attainable end rather than a window of beginning and potentiality; the prevalence of arguing in a manner not bound by truth but rather bound by constructed "reality"; the presenting of the "even" in truth while ignoring the "odd"; an ethos that permits students to think of learning as a collectable divorced from the world of meaning; and the tendency of professors to give of their form and not of their substance, their knowledge gathered from history but not their person made by history.

Education has given students too much theoretical knowledge or *about facts* that they are expected to memorize and recite back but that carry little meaning for them beyond the theory, recitation, and a good grade. This kind of teaching is form dominated. Teaching is substance dominated or substantive when it is itself an act of learning comprised of the search for meaning and when this models for students the manner in which meaning outvalues mere data. Teaching is substantive when the imprint of its "swing" is left in the groove of students' minds long after the beat is withdrawn. Teaching is substantive when learning privileges and empowers thinking capable of bringing living into maximal harmony with existence. Teaching is substantive when it reverses the trend of students being taught not to experience learning (a microcosm of their being taught not to experience life) but instead to collect data about life in order to know it theoretically rather than meaningfully. To be taught *about* (or around) something is not to know the thing itself at its center; to know something theoretically is not to know it intimately; a thing is intimately knowable only by knowing it experientially, meaningfully. Knowing something experientially means there has been an awakening of self-knowing in the light of the thing examined. This awakening of self-knowing is essential to learning, because students will not accept a professor's truth unless they have within their own experience something that already inclines them toward that truth. Thus, the slumber of not-knowing only desists when students are exposed to truth through the experience of learning, which involves an awakening of self-knowing. All else is either transparent knowledge or belief, neither of which convict and convince as regards the manner in which one lives life. In other words, the only truth is that which students themselves create through the nurture of meaning under the leadership of one whose heroicism fends off ignorance. What is ignorance? It is when one does not even react to truth that is derived from one's own meaning.

Is ignorance bliss? Certainly mere knowledge is safe to attain, while meaning lies in difficult and even dangerous places—meaning being the substance of learning, and knowledge being merely its form. Heroic teaching involves not simply the objective conveyance of information but the subjective bringing forth of meaning. The bringing forth of meaning is not learning that is ornamental to the world; it is learning that shapes the world, continuing its creation organically from within rather than formulaically from without. The bringing forth of learning is initiated or inspired from without but comes from within as probed-for meaning, activating like the body's own natural medicines, and provokes self-knowledge. This outward initiation of an inward process comes by way of the professing of a personality. Performance is the means: Like the artist, the professor nurtures a personality and performs that personality, not by force but by overflow.

It is easy enough for a professor to give of him or herself in the form of collected data. Mere data, that which students encounter in class as information but do not creatively engage, dead-ends on itself, has no beyond of meaningfulness. Form alone is insufficient for a thing to be itself in substance. Architecture is not simply the form of a structure but rather is the inner movement of space exuding outward even to the point of design and ornamentation. Religion is not outer form but rather is the inner movement of spirit exuding outward by way of spirituality embodied in personality. Form collapses on itself, form's four walls being unable to withstand the elements without something of substance propping them up from within. As a consequence of professors giving of their form and not of their substance, creative engagement in learning has been heaped over with the dirt of form and snuffed out, leaving dust and doubt. Potential, the aim of heroic teaching, can never be achieved by doubt (the *form* of learning always being a disposition of doubtful reflection), as this disposition is passive in comparison to creativity, whose nature is to pursue actively an unleashing upon the world through its particular power of personality. Creativity is like experience: one can wait for experience to come or one can pursue a way of life that is experiential. Creativity is even a certain experience—an experience of active awareness—to pursue.

For students given in to learning pessimism—namely, being grade driven and thus coming to class doubtful as regards the possibility of true learning—the attainment of creative discovery revives hope as regards the deeper value of learning: Students discover under heroic guidance that meaning comprises the road to truth, that the discovery of meaning is itself truth insofar as it is a road. Albeit neverending, this road is all along lined with lamps of wisdom, each shedding light far beyond the passageway it illuminates and onto broader regions of eye-opening landscape. Creative discovery of meaning in learning is pure joy because the attainment is always beyond expectation, beyond hopes. Although truth is always but an illumined passageway in the light of capital-t Truth, although there are many little-t truths, any truth is better than make believe and the constructions of "reality." The more truth encountered on the road of meaning, the more creativity burgeons. But even still, the hand of truth is best taken and pulled into direction by intentness of purpose—purpose being the feet and truth the eyes; otherwise, truth merely encountered and not creatively engaged dead-ends on itself, has no beyond of meaningfulness. The quest for truth on the road of meaningful learning leads to many unexpected places, and that is the purpose of having a worthy guide in a teacher of heroic proportion. Otherwise, who is to take students to "the bridge," that point of being able to say "substance of my substance" as regards the relationship between oneself and the subject of learning?

The road of meaningful learning leads to "the bridge." During the experience of learning, the inquiring and answering looks of thought begin to heighten between professor and students. The professor, always strategically ahead of the curve in the onward circular groove of learning, comes to a point of saying like James Brown, "Are you ready to go to the bridge?" If the timing is right, the class in effect answers, as does James Brown's group, "Yeah!" Knowing that each band member is to carry his and her own weight in transport to the bridge, the professor seeks certainty: "Are you ready to go to the bridge?" Again, "Yeah"—and so on. During the period of an academic course, this may be the only examination. Seeing the answer in the eyes of each student, the professor exclaims upon the bridge, in the words of James Brown's "Super Bad": "Up and down and round and round; up and down, all around"—an exegesis of the groove's circularity. Following the exegesis comes the hermeneutic: "Right on people, let it all hang out; if you don't, brothers and sisters, then you won't know what it's all about." Then James Brown beckons heroically, "Give me, give me, give me!"— the bridge transports to greater potential! When the groove gets deeper upon and subsequent to the bridge, what is happening? Students are "digging it," and that is what the experience of learning is all about. The experience of learning leads to the bridge, and the bridge leads away. Away leads to change; and under heroic teaching, everyone must change, change toward the truth, if there is to be learning.[2]

Going to the bridge is thus similar to going to the mountaintop. The mountaintop is like a tall, naked tree from whose shoulders the hawk can see. Getting there, to the mountaintop, is a learning experience, whether one is prophet, civil rights leader, or blues singer (Robert Johnson sang, "I went to the mountain, looked as far as my eyes could see").[3] At every point of a climb one sees a peak; but as one approaches that peak, one realizes that it is not the ultimate peak.

The climb continues that way, each new peak seeming to be the top but revealing other highs. Finally the summit is reached, but even from there one looks across the eye-opening landscape of sky to other mountain ranges one has not yet climbed, and one envisions yet other mountains of which there has been talk, or one looks across the world's expanse, higher and higher. But from the start of one's climb, one sees a peak that is not *the* peak, and yet one has peeked the initial peak. In other words, if a student has not yet seen the "promised land," it is because that student has not yet *made* the promised land under the guidance of an heroic professor .

There are too few students demanding heroism and creativity in their professors, and many students who get no more than what they seek: a grade. This is typical within all institutional frameworks. Members of institutions, if they even reach the minimum standards of the institution, tend not to surpass those minimum standards; they grow with the slow growth of institutions but do not grow in advance of or beyond institutional growth. As regards the radical residue in institution, that which lingers from the pre-institutionalized original, people at most strive to be comfortably uncomfortable. Getting students who have been raised in institutional education to learn beyond the four walls and low ceiling of academe, far beyond its minimum requirement of a grade but instead in the direction of potential itself, is not simply the work of getting students to accumulate more data. Students will learn more if they want to learn, and they can be influenced in this if impressed upon not merely by the subject matter of teaching but by a passionate personality, as the professor's experiences and personal sense of meaning in relationship to the subject matter are expounded upon with a voice inseparable from the subject matter. This naturally necessitates that a professor find a "voice."

What does it mean to find one's voice? It means that what is important is not simply a thing said, interesting or original as it may be, but also the voice in which a thing is said, the performance with which it is said, the manner in which the thing said is bent to the shape of one's personality. In other words, it is not just text that is important, but texture and context—not context in the sense of history as form, but context in the sense of history as substance, which involves the texture of context. Voice is substance and is related to the meaning that results from one's personal conception. As substance, voice is not reducible to objectification or a "work." One's voice can be performed but not exhibited. Nor can one's voice be sold; it can be sold no more than the soul can be sold, and the soul is neither an object nor a possession. A lecture can be published, one's voice cannot be. Just as it is not possible for an artist to say of a particular original work "Here is my creativity," neither is it possible for a professor to say of a particular class lecture "Here is my teaching," for in the heroic sense, one's teaching is one's voice. As a work comes *from* one's creativity but is not the creativity itself, so too a lecture comes from one's teaching but is not the teaching or the voice itself. The more meaning one gleans in living, the more one's voice develops for teaching. Discovering its sound is like being surprised to find that the breathing one hears is one's own: It sounds like one's own voice, although one had not remembered hearing it before.

It is the professing of a voice that is essential in performance, which again is to say that it is not text that is essential to meaning but texture and context. And it is not just any personality that is essential to performance but heroic personality. The heroic personality should enable each student to feel that the professor is there just for him or her—the kind of feeling one gets when a song sounds close, as though performed solely for the singular hearer. The professor who has developed this voice is as essential to learning as the subject matter being taught, for potential meaning in the experience of learning always comes by way of a professing personality. To understand this is to understand that the subject matter of a course is rather negligible, insofar as any given subject matter is not an end but is a means to meaning. Thus, if a student enrolls in a class expecting to study exhaustively a certain subject matter and encapsulate that subject in the form of knowledge, then at the conclusion of the class such a student may depart unsatisfied; for in the heroic model of teaching, the subject is no *matter* to teach and the professor has no matter or form to offer. But if a student comes to study with the professor to experience learning inspired by the heroic personality, then that student should depart class satisfied: That professor's voice shall always remain in his or her ear, and that is the essential lesson.

What does it take to find a voice? Woodshedding. Spending protracted time in one's woodshed practicing improvisation is not about practicing not to practice, nor is it having no standards for teaching save a whim. Rather, improvisation takes practice and discipline; it even takes the practicing of discipline. Of what is one's woodshedding comprised? Reading, studying, thinking, self-reflecting, writing, and world traveling. Retreat to the isolation of a woodshed for protracted rehearsal is a necessary means for the flow after the ebb, which is when one attains creative ascent. Yet voice itself is not something that can be practiced with talent as though voice were mere technique, because voice is substance, not form. One does not practice voice in the woodshed; one fills oneself substantively with reading, studying, thinking, self-reflecting, writing, and world traveling, and from there voice evolves of its own accord, organically.

In the same manner that voice emerges not by prescription but by improvisation, the professor having to teach from that which is prepared, that which is already ossified into form, only proceeds with creative hands tied, and this causes the professor's "work" to become labor that drags on creativity's free spirit. But creativity's free spirit, and the potential that creativity's freedom offers one to play above what one knows, to play above what anyone knows, naturally renders the professor unable to avoid those no-nos of academe—opinion and error. Heroic teaching necessitates that the professor feel comfortable teaching with that one long-living opinion that is his or her life, given that life's experiences are instructive and that genuine learning is inseparable from the living of life. Indeed, the more vital one's thoughts about life, the more essential it will be that they be explained and illustrated in the context of living life, the texture of one's voice convincing. Moreover, the deepest inspiration for teaching and learning comes not from the library and the museum but from direct contact with and experience of life itself. The consequence is that the milieu of the classroom will become less of the nature of the bookstore and more of the nature of the world, the world that the experiences of the professor help make real.

It is through the professor's shared experiences and overall autobiographical vulnerability that students are helped in contextualizing suggested meaning modeled in the teaching, and it is through students being reciprocally autobiographical that the professor is better able to guide them in determining for themselves what things potentially mean to them. Students will only truly grasp the learning of others, including professor and texts, once they have approached and embraced that learning from within their personal universe of meaning. Thus, students do not simply need to accumulate data with which to perpetuate human existence or to gain power and privilege in the societal sphere; human beings do not live by data alone. Nor is it "reality," that which data props up, that makes people feel alive; human beings live by meaning, which is why religion historically has been so important. Students must be guided in how to *make* meaning: how to put in the ingredients, stir it, cook it, let it sit, and then make a diet of it. Teaching itself has meaning when the professor helps students *make* meaning. Teaching itself has a mission when the professor helps students *make* a mission of their meaning. So then, the experience of learning is helped by the professor's subjectivity, opinion, and error, for these result from the professor's experiencing of life. The experience of learning is also the experiencing of life, and experiencing life is better than merely knowing about life theoretically with data. The experiencing of learning is a sufficient end in itself, sufficient in the same sense that a road leading to a goal is the beginning of the attainment and part of the destination.

The heroic professor is sensitive to the groaning of history, a groaning not at the level of history's form but at the level of its substance. That is, history becomes meaningful when one goes out and meets history. Meet it in what manner? In performance. How? The key to creative maturity is developing within one's "heart" an extensive spaciousness and prolific capacity to behold and hold all that is encountered in life's journey of learning in history. In the overcrowded world of four walls and low ceilings, one learns to focus on the minute—the minute in terms of space and the minute in terms of time. But as one goes out to meet history and to behold and hold all that is encountered in life's journey of learning in history, one's eyes, as one learns to behold the immenseness, necessarily adjust to the vastness, creating increasing capacity for substance. The more the professor in this wise becomes sensitive to the groaning of history, the more teaching becomes a profound act of inhibition, in which the line between professor and what is professed ceases to exist. With the subject and conveyor becoming one and the same, teaching becomes a kind of pleading in the voice of one sensitive to history's groaning. Grasped by this sensitive awareness, this heroicism, life swarms with meaning, abounds in significance, such that all life extends creatively beyond itself, transforming the world into more than what it is in the mere appearance of form. It is this vision that heroic teaching seeks to awaken in students through the experience of learning.

The relationship between professor and students might even resemble the familial concept of "provider and protector." The provider-protector is like a tree bearing the heat of the sun while yet providing cool shade. As provider, the professor is expected to be the principle bearer of the burden of maintaining a protective standard of learning, which does not mean that students need not work or contribute to the household of learning but basically that there would never be a time when the professor would cease carrying out the essential role of "bridge"-bearer. As protector, the professor is to do much more than merely open doors (of knowledge) for her or his students, more than allow them to pass through doorways first, and more than shield them from oncoming traffic when crossing the busy streets of academe; such chivalry is merely an external indicator of a deeper commitment to provide complete intellectual nurture. The heroic professor, then, may turn the "other cheek" upon personal danger, while yet it is instinctual to protect his or her students from having to take even a first blow. There are some students, however, who wish to be materially provided for but do not wish to be protected; they want their "independence" or they want to be protected only on their own terms and at their own convenience. But the two—provider and protector—go hand in hand and comprise a grave responsibility for the professor up to the heroic task. Provider-protectorship need not function in the relationship as rules and regulations; rules and regulations exist only where professor and students cannot say to each other "substance of my substance"— that is, rules and regulations exist only where the practices of providing and protecting comprise external values imposed rather than internal virtues exposed. The professor can only provide protective shade for the students who by their own will—saying to the professor "substance of my substance"—remain under the nurture of the professor's tree branches. The professor cannot otherwise force providing and protecting on students, for it then becomes the opposite of what it aims to be. Yet many students, for lack of such an educational upbringing, readily recognize themselves as needful of provider-protector nurture. They recognize that, were potentiality air, they would be suffocating; and so they are grateful when a voice of heroic stature makes them aware that there is divine air to breath: The air of learning that extends beyond and transcends the four walls of institution, the air of error as a creative door more open to infinitude than is calculation or exactitude, the air of creativity's natural force requiring them not to force it but to become aware of it and then get out of its way and merely observe its flow, the air of their own potential and of potentiality itself. Capturing creativity, which is the means of and to potentiality, simply involves developing an awareness that there is this precious air that can be breathed in such a manner as to expand the health and capacity of the lungs. Students are grateful when the experience of learning under a heroic voice awakens this truth from within.

Heroicism in teaching requires a certain humility uncustomary in the methods of academe. But if under heroic guidance students have been trained aright and those students have developed grand aspirations, perhaps to the degree where areas of learning come to surpass the learning of the professor, then how can the professor consider it respectful to continue imposing authority on those students, preventing their free flight of improvisation? Does not the maturity of students now depend on being able to try their own learning and meaning on the experience of living? After all, what does it mean for the professor to express pride in his or her students? Does it mean to have pride in the mere evidence of intelligence, that which is displayed in works and shown like a trophy in a glass window? Or does it mean to have pride in intelligence itself, the kind of pride that enables the professor to trust students' intelligence? The problem with the professor of form yet forcing authority upon students is that this dynamic disallows freedom, when freedom is a main requisite for the flourishing of creativity and, in turn, creativity is a main requisite for aspirations to and the attainment of greatness or genius. Thus, to teach is not simply to teach survival; it is to teach the aspiration to and the attainment of freedom. Freedom requires that students be taught how to observe, yes; but ultimately freedom requires that students learn to observe beyond the lessons for observation. That is to say, students must learn to see for themselves: look around and inward, and inward and around—freely and crea-tively. When the evidence sufficiently suggests that students have proven themselves to be constituted of root and branch learning through the professor's best guidance, then the professor's pride should be manifested in the granting of freedom, as opposed to the continued hold of authoritative sway. By that time, in any case, students have fallen into the momentum of the internalized intuitive professor, so that anything short of freedom itself will be, and rightly should be, shunned at all cost. If students have not proven themselves to be constituted of root-and-branch learning of which the professor may be proud, *If they holler, let them go!* Otherwise, the professor only forces in students the terrible ordeal of having to take flight. But if the professor holds genuine pride in students, seeing in them the meaningful substance of intelligence, rather than seeing outside the students the mere works of intelligence, the professor can be proud that once again the going around has come back around and that professor's best students are now ready to become the professor's best teachers. It is this coming back around that is most pride worthy on the part of the professor. The professor truly proud of such students does not keep regressing into the expression of concerns and fears as regards the student's choices and thus continue watering seeds of doubt in them. Rather, the truly proud professor displays a readiness to reap the benefit of teaching's investment by listening and learning, not resistant to the change of roles but proud! Here, at the point of professor becoming student, is where the professor's pride manifests itself in actions rather than in mere words; but the roles only seem to change because the professor is actually permitting the new roles for the sake of the new level of teaching the students. What is the new level of teaching? It is affirmation of the students as they try personal learning and meaning on the experience of living. This is important because what the matured students most need from the professor is encouragement: "Yes, yes, go out and try the wings of your own learning and meaning in the world"—knowing, as the wise professor does, that this is truly the only passageway to ultimate destiny. Even if the professor envisions that this destiny could lead to the kind of sacrifice that heroic figures of history and fiction often face, the professor also knows that a true calling to service is always greater than a students' great professor and therefore is non-negotiable and not to be tampered with under any condition. If the flow and ebb of life's tide pulls students out into swollen sea, and it is his or her will that the great sea awaits, the professor should just be grateful that those students have learned to swim and proud that they have learned and lived.

Notes

1. See, for instance C. Eric Lincoln, "Martin Luther King, The Magnificent Intruder," *The A.M.E. Zion Quarterly Review* 94 (July 1982): 3–12.
2. James Brown, *Super Bad Parts 1&2,* King Records 1127, 1971.
3. Robert Johnson, *Come in My Kitchen,* King of Spades, BMI, 1936.

5

The Lincoln Legacy:

Challenges and Considerations

Jualynne E. Dodson

It is an honor to be asked to reflect on the life and work of C. Eric Lincoln, probably the most senior African American sociologist I had heard of as I was acquiring skills and competence in the discipline. Not only was Lincoln a sociologist, he specialized in the sociology of religion, the specialization of my focus. As a graduate student at the University of California, Berkeley, I read Lincoln's works with great thirst. This was the 1970s.

When I moved to Atlanta to spend a year of research at the Institute of the Black World, I met researchers who were working with Lincoln on the Black Church Project, the project that produced the seminal book *The Black Church in the African American Experience*. I was still a graduate student acquiring knowledge and skills, so even as I observed that women were not an integral part of the Project, I didn't feel competent enough to pose more than a minor comment and critique. However, at a later conference in Baltimore, Maryland, I was on a panel with Lincoln and put forth my observation and critique about this glaring omission. As can often happen with elders, he appeared to not take my comments seriously and continued his line of discussion. I wasn't offended because I know too well the price paid by those who walked before us and made it possible for us to be where we are today. Thus, to be able to offer reflections on Lincoln's work is more than an honor. It allows me to love him and what he did for young scholars like me while simultaneously identifying what I still feel are omissions in his scholarly production. My intent is to help us improve on what C. Eric Lincoln and others have left as an important legacy.

I want to propose that within the clearly outstanding contributions C. Eric Lincoln has made to the discipline of sociology, to the field of religious studies, and to general understandings about the Black Church as a social institution, there are at least three important topics seldom found in his writing. These omitted topics are especially noteworthy because Lincoln's professional life was wholly focused on helping us to appreciate the Black Church as an important religious and social arrangement in U.S. society.

Although he opened many doors for academic and general reading audiences to better understand the Church,[1] Lincoln did not regularly consider the *intentionality* of African Americans as we continually created black religious organizations during the eighteenth and nineteenth centuries and sustained and jettisoned them throughout the twentieth century; many even predicted their demise. In addition, although Lincoln had little difficulty acknowledging that women have been regularly excluded from Black Church hierarchy, his research and writing all too rarely engaged in a deeper examination of *women's roles and significance* to the Black Church. Neither do his works give warranted discussion to how the intersection of race, gender and social class expresses itself in the work of churchwomen. Finally, I argue that Lincoln's work suffers from not attending to the *international considerations* and activities of U.S. African American churches. Allow me to begin my explorations with the issue of intentionality and its significance for better understanding the purpose and existence of the Black Church.

Intentionality

Most of our academic and scholarly knowledge about the African American in the U.S. is contained within a framework that accepts that these arrangements function as social organizational support for the African American community. This literature generally agrees that across denominational affiliation and allegiance, black congregations have acted collectively for more than 200 years to enhance the quality of social, political, economic, and cultural life for African Americans in the United States and beyond. In large and small communities, local black churches have emphasized the survival of persons of African descent and have socialized and resocialized millions for a variety of responsibilities in our society. Of course, churches have also provided their members with religious nurturance from the African American Christian tradition.[2]

C. Eric Lincoln's research and writing about religious life in the African American community has made an important contribution to the discourse on institutional roles performed by the Black Church. His volume with Lawrence Mamiya, *The Black Church in the African American Experience,* was the first in-depth sociological study since Dr. Benjamin Mays and Joseph Nicholson's work in the 1930s.[3] Despite Mays, Lincoln, and other recent authors on the social functioning of black religious institutions, there has been little research on the intentionality of the Black Church as a socially inclusive and culturally constructed creation of the African American community.

Conceptually, I define *intentionality* as *the focused or goal-oriented actions that the African American community takes as a collective and diverse body, actions of distinct African American aesthetic expression and oriented toward its survival, cultural as well as otherwise.* Such action and expression can be stylized re-statements of a U.S. cultural ethos but maintain a distinct African American style. These goals and foci are not always clear to the outsider, or easily articulated by individual members of the community, but they are intentions that reside within the accumulated wisdom acquired by the community through its historical experiences in the United States.[4]

Historian Vincent Harding began unraveling this conceptualization of *intentionality* as he explored experiences of Africa's descendants in the U.S. from first arrivals through the Civil War epoch. He proposed that despite a variety of categories in which different strata of the black community exhibited activity, a collective purpose is identifiable. His metaphor for this collective intention is that of a river, one with many tributaries, possessing a variety of depths and widths, that moves at differentiated speeds depending on terrain, but one whose combined waters flow as a single river in a similar direction with a similar goal, despite (or perhaps even because of) existing differences. The volume, *There Is A River,* is an analogous presentation for the use of *intentionality* I am employing.[5]

In other fields of research and scholarship, authors have explored the existence of a shared African American aesthetic. As a distinctive standard of beauty and cultural expression, and employed in varying strengths by different strata of the community, African American aesthetic is an existing phenomenon in both perception and behavior. Similarly, African American intentionality is not a mythical fantasy but the community's vision of itself within the United States and beyond. It is a vision whose contours, depth, dimensions, and clarity can be articulated differently by differing sectors of the community but, like the river metaphor, these contours exist and have a shared focus. Agreement about the vision is not always the first level of consciousness for every African American, but it is a shared vision that is embedded with and composed from community wisdom and knowledge, knowledge that continues living amid that body of collective information that the community accumulates through active historical experiences.

Such community knowledge and wisdom is taught and acquired as learned consciousness that guides members through the maze of behavioral options available in the socio-political circumstances of their society. This embedded body of knowledge is shared across generations to be incorporated with the learned experiences that are also part of consciousness during a particular historical period. Knowledge about societal options, accompanying behavioral possibilities, as well as consequences, whether individual or collective, is handed down through stories (oral and written, novel and short), proverbs, sermons, poetry, songs, performances, visual arts, news media, and other related means of communication. The more salient knowledge is widely known and becomes part of African American historical consciousness and wisdom. These are the lessons perpetuated over generations. It is within this body of profound knowledge, conscious and sub-conscious, that the collective *intentionality* of the community can be found. I contend that this is also the arena on which we need to focus research in order to truly understand how African Americans and other socially oppressed communities in society have prevailed individually, organizationally, and collectively. While this is not the arena from which most sociologists gather data, it is exactly within the *intentionality* of the African American community, and specifically the intentionality of the Black Church, that I believe we will find a richer understanding of consistent survival and accomplishments.

My first challenge to the work of C. Eric Lincoln stems from this conceptual perspective about intentionality and the Black Church. Rarely if ever has Lincoln included the socio-cultural or collective *intentionality* of the Black Church in his research and writing.[6] Search as I might, I have not found where his writings address those particularities, which continue to make the Black Church a distinctive social institution. I'm not looking for such inclusions because they are distinctive but because these characteristics reflect the collective intention of the community expressed in socially organized form. As a sociologist, I feel we are particularly charged to understand how such characteristics are structured into the fabric of African American social arrangements. We are in debt to Lincoln for giving us great clarity on the Black Church as an institutional response to U.S. patterns of racism and racial discrimination. As a sociologist he also helped us to understand how that response has continued to evolve and be sustained. What he does not tell us is why black congregants continue to demand particular patterns of cultural behavior within the social arrangement. These distinctive behavioral patterns identify our congregations apart from other patterns of Christian worship and practice.

Similarly, Lincoln's work does not reveal why African Americans continue the distinct organizational practices even in the face of overt and voluntary attempts to racially integrate, economically stimulate, or provide "educated" leadership to local congregations. I firmly believe that the work of the contemporary sociologist is to consider cultural meanings, behaviors, and activities if we are to achieve our professional mandate of comprehending how human activity does and does not sustain organized social life. Collective *intentionality* is interwoven into the very structures and infrastructures that continue to comprise the Black Church as social institution.

Just as Lincoln updated our baseline data about functional aspects of this important social organization, we need solid data and analysis from that body of African American knowledge that equals collective *intentionality*. From such data we can[7] begin to understand structural and institutional consequences of the community's ongoing demand for preaching styles whose foci are culturally African American, for example. From such data we can also better comprehend how and why black churches insist on a distinctive ministry of music. Scholars and researchers have yet to help us understand the organizational and individual impact of these and other rituals, rites, and ceremonies whose tone and ethos are indicatively rooted within an African American aesthetic. We know the success of maintaining these practices as they unfailingly elicit positive responses from congregants and local black churches never seem to stop multiplying. However, Lincoln's research has provided little insight into these particularities of organized African American religious life. I believe today's researchers are equally responsible for providing information about African American intentionality as well as for exploring the black community's reactive responses to racism and discrimination.

There Is No Church Without Participating Women

The second conceptual challenge I pose to C. Eric Lincoln's work revolves around his peripheral consideration of women and women's significance to the Black Church. In this arena Lincoln was, as we all are, a product of the deep social contexts within which he was socialized, live, and worked. He was raised as a male member of an entrenched U.S. patriarchy that also permeated the African American community, the Christian communions wherein he worshiped, and the discipline of sociology. As a professional academic, he learned well the existing analytical paradigms of sociology and employed them in framing his research questions, design, and analysis. He was not, however, a product of that branch of the discipline that incorporated gender and ethnographic approaches to data collection. Had this been the case, perhaps he would have been better able to approach research topics with the intent of capturing the agency or proactive participation of *all* members.

Despite the filters of his generation, Lincoln lived and worked during a time when all aspects of U.S. institutional life were being challenged, and some in sociology and other behavioral sciences were advocating a proactive inclusion of all participants of a social phenomenon. I know concretely that as Lincoln's research project was gathering data, African American women of all social categories were visible and actively demanding that their church participation be given serious and systematic attention. They challenged the idea that black women were relatively passive in contesting exclusion from church leadership and acquiesced to, even if they did not support, the patriarchy of Christian churches. Sociologist Cheryl Townsend Gilkes and I have consistently reminded the academic community of the erroneous omission of women. Perhaps the guiding assumption of the Lincoln project about the Black Church led the researchers to the exclusion of women. That assumption states:

> Since black churches are predominantly pastor-centered institutions, with the black clergy having a greater degree of authority than their white counterparts, the survey focused on the pastor as the major bearer of information about black churches.[8]

Such a "pastor-centered" approach to the Black Church led the Lincoln project to include a solitary woman "writer" to help analyze their already collected data. When she was unable to complete her written document, the project moved forward with only the barest and thinnest analysis of women's participation. To my mind, this is analogous to the "token Negro" process that European Americans employ to avoid doing the serious inclusions that accurately represent reality.

Thankfully, this and other such omissions did not deter black women and, as has been the case historically, we never doubted our significance and indispensability to the Black Church.[9] Today, the number of black women pursuing education and careers in all aspects of church life is growing rapidly. Space has also been opened and forced open for women's visible leadership in the hierarchy of several larger African American denominations. It is just a matter of time before those who continue to hold on to exclusively male-dominated leadership models will succumb to more progressive visions. Even now, the historic African Methodist Episcopal (AME) Church has elected a woman to the office of bishop, the highest position in that denomination's polity.

There are also more women than ever writing about every aspect of Black Church activities. Consider, for example, such womanist scholars as Emilie Townes, *Breaking the Fine Reign of Death*; Jackie Grant, *White Women's Christ, Black Women's Jesus*; Katie Cannon, *Black Womanist Ethics*; Evelyn Higginbotham, *Righteous Discontent*; Delores Williams, *Sisters in the Wilderness*; Cheryl Townsend Gilkes, *If It Wasn't for the Women*; Sylvia Jacobs, *Black Americans and the Missionary Movement in Africa*; and my own *Engendering Church*, that have all been published in the last decade and a half.[10] These and many other studies that prioritize black women as two-thirds and more of active church participation allow us to systematically know that social organization requires the active involvement of all segments of membership, without regard to form or fashion. Understandings about the organization of the Black Church are fundamentally incomplete when the perspective of all member segments is not factored into the presentation and analysis.

The International

My last reflection for furthering the work of C. Eric Lincoln is related to his lack of attention to the U.S. Black Church in international endeavors and presence. It is truly difficult for me to comprehend how this arena of activities could have been overlooked or left out of any investigation on the institutional nature of the Black Church. For instance, one need only remember the definitive role of the work of African American churches and denominations for missions in Africa or their domestic evangelism to support missionaries during the post-Civil War era and the early twentieth century. I have worshipped with local congregations from various African American Christian denominations and to this day they continue to support foreign missions, usually in the form of material contributions to locations with African descendants. There was the Hospitals for Haiti Programs, the fund to build Houses in Zimbabwe, the Panama Relief Fund, the South African Children's Fund, the Fund for Cuban Congregations, and the Ghanaian School Fund, not to mention clothing drives for disaster victims outside of U.S. shores. In addition, the Black Church, via several denominations, has contributed missionaries, ministers, and other workers worldwide in an effort to ensure that people of African descent are included in the Christianization process. I noted the work of Sylvia Jacobs, who along with other scholars has devoted her research to African Americans in the international context.[11] Still, the international arena received no more than generalized consideration in Lincoln's research.

It may be the case that Lincoln's Black Church Project did not have resources enough to include the international activities of any of the denominations they studied. But consider how limited our understanding and vision of the U.S. Black Church, not to mention the larger African American community, remains when we do not incorporate international issues of concern to the Church and community. Among such important subjects are our concern with PanAfricanism, Garveyism, Black Nationalism, Negritude, Afrocentricity, Black Theology, and any one of the ideas and concepts that have evolved to represent African presence in the global context. For those of us who now study African American religious expressions throughout the African Diaspora, it is imperative that there is an inclusion of the relationship of the U.S. Black Church to international perspectives and issues.

For example, my current research and writing on Africa-based religious traditions in Cuba evolves from New York's Schomburg Research Center's rich body of archival materials on the AME Church in Cuba. I once assumed that the full extent of AME development was contained in U.S. activities, notwithstanding the Church's expansion into Canada. What I discovered at the Schomburg was that the AME Church had made contact with Cuba as early as 1893 and established missionary congregations on the island soon thereafter.[12] Further exploration into the international arena of AME work revealed that it had concerns about Haiti as early as the 1830s and took action on that concern. There was also AME missionary work in Western and Southern Africa during the nineteenth century, and early in the twentieth century Bishop Henry McNeal Turner authorized missionary work in Mexico among Mexicans of African descent.[13] This bishop also helped sustain AME activities in Cuba and other parts of the Caribbean, and this is but one denomination. My final point bears repeating: We do a disservice to the extensive international work of the U.S. Black Church as well as to our own research and scholarship when we neglect or exclude the Church's activities beyond our borders.

Conclusion

In no way do I wish for anyone to misconstrue my focus on C. Eric Lincoln's omissions as representing a balanced review of his work or its significance to the sociology of religion. I know and appreciate the value of his presence in the discipline and the importance his research and writing has had for any understanding of the Black Church in the United States. By drawing attention to aspects of African American religious scholarship not appreciably addressed in Lincoln's work, I hope to renew our understanding that future research on this distinctively U.S. social institution cannot and must not present mere portions of the phenomenon. Those of us who study the Black Church and future generations of scholars are expected—no compelled—to learn from the work of our predecessors and reach beyond those enlightenments. The collective intentionality of the Black Church, the full and active participation of women, and the international scope of Church activities must be included within our data collection and descriptive presentations as well as within any analysis. Without these and other inclusions, we will do a disservice to the discipline of sociology and to the future of African America.

Notes

This speech was first presented at the C. Eric Lincoln Forum, Candler School of Theology, Emory University, Atlanta, GA, 2001.

1. My use of Church with a capital "C" is to denote the institutional arrangement, not the local congregational entity.
2. See Mechal Sobel, *Trabelin' On: The Slave Journey to An Afro-Baptist Faith* (Westport, CT: Greenwood Press, 1979).
3. I am absolutely proud that, as I was finishing undergraduate studies and Dr. Benjamin Mays spoke at a small church in Oakland, California, I drug my

sister and went to that event. I was totally in awe to meet Dr. Mays and to have him autograph my copy of his book. I felt like one of my students, who expressed on first speaking with Vincent Harding, "Do you know who you are?"

4. This conception of intentionality has begun to be employed by the African Atlantic Research Team, first of the Department of Ethnic Studies at the University of Colorado, Boulder and now of Michigan State University. We have drawn our understanding from studying Ruth Simms Hamilton's articulation of three propositions shared by those of African descent and living in the African Diaspora. She contends that the propositions are a beginning place through which solid theoretical work on common and diverse aspects of the African Diaspora can be better understood. We accept Hamilton's challenge and have begun to adjust the proposition concerning "creative organizational and individual response to oppression." We expand these creative actions beyond mere responses to oppressive conditions to include pro-active expressions of the cultural aesthetics of a community no matter its location within the African Atlantic. See Ruth Simms Hamilton, ed., *Routes of Passage: Rethinking the African Diaspora (African Diaspora Research Project)*, (Lansing, MI: Michigan State University Press, 2003).

5. Vincent Harding, *There Is a River: The Black Struggle for Freedom in America* (New York: Vintage Books, 1983).

6. On a lecture engagement at the University of Colorado, Boulder, in the spring of 1998, Lawrence Mamiya acknowledged that the sociological perspective I take in my research is "cultural" and differs from the approach used by he and Lincoln, which has a more quantitative focus for describing sociological phenomena. Even with that distinction, I contend that Lincoln's picture of the Black Church is only half complete without data on the topics to which I refer.

7. Please note that I am not saying "we will" begin to understand because the ability to understand does not always equal a willingness to understand. Similarly, understanding does not necessarily produce corrective action as action again requires a "willingness" to act according to understanding.

8. C. Eric Lincoln and Larry Mamiya, *The Black Church in the African American Experience* (Durham, NC: Duke University Press, 1990), p. 403.

9. For a profound exploration of women's indispensability to the Black Church and the African American community as a whole see Cheryl Townsend Gilkes, *If it Wasn't for the Women* (Maryknoll, NY: Orbis Books, 2001). See also Jualynne Dodson, "Encounters in the African Atlantic World: The African Methodist Episcopal Church in Cuba," in Lisa Brock and Digna Castaneda Fuertes, eds. *Between Race and Empire: African Americans and Cuban before the Cuban Revolution* (Philadelphia: Temple University Press), pp. 85–103.

10. Emilie M. Townes, *Breaking the Fine Reign of Death* (New York: Continuum, 1998); Jacqueline Grant, *White Women's Christ, Black Women's Jesus* (Atlanta, GA: Scholars Press, 1989); Katie Cannon, *Black Womanist Ethics* (Atlanta, GA: Scholars Press, 1988); Evelyn Brooks Higginbotham, *Righteous Discontent: The Women's Movement in the Black Baptist Church, 1880–1920* (Cambridge, MA: Harvard University Press, 1993); Delores S. Williams, *Sisters in the Wilderness: The Challenge of Womanist God-Talk* (Maryknoll,

NY: Orbis Books, 1993); Cheryl Townsend Gilkes, *If it Wasn't for the Women* (Maryknoll, NY: Orbis Books, 2001); Sylvia Jacobs, ed., *Black Americans and the Missionary Movement in Africa* (Westport, CT: Greenwood Press, 1983); Jualynne E. Dodson, *Engendering Church: Women, Power, and the A.M.E. Church* (Lanham, MD: Rowman Littlefield Publishers, Inc., 2002).

11. Sylvia Jacobs, ed., *Black Americans and the Missionary Movement in Africa.*
12. See Dodson, "Encounters in the African Atlantic World."
13. See Dennis Dickerson, "Bishop Henry M. Turner and Black Latinos: The Mission to Cuba and Mexico," in *A.M.E. Church Review* 108, no. 349 (January-March): pp. 51–55.

II

The Social Analysis of Religion

6

Islam in America:

Problems of Legacy, Identity, Cooperation, and Conflict among African American and Immigrant Muslims

Lawrence H. Mamiya

Introduction

Let me begin by acknowledging that my primary area of research over the past six years has focused on African American Muslim movements. I began the project on a Lilly funded national research project, Islam in the African American Experience, working with Professor C. Eric Lincoln of Duke University before his untimely death in May 2000 and Dr. Ihsan Bagby of Shaw University. Most of the research for this paper is derived from that project, which reflected Eric Lincoln's deep abiding interest in African American Muslims from the Nation of Islam and Sunni Muslims. I have also included some data on immigrant Muslims because they are very much a part of the contemporary picture of Islam in America. The data on immigrant Muslims are from a telephone survey conducted by Dr. Ihsan Bagby, who was then the director of the Islamic Resource Center in Orange County, California. Bagby's study, which was done in 1999, covered 1,500 Muslim masjids across the country, including 350 predominantly African American masjids. My own study includes face-to-face surveys and interviews with the imams of 130 African American masjids nationwide, which represents about one-third to 40 percent of total African American masjids. We also did a survey of some 400 African American congregational participants of selected masjids.[1]

The Historical Legacy of Islam in the Americas

Originating as a religion in the seventh century A.D. through the revelations, visions, and messages received by the Prophet Muhammad in Arabia, Islam spread rapidly throughout North Africa. Black African converts to Islam were called Moors, and not only helped to conquer southern Spain but also gained a reputation as skilled navigators and sailors. The Moors who accompanied the Spanish explorers in the fifteenth and sixteenth centuries were among the first to introduce the Islamic religion to the Americas. However, the greater impact of Islam in British North America occurred when African Muslims from the Islamized parts of West Africa were captured in warfare and sold to the European traders of the Atlantic slave trade.

Muslims in the Slave Era

The presence of Muslim slaves has been ignored by most historians, who have tended to focus upon the conversion of Africans to Christianity or upon the attempts to preserve aspects of traditional African religions. Yet their presence has been attested to by narrative and documentary accounts, some of which were written in Arabic. Yarrow Mamout, Job Ben Solomon, and Lamine Jay arrived in colonial Maryland in the 1730s. Abdul Rahaman, Mohammed Kaba, Bilali, Salih Bilali, and "Benjamin Cochrane" were enslaved in the late eighteenth century. Omar lbn Said, Kebe, and Abu Bakr were brought to Southern plantations in the early 1800s, while two others, Mahommah Baquaqua and Mohammed Ali ben Said, came to the United States as freedmen about 1850.[2] Abdul Rahaman, a Muslim prince of the Fula people in Timbo, Futa Jallon, became a slave for close to 20 years in Natchez, Mississippi, before he was finally freed and eventually made his way back to Africa through the aid of abolitionist groups. Court records in South Carolina spoke of African slaves who prayed to Allah and refused to eat pork. Missionaries in Georgia and South Carolina observed that some Muslim slaves attempted to blend Islam and Christianity by identifying God with Allah and Muhammad with Jesus. A conservative estimate is that there were close to 30,000 Muslim slaves who came from Islamic-dominated ethnic groups such as Mandingoes, Fulas, Gambians, Senegambians, Senegalese, Cape Verdeans, and Sierra Leoneans in West Africa.[3] However, in spite of the much larger presence of African Muslims in North America than previously thought, the Islamic influence did not survive the impact of the slave period. Except for the documents left by the Muslims named above, only scattered traces and family memories of Islam remained among African Americans, much like author Alex Haley's ancestral Muslim character, Kunta Kinte of the Senegambia, in his novel *Roots*.

By the late nineteenth century, black Christian churches had become so dominant in the religious and social life of black communities that only a few African American leaders who had traveled to Africa knew anything about Islam. Contacts between immigrant Arab groups and African Americans were almost nonexistent at this time. After touring Liberia and South Africa, Bishop Henry McNeil Turner of the African Methodist Episcopal Church recognized the "dignity, majesty, and consciousness of [the] worth of Muslims."[4] But it was Edward Wilmot Blyden (1832–1912), the West Indian educator, Christian missionary, and minister for the government of Liberia, who became the most enthusiastic supporter of Islam for African Americans.[5] Blyden, who began teaching Arabic in Liberia in 1867, wrote a book in 1888 called *Christianity, Islam and the Negro Race,* where he concluded that Islam had a much better record of racial equality than Christianity, especially after comparing the racial attitudes of Christian and Muslim missionaries whom he had encountered in Africa. Islam, he felt, could also be a positive force in improving the life conditions for African Americans in the United States. Though he lectured extensively, Blyden did not become a leader of a social movement that could establish Islam effectively in America. That task awaited the prophets and forceful personalities of the black urban migrations in the twentieth century.

Islam in America in the Twentieth Century

Islam in America in the twentieth century has been built by two major streams of Muslims: First, immigrant Muslims from usually Arab countries such as Egypt, Arabia, Syria, and Lebanon and more recently from Asian Muslim countries like Pakistan, Indonesia, and Malaysia. There have also been other Muslim ethnic groups such as Albanians, Bosnians, Iranians, Turks, Africans, Palestinians, Eastern Europeans, etc. Second, African American Muslims who converted or reverted directly to Sunni Islam from their Christian background, or those black people who became members of the early proto-Islamic movements such as Noble Drew Ali's Moorish Science Temple movement (1913 to the present), the Ahmadiyyah movement (1920s to the present), and the Nation of Islam (1930 to the present) under leaders such as Master Fard, Elijah Muhammad, and Louis Farrakhan. Unless otherwise indicated, all of my data pertain to African American Sunni Muslims and do not include the followers of Farrahkhan, Moorish Science, or the Ahmadiyyah.[6]

The exact number of Muslims in America is not known since no adequate survey has yet been undertaken.[7] However, the best estimates range from a low of one million to a high of ten million. Based on their telephone survey of religious groups, Barry Kosmin and Jeffery Scheckner place the size of the American Muslim population at no more than one million.[8] The high estimate of eight to ten million comes from Imam Warith Deen Mohammed's former American Muslim Mission. Fareed A. Numan of the American Muslim Council has given an estimate of five million.[9] Yvonne Haddad and Jane Smith support an estimate of 3.7 to 4 million American Muslims, which Dr. Ihsan Bagby of the Islamic Resource Center and I feel most comfortable with.[10] Of the four million Muslims, African Americans are estimated to be more than one million (between one-fourth to one-third of all Muslims). In his unpublished survey, Dr. Bagby gave the following ethnic breakdown of major Muslim ethnic groups: African Americans (29 percent); South Asians (29 percent); Arabs (20 percent).[11] If one looks back historically, Islam has been one of the fastest-growing sectors of religion in black communities. In 1964, when Malcolm X converted to Sunni Islam and made the Hajj to become El-Hajj Malik El-Shabazz, African American Sunni Muslims numbered in the few hundred to a few thousand. The growth to more than one million converts has largely occurred over the past 30 years.

Some Reasons for the Growth of Islam among African Americans

In a presentation, Bagby has estimated that Islam in America is growing by at least 100,000 Muslims per year, with 60,000 Muslim immigrants arriving in the country and about 40,000 African American converts annually.[12] In our study of predominantly African American masjids, the imams who were the key informants gave their reasons for converting or reverting to Islam (Note: the term "reversion" is preferred because Muslims believe that everyone is born a Muslim, i.e., submitted to Allah, so turning to Islam later in life is a "return" to an original state). Table 6.1 shows the faith background from which the Imams reverted and table 6.2 indicates the reasons they gave for their attraction to Sunni Islam. In our survey, of the 117 African American imams who responded to the question of whether they were a member of any particular religious faith before converting to Islam, 89 percent said yes, 2 percent said no, and 9 percent were raised as Muslims. Of those who replied affirmatively, all of them were members of some type of Christian group. As table 6.1 indicates, 73 (62 percent) were former Baptists, 13 (11 percent) Roman Catholics, 6 (5 percent) United Methodists, 6 (5 percent) Christian no denomination (5 percent), and 5 (4 percent) African Methodist Episcopal. Given the rigid nature of segregation in religion in American society, one can assume that the majority of imams left predominantly black churches.

Table 6.2 gives some of the main categories of reasons why the imams reverted or converted to Islam. Since some of the interview responses to the question of why they reverted to Islam contained more than one category, the total percentage of responses is 167 percent, but the total number of imams interviewed remained at 130. As table 6.2 shows, spiritual and theological reasons are the main motivation for reverting to Islam with a total of 42 percent. The subcategories include clear guidelines for spiritual growth (11 percent), Islam as a way of life (19 percent), and the strong emphasis upon the oneness of God or *tawheed* (12 percent). The stress upon Allah's oneness could also be taken as a critique or dissatisfaction with Christianity.

The next main category concerned the social recruitment and attraction by Muslim role models (31 percent). The leading subcategory involves Muslims as role models for others, admiration of those who were Muslim, including admiration of their dress code, discipline, self-help, and their sincerity, morals, and spirituality. The imams were also attracted by the unity of the Muslim community and the brotherhood/sisterhood of Muslims in whose company they felt accepted and comfortable (14 percent). It is interesting to note that exercises in direct dawah, visiting people in the neighborhood and inviting them to the masjid, were the least effective means of recruitment, at least in the experience of these imams. Muslims as role models and the feeling of brotherhood and sisterhood among Muslims appeared to be more effective in attracting new members.

The emphasis of Islam upon racial justice and nondiscrimination was another leading reason for becoming a Muslim (29 percent).

Table 6.1
Data on the Religious Background of
African American Sunni Muslim Imams

"Q. Before reverting (converting) to Al-Islam, were you a member of any particular religious faith?"

89%	Yes
2%	No
9%	Raised Muslim
100%	(n=130)

"Q. If yes, please indicate the religious faith:"

Non-Christian Faith	0%
Christian (no denom.)	5%
AME	4%
Holiness	2%
Pentecostal	1%
Baptist	62%
"Catholic, Roman"	11%
Disciples	1%
Episcopalian	2%
Lutheran	3%
Methodist	5%
Presbyterian	3%
Reformed	1%
UCC	2%
102%* (n=117)	

*Total is more than 100% because some respondents may have participated in more than one religious faith.

Twenty-two percent of the imams felt that Islam was a better religion for African Americans in particular, especially with its message of hope. Seven percent cited the nondiscrimination in Islam and its commitment to justice and equality, providing dignity to all regardless of race.

Since all of the imams surveyed were once members of Christian churches, one can expect a widespread dissatisfaction with Christianity, which was cited by 27 percent of the imams. In the subcategories, 13 percent were dissatisfied with Christian tenets such as the trinity or Jesus as son of God or felt that Christianity did not meet their needs; and 9 percent disliked Christianity because it was the religion of the oppressor. In their interviews, a few of the imams (5 percent) cited the

Table 6.2
Reasons for Reversion to Islam by African American Imams

	Subtotal	Total
Spiritual And Theological Reasons		42%
1. "Clear guidelines for spiritual growth and understanding of Allah," theological and religious questions resolved	11%	
2. Clear guidelines for healthy daily living; Islam lays out a way of life; strict discipline; moral and natural way	19%	
3. "Concept of One God is stronger, better in Islam than in Christianity;" no trinity or God in human form; Qur'an fills spiritual void	12%	
Intellectual, Mental Attraction To Islam		11%
"Islam as realistic knowledge and logical truth. Encompasses science, culture, and natural life. Islam agrees with common sense"		
Social Activism And Social Justice Of Islam		16%
"Attracted by the social activism and/or self-help programs, especially the unity of spiritual, economic, political, and social justice"		
Racial Justice And Nondiscrimination Of Islam		29%
1. Better religion for African Americans in particular; message of hope for African Americans	22%	
2. No discrimination in Islam; commitment to justice and equality; dignity to all regardless of race	7%	
Dissatisfaction With Christianity		27%
1. Dissatisfaction with Christian tenets; Christianity did not meet their needs	13%	
2. Disliked Christianity because it was the religion of the oppressor and/or the hypocrisy of Christians	9%	
3. Liked the message that the white man was/is the devil (for those who began their journey to Islam from the Nation of Islam)	5%	
Social Recruitment By And Attraction To Muslim Role Models		31%
1. Attracted by the unity of the Muslim community and the brotherhood/sisterhood of Muslims; felt accepted and comfortable	14%	
2. Result of direct evangelism (dawah): Muslims visited me and talked to me; a friend brought me to the masjid	1%	
3. "Admired others who are Muslims (dress code, discipline, self-help);" "their sincerity, morals, and spirituality"	16%	
The Fact That Islam Helps Me To Be A Better Person		11%
1. "Islam helps me to stay out of the streets, trouble, jail, drugs, drink"	1%	
2. "Personal identity problems solved by Islam, the need to belong" is fulfilled	5%	
3. Desire to improve my life and get strength from Islam	5%	

Total Percentage is 167% (respondents allowed to pick more than one choice) (n=130)

Nation of Islam's belief that whites are devils as one of the reasons that attracted them to that movement and started them on their journey to the universalism of Sunni Islam, which rejects that view.

Since the main categories do not do full justice to the interview materials, some narrative examples of reasons for reversion to Islam are presented as follow:

#0005 (former Methodist—"As a youth I tried to understand Christianity, but was disappointed. I was interested in the reality of religion. Looking for something. Looking for social answers also. I disagreed with the civil rights movement (nonviolence and turning the other cheek)."

#0020 (former Baptist)—"Allah touched my heart. I had a problem with the Trinity. I was dissatisfied with life—a spiritual void. The main attraction of Islam was the relationship between the Creator and the created. All this attracted me."

#0050 (former African Methodist Episcopal)—"I never accepted Christian teachings. Attraction to Islam was due to the utter simplicity and concept of Allah—more powerful. Struggle against oppression."

#0081 (former Baptist)—"In 1977, I saw a need for change. Studied Christianity for a means of social change but rejected it. Became a communist and rejected that too because of a lack of answers to big questions. Turned to religion. Islam answered all the questions and concern for social change. I was 21 years old in the Air Force, stationed in Turkey."

Among African Americans, the increased incarceration of black people, particularly young African American males, has had the unintended consequence of contributing to the rapid growth of Islam in prison populations. Close to one out of three young black men were in prison or in the criminal justice system in the 1990s, and many of them were attracted to Islam as a religion that resists oppression. For example, Imam Warith Deen Umar, the head Muslim chaplain of New York State prisons, has estimated that Islam is growing at the rate of 1 percent every two months, or 6 percent annually.[13] There has also been a growth of Islam among Puerto Rican inmates with the establishment of the first Puerto Rican mosque in East Harlem. We estimate that the New York–New Jersey metropolitan area has the largest number of African American Muslims in the nation, close to one-third of the total. For immigrant Muslims, the upper mid-western cities of Chicago and Detroit have the largest numbers. Other cities that have a substantial number of Muslims include Atlanta, which has the largest African

American congregation of 3,000 in Masjid Al-islam; Los Angeles; and the San Francisco Bay area.

Recent Trends of Within-Group Diversity

In regard to recent trends of within-group diversity, as mentioned above, African Americans and immigrant Arab and Asian Muslims tend to predominate in most masjids and Islamic Centers in the United States. There are very few white Americans who have been attracted to Sunni Islam; their numbers have been estimated to be less than 2 percent of the total. If Caucasian Americans join Islam, it is usually Sufism, the mystical movement of Islam that attracts them. Sufi practices and rituals, especially music, chanting, and dancing (especially the Mevlevi order or whirling dervishes) have become important parts of the New Age movement of the last decade. I attended a national Sufi conference last spring in the Bay Area and about half of the 500 participants were white Americans. There is also a small but growing attraction to Sufism among African Americans. In an interview in Philadelphia, an African American imam spoke about his concern of losing some members from his masjid to local Sufi groups. For African Americans, the Tijanniyah Sufi movement from Morocco and West Africa and the Nag Shabandia of Turkey have been the main carriers of Sufism.

Of the three sects of Islam (Sunni, Sufi, and Shia), Shiism in the United States has remained largely confined to Iranian, Arab, and Asian Muslim groups that brought the Shiite tradition with them. East Dearborn, Michigan; Chicago; Queens, New York; and Los Angeles have been the main centers for Shiites. The Shiite following is probably the smallest among African Americans. One predominantly African American Shiite masjid was recently constituted in Los Angeles during the past year and there have been some rural African American Shiite communities.

Sources and Patterns of Tensions with the Larger Society

The primary source of tensions for Muslim groups with American society is directly related to the strategic and geopolitical interests of the United States in Middle Eastern oil and its accompanying problems. A quick review to refresh our historical memories: the oil embargoes of 1973 and 1979 and the formation of the Organization of Petroleum

Exporting Countries (OPEC); the Iranian revolution of 1979 and U.S. support of the Shah through overt and covert means (Sazeman-i Ettelaat va Amniyat-i Keshvar or SAVAK, the CIA trained secret police); the American hostage crises in Iran and Lebanon; the bombings of U.S. military barracks in Lebanon and Saudi Arabia; the Gulf War; the present Iraqi crisis; the Carter, Reagan, Bush, and Clinton administrations' belief that Middle Eastern oil remains a vital strategic interest of the United States over which we would risk World War III. Other conflicts and issues could be mentioned: the long, embattled issue of Israel and the Palestinians; the bombing of Libya; Pan Am 103; the war in Afghanistan; the war in the former Yugoslavia, etc. Samuel Huntington of Harvard has added new fuel to the political flames by declaring that with the collapse of Communism, and in his vision of the clash of civilizations and cultures, the new enemy is Islam.[14]

With the bombing of the World Trade Center; the arrests of several Muslims including the blind Egyptian Sheik Omar; and the international political dimension just mentioned, the American media has unfairly portrayed Muslims as "terrorists." This is unfortunately not a new reaction; after the Oklahoma City bombing, the immediate response was to look for, arrest, and detain Muslims. The FBI pressure on local Muslim groups in the United States has been enormous (making it difficult for researchers). Both African American and immigrant Muslim groups have been the targets of constant surveillance, wire taps, visits, etc. by the FBI. Muslims have organized their own national media committee to counter the widespread negative stereotyping of Islam and Muslim groups.

Although the political tensions with the larger society have been a primary concern for all Muslims, it should be pointed out that the majority of both African American and immigrant Muslims desire to find acceptable accommodations with American society. For example, most Muslims adhere to the law of monogamous marriage in the United States even though Islam as a religion permits polygamy (up to four wives who are treated equally in all circumstances). There are a few Muslim men who do practice polygamy but are very discreet about it.

If Islam became more fully developed in the United States, the economic practices of Muslim communities would also run counter to American capitalism. In his farewell speech, the Prophet Muhammad enjoined Muslims against the practice of usury, that is, making money from the interest on loans. In other words, making money is not to become an idolatry as it has become in the West, a replacement for

Allah. In the practice of global capitalism, Muslim countries will offer interest-free loans to each other but charge interest to non-Muslims. There are a few Muslim banking groups in the United States that will offer interest-free loans to their Muslim members.

Other points of Muslim tension with American society are very similar to the concerns of orthodox Jews and Roman Catholics, namely the need for a parochial education separate from the public schools, and medical and other kinds of social services that respect Islamic values. Like the orthodox Jews, Muslims emphasize gender separation (except for families) in all spheres of life, particularly in worship, education, and everyday social interaction. Men and women should dress modestly and both should cover their heads, especially in worship. Again, like their Jewish and Catholic coverts, Muslims tend to be very conservative in matters of sexuality, preferring traditional roles for women and excluding them from religious leadership roles such as imam (the rabbinate for Jews and priesthood for Catholics). In their concern for dietary laws, Muslims support halal meat products (no pork) and a ban on consumption of alcohol and other intoxicants, both of which put them outside the mainstream of American culture.

Besides their concern for parochial education, Muslims also desire to have their holy days recognized, particularly Eid al Fitr at the end of Ramadan and Eid al Adha at the end of the Hajj (Pilgrimage). Recognizing that they are not in an Islamic milieu, Muslims would like some accommodation with their day of worship on Fridays, particularly for attendance at the Jumu'ah prayer service, which is usually from 1 to 3 P.M. For immigrant Muslims, being a part of a religious minority is a strange situation for them since many have come from predominantly Muslim societies where Islamic practices and beliefs are widely supported.

Sources and Patterns of Within-Group Tensions

It should be pointed out at the outset that African American and immigrant Muslims have very good relationships with each other. In every predominantly African American masjid there are usually immigrant Muslims in attendance, too. Having observed both black churches and African American masjids in action over the past five years, I would say that the different Muslim groups tend to relate better to each other than black and white Christians do. There is a deeper sense of brotherhood (and sisterhood) among African American and immigrant Muslims. However, there are also points of tension.

In a khutbah (sermon) on August 1, 1997, Imam Abu Muslimah of the Islamic Center of East Orange, New Jersey, preached about racism against Black Muslims. In his khutbah, Imam Muslimah focused on the issue of racism from Arab Muslims against "blacks" or African American Muslims. He first gave a historical summary of some of the racial problems that black Africans such as Bilal lbn Rabah, the former Ethiopian slave and member of the first Muslim community, encountered from Arab Muslims in Medina. (Bilal became the first muezzin in Islamic history, using his powerful melodic chant to call worshipers to prayer, the Adan). Imam Muslimah then proceeded to give two contemporary examples of racism by Arab Muslims against African American Muslims. The first example concerned the criticism that Muslims who are black "mismanage their money . . . waste their money, and they're always asking for more money than they need."[15] The second example related to the often-cited criticism by Arabs that African American Muslims, especially their imams, are ignorant of the Arabic language and the "deen" (loosely translated as the "religion" or the fundamentals of Islam). In response to these two examples of racism, Imam Muslimah in fluent Arabic replied by saying that this kind of criticism of a lack of knowledge of Arabic and the deen tends to drive African American Muslims away from ever wanting to learn the basic fundamentals and is ultimately detrimental to the Islamic Ummah. On the charge of the financial mismanagement of money, Imam Muslimah said, "Are we not aware that a masjid was built in America with no schools and no business offices attached to the masjid that holds only 800 Muslims. That it was built for over $33 million. Do you want to talk about the issue of mismanagement?" Muslimah was referring to the masjid that is colloquially called the "Diplomats Mosque," which was built by United Nations diplomats from Muslim countries and located at 96th Street and First Avenue in Manhattan.[16] For Imam Muslimah, the eventual goal beyond racial and ethnic divisions is stated by the Qur'an: "Oh humanity, We have created you from a male and a female and We've made you into nations and tribes so that you may know one another. Indeed the most noble in the sight of Allah is the one with the most taqwa" ("taqwa" is translated as "faith").

There is also the complaint by African American Muslims that immigrant Muslims may worship in masjids in black communities but don't want to get involved in the community problems there. For a long time immigrant Muslims were content to remain aloof from community outreach programs or instituted programs that only served their immigrant ethnic community. Confronted by such attitudes, a number of young African American Muslim activists withdrew from immigrant masjids, started their own places of worship, and began community outreach programs. The Darul Islam movement and the Islamic Party of the late 1960s and early 1970s were examples of this kind of separation.

Another source of tension concerns the issue of intermarriage between immigrant and African American Muslims. A complaint often heard in conversation and in field interviews related to the fact that African American Muslims were often treated as brothers in the faith during worship but were rejected in their attempts to marry the daughters of immigrant Muslims. While cultural differences and ethnic traditions certainly play a role in such decisions, many African Americans felt that their immigrant brothers had been influenced by the racism and prejudice of American society. In any case, the universalism of Islam was not able to overcome such barriers.

A final source of within-group tension may be related to the patterns of accommodation developed by immigrant and African American Muslims. Immigrant Muslims have largely sought to assimilate and diffuse into the American mainstream as Arab Americans, Pakistani Americans, etc. Long accustomed to the racial separation and racial isolation of American society, African American Muslims have sought to form identifiable Islamic neighborhoods. African American imams often encourage their members to buy homes or rent apartments in the neighborhood of the masjid, and Muslim merchants to set up their shops and businesses nearby. Besides the masjid, the building of an Islamic school is the goal of such neighborhoods.

Coming from Islamic societies where the government provided for both educational and social services, masjids for most immigrants were only places of prayer. In the United States, immigrant Muslims have sought to found "Islamic Centers" that contain a masjid but also a school and also function as a community center. Meanwhile, following the pattern of black churches,[17] African American Muslims have called their places of prayer "masjids." The masjid can also serve a variety of other functions, making it an educational, social service, and political space. The class differences between immigrant and African American Muslims also play a role in these differing institutions. Many immigrant Muslims tend to be somewhat wealthier and more middle class than their African American counterparts. Thus, they have the resources to build an Islamic Center from the ground up, whereas many African American masjids are in essence storefront operations.

Changing Structural Characteristics

Since we have very little economic and financial data on immigrant Muslims, we can only make some educated guesses in terms of their internal resources and power. As mentioned above, immigrant Muslims in America generally tend to be more middle class, because the immigration laws of the Immigration and Naturalization services (INS) make it extremely difficult for poor people to receive permission to immigrate. Further, very few Muslims have received refugee status as a result of political persecution. In order to get a work visa, too, one must demonstrate a skill or occupational category that is needed in the American labor force. Hence, there is a disproportion of physicians, engineers, and other high-tech and professional personnel among immigrant Muslims. While there are some poor and working-class Muslims doing things such as driving cabs, the majority are in the middle-class categories, probably middle-middle to upper-middle class.

The economic power of immigrant Muslims has meant that they have been able to effectively establish national organizations such as the Islamic Circle of North America (ICNA) and the Islamic Society of North America (ISNA), both of which are dominated by Pakistani Muslims who run educational programs and hold an annual meeting for all Muslims. ISNA has been able to build a large masjid and Islamic Center in Plainfield, Indiana. Rather than selecting any qualified male member from within their congregations to serve as the imam, immigrant Muslims also tend to hire trained imams from their home country, for example, Lebanese Shiites in Linda Wallbridge's study hired two imams from Lebanon to staff their Islamic Center and Islamic Institute in East Dearborn.[18] In contrast, African American Muslims tend to select their imams from within their congregations. However, the longevity of African American imams in their positions tend to parallel the long-term pastorates of many black clergy.

According to our study, about 74 percent of 130 predominantly African American masjids had annual budgets of $40,000 or less. Only 10 (8 percent) reported incomes over $100,000. In response to the question "how would you describe the economic background of the majority of Muslims who regularly attend community activities?" the imams estimated the following: 69 (53 percent) said most of their members were in the lower-middle income bracket ($20,000 to $35,000), and 47 (36 percent) in the lower income bracket (below $20,000). Only 12 (9 percent) were in the middle-middle income bracket ($35,000 to

$49,999), and 2 (2 percent) were in the upper-middle income bracket (over $50,000).

In a similar fashion, the imams reported their own annual income last year with the following breakdown: 17 (13 percent) at lower income (below $20,000); 39 (30 percent) at lower middle income ($20,000 to $34,999); 49 (38 percent) at middle income ($35,000 to $49,999); and 21 (16 percent) at upper-middle income ($50,000 to $99,999). No imam reported an income of more than $100,000.

While African American masjids lack the economic clout of immigrants, African American imams and their followers are much more savvy about using the American political system to their advantage. On the whole, African American Muslims are much more socially and politically active in their communities, sponsoring programs ranging from drug patrols to feeding programs to 12-step substance abuse programs. Nationally, there is a "majlis ashura," or Islamic Council, comprised of the leaders of African American and immigrant Muslim groups. Islam in America is still in an institution-building phase. In America, compared to its Jewish and Christian counterparts, Islam is a relatively young religion, with much of its activities and growth occurring during the past 40 years.

Changing Cultural Characteristics

For the majority of immigrant Muslims, the goal is to preserve Islamic and ethnic cultural traditions and practices. Much of the task of their Islamic Centers is focused on the institutional maintenance of families and kin relations, to make sure that their young people are raised with Islamic culture and knowledge and some traditions from the old country. On the other hand, African American Muslims are much more focused on spreading Islam, seeking converts, and attempting to create an Islamic milieu and environment. As in other religions, the recent converts are much more fervent and enthusiastic about the faith. African American imams preach more often about the need to undertake *dawah* (propagation of the faith).

Secularization is certainly a major concern for both immigrant and African American Muslims. This concern is mainly focused on young people, developing the next generation of Muslims in America. The permissive atmosphere of most public schools and college campuses; the loose sexual mores, and immodest dress; the consumption of tobacco, alcohol, and drugs; the lyrics of rock and rap music; the pervasive influence of television; and the trend of living together before marriage create great anxieties for Muslim parents and adults. In our survey of 130 African American masjids, 71 percent of the imams answered "yes" to the question of whether "their organization had any difficulty in recruiting and maintaining young adults—between the ages of 17 to 30." In answering why this difficulty exists, about one-third of the imams responded by pointing to the "pressure from the larger society, especially of their non-Muslim peers."

While there are secularizing pressures from the larger society and some difficulty in recruiting and maintaining young adults in the religion, there is also an atmosphere of Islamic revivalism, especially among African Americans. For some young Muslims, wearing a veil or a kufi or fasting during Ramadan is a statement about their faith and their affirmation of difference. "For some young women, the veil in America works a bit like the Afro during the black-power era," said Mohja Kahf, a professor at the University of Arkansas. Amira Al-Sarraf, 34, a teacher at an Islamic School in Los Angeles, explains: "I don't have men flirting with me. I enjoy the respect I get."[19]

Conclusion

The future challenges for Islam in America are twofold: First, the need to increase the numbers of Muslims participating in masjids, especially at the Friday Jumu'ah prayer service. Bagby estimates that only about 10 to 20 percent of all Muslims are regular participants in masjids. This participation rate tends to be on the low side compared to other American religious groups. The reasons for the low participation include the fact that the main worship time for Muslims is on Friday afternoon (usually between 1 and 3 P.M.), and many American businesses have not made accommodations for Muslims desiring to participate in worship services. Second, the need to find stable financial means of supporting masjids, their programs, and imams. In answer to our survey question "what do you consider to be the major problem facing your organization today?" 42 percent of the imams responded "enough revenue, finances," the largest single category. Following the practice of black churches, some African American imams have taken to passing the plate, or, in most cases, a box, for offerings during the service. However, the majority of immigrant and African American masjids tend to support themselves via zakat or the 2.5 percent annual charity tax and sadaqa contributions to support the masjid. Most of these masjids subsist, as reported above, on the economic margins. More than 90 percent of the imams work at another job, and much of their work as imams is unpaid. Some immigrant masjids can rely on the contributions of one or a few wealthy merchants or professionals who usually make a sizable donation to their masjids; these wealthy individuals also have a lot of clout in the governance of the masjid.

In spite of a relatively hostile climate toward Islam and Muslims in the United States, the religion is thriving and growing in certain sectors of American society. Its greatest influence will come when it begins to make inroads among white Americans.

Notes

This speech was first presented at the C. Eric Lincoln Forum, Candler School of Theology, Emory University, Atlanta, GA, 2001.

1. The masjids selected for on-site surveys of congregational participants coincided with our interviews with the imam of the masjid prior to the Friday Jumu'ah service. With the consent of the imam, an announcement was made about the survey, and the questionnaires were passed out and filled out at the end of the service.
2. Allan D. Austin, *African Muslims in Antebellum America: A Sourcebook* (New York: Garland, 1984), p. 9.
3. Ibid., p. 38.
4. Adelaide Cromwell Hill and Martin Kilson, eds., *Apropos of Africa: Afro-American Leaders and the Romance of Africa* (Garden City, NY: Anchor Books, 1971), p. 63.
5. Ibid., pp. 183–191.
6. The Ahmadiyyah movement was an Islamic missionary movement stemming from India (now Pakistan). It is a sectarian group founded in the late nineteenth century that followed the teachings of Ghulam Ahmad, who among other things claimed to be the Mahdi and prophet. The movement is considered to be outside the bounds of Sunni Islam. Ahmadiyyah missionaries were important to the spread of Islam in black communities beginning in the 1920s.
7. The studies that have been done have usually relied on telephone surveys, which can be problematic in assessing numbers of Muslims. Telephone surveys usually miss about 20 percent of the population, especially those who are poor and cannot afford a phone. Some African American and immigrant Muslims are poor. Furthermore, the American media bias against Muslims has also produced a reluctance to answer questions of religious identification, especially to strangers on a phone.
8. Barry A. Kosmin and Egon Mayer, "Profile of the U.S. Muslim Population" (New York: The Graduate Center, City University of New York, 2001).
9. Fareed A. Numan, *The Muslim Population of the United States: "A Brief Statement"* (Washington D.C.: The American Muslim Council, 1992).

10. Yvonne Yazbeck Haddad and Jane Idelman Smith, eds., *Muslim Communities in North America* (Albany: State university of New York Press, 1994).

11. Ihsan Bagby, "Masjid Survey Results," unpublished survey, Islamic Resource Institute of Orange County, California, 1992.

12. Ihsan Bagby, presentation of his survey results to a meeting of the New England Religion Discussion Society (NERDS), Hartford, CT, September 19, 1997.

13. Interview with Imam Warith Deen Umar, Director of Muslim Chaplaincy Services, New York State Correctional Facilities, at the annual Islamic Conference, Poughkeepsie, NY, November 1, 1997.

14. Samuel Huntington, *The Third Wave: Democratization in the Twentieth Century* (Norman, OK: University of Oklahoma Press, 1991).

15. Khutbah by Imam Abu Muslimah, "Racism Against the Black Muslims," taped sermon transcribed by Mrs. Waheedah Bagby, Islamic Center of East Orange, NJ, 1997, p. 5.

16. Ibid., p. 6.

17. Black churches have been multi-dimensional institutions, focusing on worship but also serving a variety of other needs, including social, political, and economic ones. As C. Eric Lincoln has summed it up, the Black Church was both "lyceum and gymnasium, as well as sanctum sanctorum"; it was also the art gallery, concert hall, and place for mass meetings. See the foreword to Lincoln, *The Black Experience in Religion* (New York: Doubleday, 1974).

18. See Linda Wallbridge, *Without Forgetting the Imam: Lebanese Shism in an American Community* (Detroit: Wayne State University Press, 1997).

19. Carla Power, "The New Islam," *Newsweek* (March 16, 1998), p. 34.

7

W. E. B. DuBois and the Struggle for African America's Soul

Alton B. Pollard, III

It is but human experience to find that the complete suppression of a race is impossible.... This the American Black knows: our fight here is a fight to the finish. Either we die or we win.... We will enter modern civilization here in America as Black people on terms of perfect and unlimited equality with white people, or we will not enter at all. Either extermination root and branch, or absolute equality. There can be no compromise. This is the last great battle of the West.

—*W. E. B. DuBois*

The news of W. E. B. DuBois's death in Ghana at the age of 95 reached the United States early on the morning of August 28, 1963, the day of the historic March on Washington. Roy Wilkins, executive secretary of the NAACP, urged the vast assemblage on the Lincoln Memorial lawn to "remember that this has been a long fight. We were reminded of it by the news of the death yesterday in Africa of Dr. W. E. B. DuBois. . . . [I]t is incontrovertible that at the dawn of the twentieth century his was the voice that was calling to you to gather here today in this cause."[1]

DuBois was indeed a prophet—for the early decades of the twentieth century, for the burgeoning Civil Rights and Black Consciousness movement of the 1960s and, I would argue, for these formative years of the twenty-first century. His social thought represents a moral and intellectual call to arms in the fight against imperialism, antisemitism, and oppression based on race and gender. Equally important for our moment, as a proponent of African Diasporic pride, DuBois celebrated cultural pluralism as a tenet of his faith in the democratic ethos.

DuBois reached maturity during some of the most long and lean years of African American struggle and despair. The hope to which emancipation and Reconstruction had given rise shattered against the racism rife across the land. In the South and border states anti-Negro hate groups maimed, lynched, raped, and rioted in bigoted fury. Social and political deconstruction, North and South, denied black people the vote and offered them educational opportunities that were deficient at best; the courts gave them civil injustice, and discrimination barred them from decent housing; those who could find jobs had to withstand subhuman working conditions. White American society as a whole saw blacks as lazy, insolent, libidinous, ignorant, irresponsible, uncultured, criminal—and in the final analysis, irredeemable. And, by and large, the scientific community concurred: The social Darwinists proclaimed that the Negro's culture was deficient and their inferiority innate, that those who were of darker hue were unfit for full and equitable participation in the modern competitive world.

This was the context within which DuBois declared in *The Souls of Black Folk* that the central problem of the twentieth century would be "the relation of the darker to the lighter races of humankind in Asia and Africa, in America and the islands of the sea."[2] Events—from the advent of Martin Luther King, Jr., and Malcolm X to the emergence of the Two-Thirds World—have proved DuBois right.

In 1903, 60 years before the names of King and Malcolm became familiar, DuBois described in *The Souls of Black Folk* the essential problematic of African American life (and if DuBois were writing today he would no doubt write in gender inclusive ways):

> One ever feels his twoness—an American, a Negro; two souls, two thoughts, two unreconciled strivings; two warring ideals in one dark body, whose dogged strength alone keeps it from being torn asunder. The history of the American Negro is the history of this strife—this longing to attain self-conscious manhood, to merge his double self into a better and truer self. In this merging he wishes neither of the older selves to be lost. . . . He simply wishes to make it possible for a man to be both a Negro and an American, without being cursed and spit upon by his fellows, without having the doors of opportunity closed roughly in his face.[3]

Regrettably, DuBois's insights are now largely neglected, to the peril of African America and society at large. Both the civil rights and black consciousness components of the movement for African American freedom—both the descendents of King and the followers of Malcolm—their own future shrouded in doubt, would do well to remember DuBois's call to African Americans that they merge their double selves into new and better selves with "neither of the older selves to be lost." DuBois's great fear was that his people—women, children, and men, conveyers and purveyors of soul throughout the modern history of the Western hemisphere—would relinquish their birthright for a mess of pottage, renouncing their illustrious heritage of strident social protest and rich cultural gifts:

> What if the Negro people be wooed from a strike for righteousness, from a love of knowing, to regard dollars as the be-all and end-all of life? Whither, then, is the new-world quest for goodness and Beauty and Truth gone glimmering? Must this, and that fair flower of freedom which . . . sprung from our fathers' blood, must that too degenerate into a dusky quest of gold?[4]

With only the slightest rewriting, those questions might well be asked of any group in the United States, no matter its heritage.

Decades later, DuBois could still be found struggling valiantly with the cultural and political implications of black social division as it spread slowly but surely through his community of origin. Issues of communal care, he believed, were inseparable from the moral imperatives of justice. His identification with his race and his opposition to racism—as well as colonialism, capitalism, militarism, and sexism—derived from his own most intimate experience of the African American attempt to wrest selfhood from a supposedly ignominious past. What does it mean, finally, to be both a person of African descent *and* a seeker of the kingdom beyond caste? In a 1933 essay, "On Being Ashamed of Oneself," DuBois recoils from the view that racial equality could be realized within the hegemonic structures of Western capitalist industrial society. He challenges his people, Black people, African American people, African descended people, African Diasporic people, with this plaintive warning:

> What are we really aiming at? The building of a new nation or the integration of a new group into an old nation? The latter has long been our ideal. Must it be changed? Should it be changed? If we seek new group loyalty, new pride of race, new racial integrity—how, where, and

by what method shall these things be attained? A new plan must be built up.[5]

DuBois's "new plan" required group action involving "the organization of intelligent and earnest people of Negro descent for their preservation and advancement in America, in the West Indies and in Africa; *and no sentimental distaste for racial . . . unity can be allowed to hold them back from a step which sheer necessity demands.*"[6]

Prior to the *Brown vs. Topeka Board of Education* decision of 1954, no one in the United States could have foreseen the full implications of DuBois's endarkening and prophetic stance. Nevertheless, the desire of some African Americans "to escape from [them]selves" and "the trammels of race" had surfaced as a significant if muted social theme since the end of the Civil War.[7] Once a breech appeared in the wall of desegregation, more and more blacks seized the educational opportunity it offered—and many of them never returned: The social advancement of a relatively few individuals gradually, almost imperceptibly, began to take precedence over the welfare and concerns of the community. To a saddening extent, DuBois's worst fears became reality; African Americans with a distaste for racial unity found due inspiration instead in the quest for gold.

Belief in "color-blindness"—a sense of self or identity that implies certain rites (and rights) of social entry without regard to race —has for the most part emerged since the time of DuBois. Many who support efforts to erase racial and ethnic distinctions suspect as an odious and irrational deception progressive rainbow declarations in praise of a "color-full" society. They have little use for the post-modern recognition of alterity, social heterogeneity, cultural difference, or distinctive gendered or sexual views. They consider any race-conscious solution— such social initiatives as affirmative action and the Head Start program or such community efforts as independent African American social and economic institutions—to be outmoded and repressive, an albatross around the neck of the upwardly mobile. They trumpet equality of opportunity (access to the barbarism of naked capitalism?) and pay little regard to equality of conditions for the poor, the exploited, the violated, and the dispossessed. The familiar refrain they sing is as distressingly simple as it is symptomatic: "Rather than cast our lot with the race, we race to leave the caste."

The historic spirit of African American protest culminated during the 1950s, 1960s, and early 1970s, in the Civil Rights and Black

Consciousness movement. The processes that for the better part of three centuries had quarantined African Americans were powerfully challenged, widely implicated, and, to an unparalleled extent, overcome. Desegregation rulings forced public facilities to end juridical (but not extrajudicial) discriminatory practices. Public school systems had to extend a measure of educational equality, and the private sector was compelled to take black job applicants seriously. By almost any criteria, conditions in the African American community improved as a result of movement efforts.

There was emerging, however, a dissonant reality, a contentious caveat of major moral and social consequence. Social gains confronted African Americans who wished to move beyond segregation with the need to accept larger societal values that had, often if not always, served to buttress the oppression of their race. In short, legal desegregation was producing its own peculiar wrenching of the African American soul. DuBois had predicted as much in this 1947 essay, "Can the Negro Expect Freedom by 1965?":

> It [freedom] will bring, however, certain curious problems. How far will . . . young Negroes consider that their primary duty is toward the cultural group which they represent and which created them? If they had been born in Russia or England, in France or Japan, in white America, such a question would not arise.
>
> On the other hand, Negroes in the United States, being on the one hand American, and on the other hand members, more or less integrated, of the Negro group, will not have so clear a duty before their eyes. They may think of their preferment chiefly as their personal accomplishment and therefore as a chance to escape an unpleasant environment and hateful conditions. They may look upon their careers as American, not Negro; withdrawing themselves from the Negro group as far as possible.[8]

In time, the rewards of civil rights integrationism while critical proved considerably smaller than had been anticipated. Moreover, they came with a high and unanticipated cost: the (usually) unquestioning acceptance of general societal values inimical to those who remained unintegrated, those kith and kin who remained beyond the pale.

Civil rights orthodoxy in the 1960s assumed that African Americans were entitled to participate fully in the socio-economic benefits of the American dream. With the notable exceptions of such public figures as Martin Luther King, Jr., and Malcolm X, however, there was little sustained discussion of what kind of people, in moral and social terms, such "progress" might produce—middle-class, white-collar African Americans disdainful of their community and amnesiac concerning their culture. *Crossing over*—as opposed to *passing*—became a prize of great worth. DuBois, because he recognized that to be authentic, social equality would have to preserve and embrace African American cultural patterns, warned against complete capitulation to racial assimilation: "American Negroes must remember that voluntary organization for great ends is far different from compulsory segregation for evil purposes."[9]

Many African Americans came to reject voluntary racial organization for great ends. They accepted instead the social attitudes and arrangements that relegated the majority of African Americans, Latinos, Native Americans, and women to lives of involuntary serfdom or hapless dependence on government largess. As early as 1960, DuBois believed that the pursuit of economic success so preoccupied African Americans "that they are no longer a single body. They are different sets of people with different sets of interests."[10] He was already convinced that, in the words of Vincent Harding, African Americans had been successfully "bribed to trade equal status in the United States for the slavery of the majority of humankind."[11]

DuBois's greatest fear—racial fragmentation and assimilation—finds disturbing fulfillment in some of the more prominent African American voices of our day. There is little need to elaborate on the activities of those who figure so prominently (or at least publicly) in the struggle of which I speak. Some selfishly proclaim "self-help," while others espouse the common good of "the race."[12] The loudest voices belong to those whose vision of self-help leads them to attack the very educational and professional forms of affirmative action that enabled them to climb the ladder of success in the first place. Meanwhile, the general condition of many of America's African progeny continues to deteriorate sharply.

Clarence Thomas, a product of the rural South (Pin Point, Georgian to be exact), and acknowledged beneficiary of the Civil Rights movement, is an infamous case in point. With his appointment as an associate justice of the Supreme Court in 1991, he reached the pinnacle of his profession. Determination and achievements of his caliber usually draw commendation and accolade. But how was Justice Thomas, one of a growing number of black political and economic conservatives ("But what do African Americans have to conserve?" one disbelieving African observer asked), able to become so oblivious to the painful memories of the race? How is it that he was so easily able to separate himself from the events of recent history? If, as DuBois maintained, the goal of the black struggle is merging the "double self into a better and truer self" with "neither of the older selves to be lost," then Thomas offers hope only to himself, for he has lost—one may even say dispensed with—his African American soul.

This may be the reason that Judge Thomas was caught off guard during his televised Senate Judiciary Committee hearings, seemingly unaware that he too could get his racial comeuppance. The confirmation hearings were, as Thomas rightfully described them, a "high-tech lynching" of his person, but they were even more so a public case of high-tech rape.[13] Again, the words of DuBois give us reason to pause, this time before the salacious and acrimonious debate that accompanied the testimony of Anita Hill, an African American professor of law who had worked for Thomas during the 1980s and accused him of sexual harassment: "The present mincing horror at free womanhood must pass if we are ever to be rid of the bestiality of free manhood. . . . The world . . . forgets its darker sisters. They seem in a sense to typify that veiled melancholy" that is among the fruits of injustice.[14]

At the time, numerous commentators attempted to put the best face on the Thomas-Hill debacle, referring to the excellent credentials and admirable composure that each displayed. The pertinent question is, of course, so what? Essentially, all of African America was placed on trial and, as has been the case in virtually every high-profile case in the United States involving a person of African descent before and after, justice was found wanting. Such a verdict, DuBois somberly declares, is the inevitable consequence of this nation's sins. "A group, a nation, or a race, commits murder and rape, steals and destroys, yet no individual is guilty, no one is to blame, no one can be punished. The black world squirms beneath the feet of the white in impotent fury or sullen hate."[15] Our system of legal jurisprudence still serves to remind us that, even for apostles of self-help preaching their faith in a self-proclaimed color-blind society, admittance is no guarantee of acceptance.

W. E. B. DuBois's legacy is not offered here as the blueprint for how America and its communities of African descent should move into the twenty-first century. However, his way of seeing—his way of approaching social justice and the common good—can help in our search for answers to the numerous questions that yet remain to be answered. Will the hopes and aspirations of African Americans continue to be founded largely on the goals, strategies, and purviews associated with the Civil Rights and Black Consciousness movement? Have we who center our concern on the African American community as a whole become, as many proponents of self-help would charge, unquestioningly mimetic in our current praxis—incapable of expanding perspectives that, though liberating in an earlier era, no longer suffice to sustain hope and ensure well-being? Are there prospects for new modes of black activism that are capable of simultaneously nourishing the African American soul while moving the nation beyond divisive social realities? Is it possible that a prophetic African American consciousness is emerging, one that can emancipate, elevate, and liberate—collectively?

In that last question lies the challenge. And more than a measure of hope. Much of the evidence to date—the emergence of contemporary rap and hip-hop; African-centered worldviews and womanist expressions; the proliferation of African American cultural groups; the resurgence of historically black colleges and universities; political identification with South Africa, Cuba, Mauritania, Grenada, Haiti, Palestine, and other peoples of the Two-Thirds World—all these reflect changes of major moment, the growth of a new prophetic consciousness. On the other hand, consider the fracturing of African America into two extremes—the prosperous and the desperate, the haves and the have-nots, the already-haves and the never-will-haves. To observe this dichotomy is to realize that even the evidence for hope may not suffice in the African American soul-quest for dignity, well being, freedom, and justice.

It is difficult to determine the depth and extent of the new prophetic consciousness, nor can we discern with absolute certitude the condition of the contemporary African American soul. Still, the evidence of its stamina is beyond refute. There is abroad in the land a contagious pride and a dogged determination that confirms the DuBoisian dictum: "We must accept equality or die."[16] No apologies are heard being offered, no invectives hurled, no denial of our best selves, just progress—the renewed sense of our own humanity—born of struggle. Yes, I hear the dedication of America's African communities as it reverberates in the spiritual's soaring refrain:

> Done made my vow to the Lord,
> And I never will turn back.
> I will go. I shall go.
> To see what the end will be.

Notes

This speech was first presented at the C. Eric Lincoln Lectureship Series, Clark Atlanta University, Atlanta, GA, 1991.

1. Recounted in Manning Marable, *W.E.B. DuBois: Black Radical Democrat* (Boston: Twayne Publishers, 1986), p. 214. Other excellent perspectives are Arnold Rampersad, *The Art & Imagination of W.E.B. Du Bois* (Cambridge, MA: Harvard University Press, 1976); Gerald Horne, *Black & Red: W.E.B. DuBois and the Afro-American Response to the Cold War, 1944–1963* (New York: State University of New York Press, 1986), and David Levering Lewis, *W.E.B. DuBois: Biography of a Race, 1868–1919* (New York: Henry Holt & Co., 1994) and *W.E.B. DuBois: The Fight for Equality and the American Century 1919–1963* (New York: Henry Holt & Co., 2000).

2. W. E. B. DuBois, *The Souls of Black Folk* (Greenwich, CT: Fawcett Publications, 1961), p. 23. First published in 1903, this is widely regarded as DuBois's masterpiece. Outstanding among his numerous other works are *Suppression of the African Slave Trade* (1896); *The Philadelphia Negro* (1899); *Darkwater* (1920); *The Gift of Black Folk* (1924); *Dark Princess* (1928); *Black Reconstruction* (1935); *Color and Democracy* (1945); and *The World and Africa* (1947).

3. DuBois, *Souls of Black Folk*, p. 17.

4. Ibid., p. 69.

5. Meyer Weinberg, ed., *W.E.B. DuBois: A Reader* (New York: Harper & Row, 1970), p. 13.

6. Ibid., p. 15, emphasis added.

7. Ibid., pp. 11–12.

8. Ibid., pp. 332–33.

9. Cited in Manning Marable, *Black American Politics: From the Washington Marches to Jesse Jackson* (London: Verso, 1985), p. 101.

10. W. E. B. DuBois, "Wither Now and Why," in Herbert Aptheker, ed., *The Education of Black People: Ten Critiques, 1906–1960* (New York: Monthy Review Press, 1973), pp. 149–58.

11. Vincent Harding, "W.E.B. DuBois and the Black Messianic Vision," in John Henrik Clarke, ed., *Black Titan: W.E.B. DuBois* (Boston: Beacon Press, 1970), p. 67.

12. The political classifications are wide-ranging, from Americanists, assimilationists, bourgeoisie, neoconservatives, and reactionaries, on the one hand, to Africanists, womanists, subversives, leftist radicals, and separatists, on the other.

13. Controversial from the start, Judge Clarence Thomas's nomination became a media sensation when it was leaked to the press that law professor Anita Hill was willing to testify that Thomas harassed her while she served under him at the Equal Employment Opportunity Commission (EEOC) during the 1980s. Following days of extensive coverage on every major television network, the hearings came to a climax when Thomas cast himself as the "victim" of a

"high-tech lynching" in an effective displacement of attention from his own guilt or innocence to that of the Judiciary Committee's. In the end, Thomas was confirmed by a full Senate vote of 52–48. See Jack E. White, "The Stereotypes of Race," *Time Magazine* (October 21, 1991): 66.

14. W. E. B. DuBois, *Darkwater: Voices from within the Veil* (New York: Schocken, 1969), p. 165.

15. Cited in Truman Nelson, "W.E.B. DuBois as a Prophet," in Clarke, ed., *Black Titan*, p. 141.

16. DuBois, "Wither Now and Why," pp. 149–58.

8

Martin, Malcolm, and Black Theology

James H. Cone

America, I don't plan to let you rest until that day comes into being when all God's children will be respected, and every [person] will respect the dignity and worth of human personality. America, I don't plan to let you rest until from every city hall in the country, justice will roll down like waters and righteousness like a mighty stream. America, I don't plan to let you rest until from every state house ... [persons] will sit in the seat who will do justly, who will love mercy, and who will walk humbly before their God. America I don't plan to let you rest until you live it out that "all [persons] are created equal and endowed by their creator with certain inalienable rights." America, I don't plan to let you rest until you live it out that you believe what you have read in your Bible, that out of one blood God made all [people] to dwell upon the face of the earth.[1]

—Martin Luther King, Jr.

All other people have their own religion, which teaches them of a God whom they can associate with themselves, a God who at least looks like one of their own kind. But we, so-called Negroes, after 400 years of masterful brainwashing by the slave master, picture "our God" with the same blond hair, pale skin, and cold blue eyes of our murderous slave master. His Christian religion teaches us that black is a curse, thus we who accept the slave masters' religion find ourselves loving and respecting everything and everyone except black, and can picture God as being anything else EXCEPT BLACK.[2]

—Malcolm X

The prophetic and angry voices of Martin Luther King, Jr., and Malcolm X together revolutionized theological thinking in the African American community. Before Martin and Malcolm, black ministers

and religious thinkers repeated the doctrines and mimicked the theologies they read and heard in white churches and seminaries, grateful to be
allowed to worship God in an integrated sanctuary and to study
theology with whites in a seminary classroom.

I remember my excitement when I was accepted as a student at
Garrett Theological Seminary more than 35 years ago. It was my first
educational experience in a predominantly white environment. Like
most blacks of that time who attended white colleges and graduate
schools, I tried hard to be accepted as just another student. But no
matter how hard I tried, I was never just another student in the eyes of
my white classmates and my professors. I was a *Negro* student—which
meant a person of mediocre intelligence (until proven otherwise) whose
history and culture were not worthy of theological reflection.

No longer able to accept black invisibility in theology and getting
angrier and angrier at the white brutality meted out against Martin
King and other civil rights activists, my southern, Arkansas racial
identity began to rise in my theological consciousness. Like a dormant
volcano, it soon burst forth in a manner that exceeded my intellectual
control. "You are a racist!" I yelled angrily at my doctoral advisor, who
was lecturing to a theology class of about 40 students. "You've been
talking for weeks now about the wrongdoings of Catholics against
Protestants in sixteenth- and seventeenth-century Europe," I continued,
raising my voice even higher, "but you've said absolutely nothing about
the monstrous acts of violence by *white* Protestants against Negroes in
the American South today in 1961!"

Devastated that I—who was a frequent presence in his office and
home—would call him a racist, my advisor, who was a grave and staid
English gentleman, had no capacity for understanding black rage. He
paced back and forth for nearly a minute before he stopped suddenly
and stared directly at me with an aggrieved and perplexed look on his
face. Then he shouted, "That's simply not true! Class dismissed."

He stormed out of the classroom to his office. I followed him. "Jim,"
he turned in protest, "you know I'm not a racist!" "I know," I said with
an apologetic tone still laced with anger. "I'm sorry I blurted out my
frustrations at you. But I am angry about racism in America and the rest
of the world. I find it very difficult to study theology and never talk
about it in class." "I'm concerned about racism too," he retorted with
emphasis. We then talked guardedly about racism in Britain and the
United States.

The more I thought about the incident, then and later, the more I
realized that my angry outburst was not about the personal prejudices

of my advisor or any other professor at Garrett. It was about how the discipline of theology had been defined so as to exclude any engagement with the African American struggle against racism. I did not have the words to say to my advisor what I deeply felt. I just knew intuitively that something was seriously wrong with studying theology during the peak of the civil rights era and never once reading a book about racial justice in America or talking about it in class. It was as if the black struggle for justice had nothing to do with the study of theology—a disturbing assumption that I gradually became convinced was both anti-Christian and racist. But since I could not engage in a disinterested discussion about race as if I were analyzing Karl Barth's christology, I kept my views about racism in theology to myself and only discussed them with the small group of African American students who had similar views.

After I completed a Ph.D. in systematic theology in the fall of 1964, I returned to Arkansas to teach at Philander Smith College in Little Rock. No longer cloistered in a white academic environment and thus free of the need for my professors' approval, I turned my attention to the rage I had repressed during six years of graduate education. Martin Luther King, Jr., and the Civil Rights movement helped me to take another look at the theological meaning of racism and the black struggle for justice. My seminary education was nearly worthless in this regard, except as a negative stimulant. My mostly neo-orthodox professors talked incessantly about the "mighty acts of God" in biblical history. But they objected to any effort to link God's righteousness with the political struggles of the poor today, especially among the black poor fighting for justice in the United States. God's righteousness, they repeatedly said, can never be identified with any human project. The secular and Death of God theologians were not much better. They proclaimed God's death with glee and published God's obituary in *Time* magazine. But they ignored the theological significance of Martin King's proclamation of God's righteous presence in the black freedom struggle.

Although latecomers to the Civil Rights movement, a few white theologians in the North supported it and participated in marches led by Martin Luther King, Jr. But the African American fight for justice made little or no impact on their intellectual discourse about God, Jesus, and theology. Mainstream religion scholars viewed King as a civil rights activist who happened to be a preacher rather than as a creative theologian in his own right.

It is one thing to think of Martin King as a civil rights activist who transformed America's race relations and quite another to regard the struggle for racial justice as having theological significance. Theology, as I studied it in the 1960s, was narrowly defined to exclude the practical and intellectual dimensions of race. That was why Albert Camus, Jean-Paul Sartre, and Susan Sontag were read in theology courses but not Richard Wright, Zora Neale Hurston, W. E. B. DuBois, and James Baldwin. Likewise Harry Emerson Fosdick and Ralph Sockman figured high on the reading lists in homiletics courses but not Howard Thurman and Martin King. White theologians reflected on the meaning of God's presence in the world from the time of the exodus of Israelite slaves out of Egypt to the civil rights revolution of the 1950s and 60s and never once made a sustained theological connection between these two liberation events. The black experience was theologically meaningless to them.

Unfortunately, black ministers and theologians were strongly influenced by the white way of thinking about God and theology. When Richard Allen and other black Christians separated from white churches in the late eighteenth and early nineteenth centuries they did not regard their action as having *theological* meaning. They thought of it as a social act, totally unrelated to how blacks and whites think about God. That was why they accepted without alterations the confessions of faith of the white denominations from which they separated. But how is it possible to enslave and segregate people and still have correct thinking about God? That was a question that black ministers did not ask.

Even Martin King did not ask that question so as to expose the flawed white liberal thinking about God that he had encountered in graduate school. King thought his theology was derived primarily from his graduate education, and to a large degree, it was, especially his ghost-written books and speeches to white audiences. As a result, he was unaware of the profoundly radical interpretation of Christianity expressed in his civil rights activity and proclaimed in his sermons.

But what King *did* in the South and later the North and what he *proclaimed* in sermons and impromptu addresses profoundly influenced our understanding of the Christian faith. King did not do theology in the safe confines of academia—writing books, reading papers to learned societies, and teaching graduate students. He did theology with his life and proclaimed it in his preaching. Through marches, sit-ins, and boycotts and with the thunder of his voice, King hammered out his theology. He aroused the conscience of white America and made the racist a moral pariah in the church and the society. He also inspired passive blacks to take charge of their lives, to believe in themselves, in God's creation of them as a free people, as equally deserving of justice as whites.

King was a public theologian. He turned the nations' television networks into his pulpit and classroom, and he forced white Christians to confront their own beliefs. He challenged all Americans in the church, academy, and every segment of the culture to face head-on the great moral crisis of racism in the United States and the world. It was impossible to ignore King and the claims he made about religion and justice. While he never regarded himself as an academic theologian, he transformed our understanding of the Christian faith by making the practice of justice an essential ingredient of its identity.

It could be argued that Martin King's contribution to the identity of Christianity in America and the world was as far-reaching as Augustine's in the fifth century and Luther's in the sixteenth.[3] Before King no Christian theologian showed so conclusively in his actions and words the great contradiction between racial segregation and the gospel of Jesus. In fact, racial segregation was so widely accepted in the churches and societies throughout the world that few white theologians in America and Europe regarded the practice as unjust. Those who did see the injustice did not regard the issue important enough to even write or talk about it. But since King, no theologian or preacher dares to defend racial segregation. He destroyed its moral legitimacy. Even conservative white preachers like Pat Robertson and Jerry Falwell make a point to condemn racial segregation and do not want to be identified with racism. That change is due almost single handedly to the theological power of King's actions and words.

Martin King was extremely modest about his political achievements and rather naive about the intellectual impact he made on the theological world. Theologians and seminarians have also been slow to recognize the significance of his theological contribution. But I am convinced that Martin Luther King, Jr., was the most important and influential Christian theologian in America's history. Some would argue that the honor belongs to Jonathan Edwards or Reinhold Niebuhr or even perhaps Walter Rauschenbusch. Where we come down on this issue largely depends upon how we understand the discipline of theology. Those who think that the honor belongs to Edwards or Niebuhr or Rauschenbusch regard intellect as more important than character in the doing of theology and thus do not think that the disparity between morality and intelligence affects theological insight. To place Edwards, Niebuhr, and Rauschenbusch over King means that one cannot possibly regard the achievement of racial justice as a significant theological issue, because none of them made justice for black people a central element of his theological program. Edwards, Rauschenbusch, and Niebuhr were *white* theologians who sought to speak only to their racial community. They did not use their intellectual power to support people of color in their fight for justice. Blacks and the Third World poor were virtually invisible to them.

I am a black liberation theologian. No theologian in America is going to receive high marks from me who ignores race or pushes it to the margin of their theological agenda. But my claim about the importance of race for theology in America does not depend on one being a black liberation theologian. *Any* serious observer of America's history can see that it is impossible to understand the political and religious meaning of this nation without dealing with race. Race has mattered as long as there has been an America. How then can one be a serious Christian theologian in this land and not deal with race?

Martin King is America's most important Christian theologian because of what he said and did about race from a theological point of view. He was a liberation theologian before the phrase was coined by African American and Latin American religious thinkers in the late sixties and early seventies. King's mature reflections on the gospel of Jesus emerged primarily from his struggle for racial justice in America. His political practice preceded his theological reflections. He was an activist-theologian who showed that one could not be a Christian in any authentic sense without fighting for justice among people.

One can observe the priority of practice, as a hermeneutical principle, in his sermons, essays, and books. *Stride Toward Freedom* (1958), *Why We Can't Wait* (1964), and *Where Do We Go From Here?* (1967) were reflections on the political and religious meaning (respectively) of the Montgomery bus boycott (1955–56), the Birmingham movement (1963), and the rise of Black Power (1966). In these texts, King defined the black freedom movement as seeking to redeem the soul of America and to liberate its political and religious institutions from the cancer of racism. I contend that as a theologian to America he surpassed the others, because he addressed our most persistent and urgent sickness.

But two other features of King's work elevate him above Edwards, Rauschenbusch, and Niebuhr. The first is his international stature and influence. I do not mean his Nobel Prize, but his contribution beyond the particularity of the black American struggle. He influenced liberation movements in China, Ireland, Germany, India, South Africa, Korea, and the Philippines, and throughout Latin America and the

Caribbean. Hardly any liberation movements among the poor are untouched by the power of his thought.

Second, King was North America's most courageous theologian. He did not seek the protection of a university appointment and a quiet office. One of his most famous theological statements was written in jail. Other ideas were formed in brief breathing spaces after days of exposure to physical danger in the streets of Birmingham, Selma, and Chicago and the dangerous roads of Mississippi. King did theology in solidarity with the least of these and in the face of death. If physical death, he said, is the price I must pay to free my white brothers and sisters from the permanent death of the spirit, then nothing could be more redemptive. Real theology is risky, as King's courageous life demonstrated.

From King black liberation theology received its Christian identity, which he understood as the practice of justice and love in human relations and the hope that God has not left the least of these alone in their suffering. However, that identity was only one factor that contributed to the creation of black liberation theology. The other was Malcolm X, who identified the struggle as a *black* struggle. As long as black freedom and the Christian way in race relations were identified exclusively with integration and nonviolence, black theology was not possible. Integration and nonviolence required blacks to turn the other cheek to white brutality, join the mainstream of American society, and do theology without anger and without reference to the history and culture of African Americans. It meant seeing Christianity exclusively through the eyes of its white interpreters. Malcolm prevented that from happening.

I remember clearly when Malcolm and Black Power made a decisive and permanent imprint upon my theological consciousness. I was teaching at Adrian College (a predominantly white United Methodist institution) in Adrian, Michigan, trying to make sense out of my vocation as a theologian. The black rage that ignited the Newark and Detroit riots in July 1967, killing nearly 80 people, revolutionized my theological consciousness. Nothing in seminary prepared me for this historic moment. It forced me to confront the blackness of my identity and to make theological sense of it.

Martin King helped to define my *Christian* identity but was silent about the meaning of blackness in a world of white supremacy. His public thinking about the faith was designed to persuade white Christians to take seriously the humanity of Negroes. He challenged whites to be true to what they said in their political and religious documents of freedom and democracy. What King did not initially realize was how deeply flawed white Christian thinking is regarding race and the psychological damage done to the self-image of blacks.

To understand white racism and black rage in America, I turned to Malcolm X and Black Power. While King accepted white logic, Malcolm rejected it. "When [people] get angry," Malcolm said, "if they aren't interested in logic, they aren't interested in odds, they aren't interested in consequences. When they get angry, they realize that the condition that they're in—that their suffering is unjust, immoral, illegal, and that anything they do to correct it or eliminate it, they're justified. When you develop that type of anger and speak in that voice, then we'll get some kind of respect and recognition, and some changes from these people who have been promising us falsely already for far too long."[4]

Malcolm saw more clearly than King the depth and complexity of racism in America, especially in the North. The North was more clever than the South and thus knew how to camouflage its exploitation of black people. White northern liberals represented themselves as the friends of the Negro and deceived King and many other blacks into believing that the liberals really wanted to achieve racial justice in America. But Malcolm knew better and he exposed their hypocrisy. He called white liberals "foxes" in contrast to southern "wolves." Malcolm saw no difference between the two, except that one smiles and the other growls when they eat you. Northern white liberals hated Malcolm for his uncompromising, brutal honesty. But blacks, especially the young people, loved him for it. He said publicly what most blacks felt but were afraid to say except privately among themselves.

I first heard Malcolm speak while I was a student at Garrett, but I did not really listen to him. I was committed to Martin King and even hoped that he would accept the invitation offered him to become a professor of theology at Garrett. I regarded Malcolm as a racist and would have nothing to do with him. Malcolm X did not enter my theological consciousness until I left seminary and was challenged by the rise of the Black Consciousness movement in the middle of the 1960s. Black Power, a child of Malcolm, forced me to take a critical look at Martin King and to discover his limits.

It is one thing to recognize that the gospel of Jesus demands justice in race relations and quite another to recognize that it demands that African Americans accept their blackness and reject its white distortions. When I turned to Malcolm, I discovered my blackness and realized that I could never be who I was called to be until I embraced my

African heritage—completely and enthusiastically. Malcolm put the word "black" in black theology. He taught black scholars in religion and many preachers that a colorless Christianity is a joke—only found in the imaginary world of white theology. It is not found in the real world of white seminaries and churches. Nor is it found in black churches. That black people hate themselves is no accident of history. As I listened to Malcolm and meditated on his analysis of racism in America and the world, I became convinced by his rhetorical virtuosity. Speaking to blacks, his primary audience, he said:

> Who taught you to hate the color of your skin? Who taught you to hate the texture of your hair? Who taught you to hate the shape of your nose? Who taught you to hate yourself from the top of your head to the sole of your feet? Who taught you to hate your own kind? Who taught you to hate the race you belong to so much that you don't want to be around each other? You should ask yourself, "Who taught you to hate being what God gave you?"[5]

Malcolm challenged black ministers to take a critical look at Christianity, Martin King, and the Civil Rights movement. The challenge was so deep that we found ourselves affirming what many persons regarded as theological opposites: Martin and Malcolm, civil rights and Black Power, Christianity and blackness.

Just as Martin King may be regarded as America's most influential theologian and preacher, Malcolm X may be regarded as America's most trenchant race critic. As Martin's theological achievement may be compared to Augustine's and Luther's, Malcolm's race critique is as far-reaching as Marx's class critique and the current feminist critique of gender. Malcolm was the great master of suspicion in the area of race. No one before or after him analyzed the role of Christianity in promoting racism and its mental and material consequences upon the lives of blacks as Malcolm did. He has no peer.

Even today, whites do not feel comfortable listening to or reading Malcolm. They prefer Martin because he can easily be made more palatable to their way of thinking. That is why we celebrate Martin's birthday as a national holiday, and nearly every city has a street named in his honor. Many seminaries have a chair in his name, even though their curriculums do not take his theology seriously. When alienated blacks turn to Malcolm, whites turn to Martin, as if they really care about his ideas, which most do not. Whites only care about Martin as a way of undermining the black allegiance to Malcolm.

When Malcolm X was resurrected in Black Power in the second half of the 1960s, whites turned to Martin King. White religious leaders tried to force militant black ministers to choose between Martin and Malcolm, integration and separation, Christianity and Black Power. But we rejected their demand and insisted on the importance of both. The tension between Martin and Malcolm, integration and separation, Christianity and blackness, created black theology. It was analogous to the "double-consciousness," the "two unreconciled strivings," that W. E. B. DuBois wrote about in *The Souls of Black Folk* in 1903.[6]

Martin King taught black ministers that the meaning of Christianity was inextricably linked with the fight for justice in society. That was his great contribution to black theology. He gave it its Christian identity, putting the achievement of social justice at the heart of what it means to be a Christian. He did not write a great treatise on the theme of Christianity and justice. He organized a movement that transformed Christian thinking about race and the struggles for justice in America and throughout the world.

Malcolm X taught black ministers and scholars that the identity of African Americans as a people was inextricably linked with blackness. This was his great contribution to black theology. Malcolm gave black theology its *black* identity, putting blackness at the center of who we were created to be. Like Martin, Malcolm did not write a scholarly treatise on the theme of blackness and self. He revolutionized black self-understanding with the power of his speech.

The distinctiveness of black theology is the bringing together of Martin and Malcolm—their ideas about Christianity and justice and blackness and self. Neither Martin nor Malcolm sought to do that. The cultural identity of Christianity was not important to Martin because he understood it in the "universal" categories he was taught in graduate school. His main concern was to link the identity of Christianity with social justice, oriented in love and defined by hope.

The Christian identity of the black self was not important to Malcolm X. For him, Christianity was the white man's religion and thus had to be rejected. Black people, Malcolm contended, needed a black religion, one that would bestow self-respect upon them for being black. Malcolm was not interested in remaking Christianity into a black religion.

The creators of black theology disagreed with both Martin and Malcolm and insisted on the importance of bringing blackness and Christianity together. The beginning of black theology may be dated with the publication of the "Black Power" statement by black religious leaders in the *New York Times*, 31 July 1966, a few weeks after the rise of Black Power during the James Meredith March in Mississippi. Soon afterward the National Committee of Negro Churchmen was established as the organizational embodiment of their religious concerns. It did not take long for the word "Black" to replace the word "Negro," as black ministers struggled with the religious meaning of Martin and Malcolm, Christianity and blackness, nonviolence and self-defense, "freedom now" and "by any means necessary."

I sat down to write *Black Theology and Black Power* in the summer of 1968. Martin and Malcolm challenged me to think deep and long about the meaning of Christianity and blackness. Through them, I found my theological voice to articulate black rage against racism in the society, the churches, and in theology. It was a liberating experience. I knew that most of my professors at Garrett and Northwestern would have trouble with what I was saying about liberation and Christianity, blackness and the gospel. One even told me that all I was doing was seeking justification for blacks of the South side of Chicago to come to Evanston and kill him. But I could not let white fear distract me from the intellectual task of exploring the theological meaning of double-consciousness in black people.

Martin and Malcolm symbolize the tension between the African and American heritage of black people. We are still struggling with the tension, and its resolution is nowhere in sight. We can't resolve it because the social, political, and economic conditions that created it are still with us today. In fact, these conditions are worse today for the black poor, the one-third of us who reside primarily in the urban centers of Chicago and New York.

It is appalling that seminaries and divinity schools continue their business as usual—analyzing so many interesting and irrelevant things but ignoring the people who could help us to understand the meaning of black exploitation and rage in this society. Why are two of the most prophetic race critics of the church and society marginal in seminary curriculums? If we incorporated Martin's and Malcolm's critique of race and religion into our way of thinking, it would revolutionize our way of doing theology, just as class and gender critiques have done.

But taking race seriously is not a comfortable task for whites or blacks. It is not easy for whites to listen to a radical analysis of race because blackness is truly *Other* to them—creating a horrible, unspeakable fear. When whites think of evil, they think of black. That is why the word "black" is still the most potent symbol of evil. If whites want to direct attention away from an evil that they themselves have committed, they say a black did it. We are the most potent symbols of crime, welfare dependency, sexual harassment, domestic violence, and bad government. Say a black did it, whites will believe you. Some blacks will, too.

With black being such a powerful symbol of evil, white theologians avoid writing and talking about black theology. Even though black theologians were among the earliest exponents of liberation theology, we are often excluded when panels and conferences are held on the subject. One could hardly imagine a progressive divinity school without a significant interpreter of feminist and Latin American liberation theology. But the same is not true for black theology. The absence of a serious and sustained engagement of black theology in seminaries and divinity schools is not an accident. It happens because Black is the Other—strange, evil, and terrifying.

But theology can never be true to itself in America without engaging blackness, encountering its complex, multilayered meaning. Theology, as with American society as a whole, can never be true to itself unless it comes to terms with Martin and Malcolm together. Both spoke two different but complimentary truths about blackness white theologians do not want to hear but must hear if we are to create theologies that are liberating and a society that is humane and just for all of its citizens. Only then can we sing, without hypocrisy, with Martin King, along with Malcolm X, the black spiritual, "Free at last, free at last, thank God almighty, we are free at last."

Notes

This speech was first presented at the C. Eric Lincoln Lectureship Series, Clark Atlanta University, Atlanta, GA, 2001.

1. Martin Luther King, Jr., "Which Ways Its Soul Shall Go?" address given August 2, 1967, at a voter registration rally, Louisville, Kentucky, in Martin Luther King, Jr., Papers, Martin Luther King, Jr., Center for Nonviolent Social Change, Atlanta, Georgia.
2. Malcolm X, "God's Angry Men," *Los Angeles Herald Dispatch,* 1 August 1957.
3. Theologian Langdon Gilkey of the University of Chicago made that observation to me in a private conversation. It is unfortunate that he never made a disciplined argument about King's theological importance in his published writings. If he had done so, perhaps American white theologians would not have been as hostile as they were to the rise of black liberation theology
4. George Breitman, ed., *Malcolm X Speaks* (New York: Grove Press, 1965), pp.107–108.
5. Mary Ann French, "Don't Kill the Messenger: A New Documentary Examines Malcolm X's Message—and Why It Still Matters," *Washington Post,* 23 January 1994, p. G6.
6. W. E. B. DuBois, *The Souls of Black Folk* (Greenwich, CT: Fawcett Publications, 1961), pp. 16–17.

9

"There Is a Work for Each One of Us":

The Socio-Theology of the Rev. Florence Spearing Randolph

Cheryl Townsend Gilkes

African American women are significant forces in the religious and political histories of their communities—in all of African America.[1] Until recently phrases such as "the backbone of the church" and "the power behind the throne" have been the most generous assessments of black women's roles in their churches. Such assessments did not attribute agency to their roles in the churches. Their religious leadership has been evaluated largely in terms of the *influence* they have exerted from their missionary societies and auxiliary conventions. In contrast to influence, other forms of power and authority are not attributed to women's leadership in the church. Women are not immediately linked to the direct creation and proclamation of religious ideas. As a result, the power of women in institutions and organizations has been more difficult to imagine and explore.

Because of the prominence of male ministers in the public leadership of the Civil Rights movement, that leadership has been extrapolated to all sectors of African American political life. Charles V. Hamilton, in his book *The Black Preacher in America,* pointed to the lives of Martin Luther King, Jr., Adam Clayton Powell, Leon Sullivan, and others to illustrate the pivotal political role of black male preachers and the recognition of that role by white political interests.[2] Although women were vital to the prosecution and success of the Civil Rights movement, they are not automatically linked to the standard lists of movement exemplars. Gloria Richardson, Daisy Bates, Fanny Lou Hamer, and Ella Baker often must be invoked by particularly conscious women in order to be included. Since most of the women involved in the Civil Rights movement were educators rather than ministers, their absence and marginalization were compounded. Thus there were no women among Hamilton's composite of the black preacher.

The life and thought of Florence Spearing Randolph provides a special opportunity to explore a life whose leadership spanned two major institutional settings—the church and the club movement. Rev. Randolph was a preacher, elder, and pastor of the African Methodist Episcopal Zion African Methodist Episcopal Zion (AMEZ) Church, pastoring most of her career in Summit, New Jersey. She was also the founder of the New Jersey Federation of Colored Women's Clubs. Although we are talking about one life, like many of the male lives we see as paradigmatic, Rev. Randolph's life is embedded in a crucial matrix of affiliations.

Florence Spearing Randolph began her life in Charleston, South Carolina, in 1866. She was graduated from the Avery Institute and utilized her training as a dressmaker to teach. She was influenced by the holiness teaching and preaching of AMEZ preacher Julia Foote, a pioneer woman preacher of the nineteenth century.[3] Rev. Randolph was ordained a deacon of the AMEZ Church in 1901 and in 1903 was ordained an itinerant elder of that Church. After several appointments Rev. Randolph was appointed pastor of the Wallace Chapel AMEZ church in Summit, New Jersey, in 1925. She retired from that appointment in1946, continuing as pastor emeritus until her death in 1951.[4]

Like many other activist black women, Florence Spearing Randolph had a complicated organizational life both within the Church and outside of it.[5] According to Bettye Collier-Thomas, Randolph worked in Christian Endeavor and was the state president of the Women's Home and Foreign Missionary Society for 17 years. She also became national president of that body in 1916. Her activism outside the church involved the suffrage movement, the National Association of Colored Women's Clubs, and the Women's Christian Temperance Union, for which she served as a lecturer. The black women's club movement organized black women all over the United States, and Randolph organized the New Jersey Federation of Colored Women's Clubs. She was the chaplain for the northeast region during the years 1918 and 1919, and she chaired the National Association's religion department from 1919 to 1927. While serving in the unusual and distinctive role of pastor of a church in a mainline African American denomination, Rev. Randolph remained embedded and engaged in the central movements and organizations involving black women, especially the vitally important National Association of Colored Women's Clubs, a movement that propelled black women to leadership in other organizations at the local and national levels. Indeed, it is the work in clubs outside the church and in missionary societies within the church that much of the organizational infrastructure of black communities has been constituted and maintained.

W. E. B. DuBois, in his much-neglected book *The Gift of Black Folk*, pointed to the utter centrality of women to the institutional life and cultural sensibilities of African Americans.[6] DuBois also highlighted the way in which African American women in their work roles provided a liberating tradition that redounded to benefit other women and other workers, male and female. Black women's material deprivation, in spite of their hard work, led to what DuBois considered a more valuable contribution to the overall life of the community than they were credited with. Because they had no wealth to lean on, black women generated a web of organizational and interpersonal connections through multiple affiliations in churches, missionary societies, uplift organizations, clubs, burial societies, and political organizations. At the time he was writing, DuBois had already been able to observe the way women's groups provided the foundation of national organizations such as the Urban League and the NAACP. Throughout his analysis, he recognized that what we now call "networks of women" undergird whatever political and social cohesion have characterized the African American experience at any historical moment. The life and work of Florence Spearing Randolph placed her squarely in this tradition of vitally connected and affiliated activist lives.

Rev. Randolph's affiliations or connections point to the importance of centering our analysis of African American church history in the lives and webs of affiliations of women. Florence Spearing Randolph, because she was a preacher and a pastor in a mainline African American denomination and because she was a leader in the mainstream of black women's activist traditions, points to the way in which women and religion combine to create a motivating force in African American religious history.

We presume, because most black women activists are churchwomen, that the church plays a vital role in shaping their values and practices. While we discern the patently Christian understandings embedded in African American women's emphases on social uplift and the redemption of communities, we find it more difficult to point to the ways in which women's values and sensibilities directly shape the proclamations that are centered in Christian churches. A limited amount of tokenism through women's speaking at women's days and missionary Sundays does provide for the occasional foregrounding of women's voices. In spite of the women's days and the missionary Sundays, the African American mainstream preachers are men. Indeed, the preaching event is so gendered that many men and women insist upon calling women's proclamation from pulpits "speaking" in contrast to the men's "preaching." The impact of women on these men must often be discerned inductively. We hear women's voices in the prayer, testimony, and music traditions of African American churches and we hear women's discourses from these traditions appropriated into male preaching.[7] Regardless, we find it hard to imagine women's direct impact or agency in the most powerful dimensions of African American religious life—preaching and pastoral leadership.

Florence Spearing Randolph was clearly an agent of religious knowledge. She left behind an important collection of papers, the core of which is a collection of her sermons. A partial examination of these sermons reveals an intricate linkage among themes focused on basic Christian doctrine, cultural criticism, basic theology, Christian practice, and ethics. Like many African American Christian preachers, her sermons contained powerful critiques of racism based on her reading of Jesus' admonitions to love and to heal and John's insistence that hatred of others was incompatible with Christian faith—that professing to love God while hating another human being rendered the person essentially a liar. There were also themes of direct social criticism. Her race relations Sunday sermon before a white congregation was titled "If I Were White."[8] Another sermon, "Two American Gods: Money and Self,"[9] was a very clear cultural critique.

Rev. Randolph exhorted her congregation to be activist Christians, reminding them that they were missionaries, stewards, seekers, called to "make our own world." What she considered to be "the gracious privilege of knowing Christ" evoked in her a response that saw service as "beauty" and "joy."[10] Her sermon on the parable of the talents, where Jesus rewards the stewards who take risks in order to make their talents grow while chastizing the steward who buried his talent, focused on "the punishment of unused talent and opportunity."[11]

The convergence of her roles as pastor and community leader are evident in her preaching of Christian actualization. In her sermon on freedom, she insisted, "There is a work for each one of us." As free people in Christ, Randolph saw an empowered opportunity for action:

As a race of people we are in the midst of a great struggle as American citizens. But [we must] remember the foe within is greater than the foe without and hence [the foe without] must [eventually] be overpowered. First it is not enough to come and worship sabbath after sabbath, and listen to sermons [about] strong men and women, but we must digest the truths we hear and strive to put them in practice. There is a work for each one of us to do to better the condition of the home life and the community life of the great masses of our people.[12]

The great work "for each one of us" could be accomplished, according to Randolph, by the aid of the Holy Spirit. The person and work of the Holy Spirit were central to her preaching. Although not formally a part of the Holiness and Pentecostal movements, Randolph preached and wrote about the Holy Spirit, sanctification, and their importance in our lives. Such a position was more consistent with the thinking of the Holiness and Pentecostal movements that was part of the public religious conversations characterizing the African American community. Rev. Randolph's position on the Spirit was such that her pneumatology informed her christology. Traditional or orthodox Christian approaches to theology and doctrine emphasized christology as the critical point of doctrinal and dogmatic departure. Rev. Randolph almost seemed to reverse that tradition when, at one point she asserts that the person of Christ is really a blessing from the Holy Spirit. Because of that blessing, humanity embodies more perfectly the image of Christ.

In her sermon "Every Christian a Missionary," one of her messages exhorting Christian activism, she presumes that every committed Christian is a disciple and is therefore sent "with an inspiration and authority similar" to what God had invested in Jesus.[13] As "divine agents" people needed to be "not only . . . instructed but empowered. . . ."[14] The source of power, of course, is "the comforter, which is the Holy Ghost."[15] Such an emphasis was not only a theology that was a heightened and foregrounded pneumatology but it was also a liberation theology/pneumatology. The emphasis on the person of the Spirit as a source of power was a radical reflection on the gospel to a congregation that was more or less powerless in its economic and political situation. Summit, New Jersey, as a suburb of New York City contained and still contains a black community full of service workers to the affluent and powerful whites in control of that community. A *kerygma* or theory of preaching that focused on empowerment was a persistent if unacknowledged challenge to these political and economic relations.

Not only was Rev. Randolph an agent of religious knowledge—a creative, productive, moving force—but she was also, like so many African American women, an advocate for the Spirit (or Holy Ghost). Some observers have argued that the distinctiveness of African American Christianity and other religions of the African Diaspora is their members' emphasis on "the Spirit." Joseph M. Murphy in his book *Working the Spirit: Ceremonies of the African Diaspora,* summarized this unity:

> The religions of the African diaspora are different from each other in that each possesses a unique heritage from African, European, Native American, and still other sources. Yet they are like one another in that all recognize the special priority of their African roots.[16]

In spite of unique challenges and diverse contexts within which each religion arose, "each tradition construct[ed] a code of relationships between human beings and 'spirit.' . . ." Murphy emphasized that in spite of their differences, "Each diasporan community celebrates the spirit in ceremonies, and shows in various ways, through the arrangement of symbolic objects and actions, a spirituality of interdependence between the community and the spirit."[17] For the African American Christians in North America, that spirit is the Holy Spirit or the Holy Ghost.

One cannot help but notice that in those African American churches where the movement and the power of the Holy Spirit are explicitly recognized and praised, there are far more women than men. While some have theorized that the overabundance of black women in such churches when compared to men is an outcome either of men's damage or failure in spiritual development and religious attachment or of women's sexual ardor for their pastors, or some of both, I am convinced that the exploration of the African American religious experience from a perspective that centers or foregrounds African American women's church history demonstrates that African American women have been pivotal sources of religious knowledge, particularly about the Holy Spirit or Holy Ghost. As more observers and researchers center their focus on women, themes that highlight the importance and power of the Holy Spirit persist. Whether the focus is on spiritual biographies, on the structures in which women choose to exercise their faith and institutional commitments, or on the streams of history in which women are publicly involved, one can argue that African American women, in their choices of Christian practice and belief, can be viewed as agents and advocates for the Holy Spirit or Holy Ghost. Even in her exceptional role as preacher and pastor, Rev. Randolph can be placed squarely in this tradition.

Any discussion of emphases on the Holy Spirit elicits immediate questions about whether or not such beliefs are fully Christian. Because the traditional creeds and confessions of Christian churches tend to attach the Holy Spirit/Holy Ghost to the Father and the Father's begotten Son, the Holy Spirit or Holy Ghost is presumed to be a later appendage, a sort of substitute for the risen Christ. The Spirit proceeds from either the Father or the Father and Son together. The ecclesiological consequences of such beliefs are the subordination of manifestations of the indwelling Spirit to the authority and discipline of the established church and her agents, usually the overwhelmingly male clergy. In such an institutional matrix, the radical implications of ordinary women and men guided by the Holy Spirit or Holy Ghost are suppressed. For Randolph, the radical implications of Christians filled with the Holy Spirit or Holy Ghost, taking seriously their individual calls and spiritual empowerment to work, are plainly articulated. That which is a source of horror to conservative religious patriarchy is a source of hope to women like Florence Spearing Randolph.

Such an understanding has important consequences for social, historical, and theological perspectives on African American Christianity. The central theological presumptions of so-called mainline Christianity exalt the person of Christ. And in this, Randolph's preaching is no different. Regardless of the biblical text upon which a sermon was based, references to the Johannine literature (the Gospel of John, I John, II John, and III John) abound in her sermons. My reading of a portion of the collection also indicates that Rev. Randolph included Revelation in the Johannine corpus, although contemporary biblical scholars do not. Her reading is totally consistent with the general African American emphasis of Jesus' assertion to the Samaritan woman at the well articulated in John 4:24: "God is a spirit and they that worship him must worship him in spirit and in truth." Florence Spearing Randolph's linkages with the Holy Spirit are clearly and decidedly Jesus centered.

African sensibilities concerning the spirit world and consequently the Holy Spirit (or Holy Ghost) tended to throw such long-established understandings of theological order into debate. The African American experience, shaped by a significant encounter between European and African worldviews, led to the emergence of a religious ethos that gave primacy to the person of the Holy Spirit or Holy Ghost and endowed the individual's encounter with the Holy Spirit or Holy Ghost, an encounter grounded in the normative constraints of the believing community, with a special authority. To truly know Jesus, in traditional African American Christianity, was to have met Jesus in the Spirit. Such meetings in the Spirit carried with them visionary and ecstatic experiences that could be shared in some way by the larger community. During slavery and on into the early part of the twentieth century, people were expected to "mourn" and seek such experiences in order to be accepted into the church and to be considered ready for baptism. Within the walls of their churches and in their homes, women's voices as agents of socialization and of traditional knowledge are heard in religious accounts. In addition to shaping the norms of religious practice or belief, Rev. Randolph's preaching is clear evidence that the creation of an alternative Christianity that emphasized the person of God as Spirit, and the transformation that ensued from an encounter with that Spirit, was shaped by the religious agency of women as well as men.

In the study of religion and culture—the interface of which we often call "worldview"—the relationship between mythos and ethos is a critical factor in understanding the emergence of institutions and practices. More specifically, it is important to account for the ways in which myths or corporately remembered stories inform values and actions. The practical organization of religious knowledge is an important part of this process. The contributions to religious knowledge of women who emphasized the person of the Holy Spirit or Holy Ghost and its operation in their lives and their churches—women such as Fannie Lou Hamer, Bessie Jones, Jarena Lee, Zilpha Elaw, Julia Foote, Amanda Berry Smith, and Sojourner Truth—are critical to our understanding of the African American religious experience. The life of Florence Spearing Randolph enables us to understand that the voices of African American women extended to all levels of African American Christianity, practical and intellectual, while a distinctive religious experience was being forged in the heat of racial oppression. The inseparability of Rev. Randolph's Christ and Rev. Randolph's Holy Ghost forcefully answers the question concerning the African American emphasis on the Spirit—it *is* Christian. Rev. Randolph's love of the Holy Spirit or Holy Ghost places her squarely in the tradition of community commitment, historical embeddedness, and cultural grounding that Alice Walker has identified as "womanist."[18] It is here, at the nexus of Spirit, church, and community, where Florence Spearing Randolph invites us to center and foreground African American women's church history as a way of understanding the African American Christian experience and its distinctive and empowering emphasis on the Holy Spirit or Holy Ghost.

Notes

1. Earlier versions of this paper were presented on programs of the Association for the Study of AfroAmerican Life and History, Drew University, and the Temple University Center for African American History and Culture Research Seminar. Research for this paper was made possible by a Summer Fellowship award by the Temple University Center for African American History and Culture. The author would like to thank Dr. Bettye Collier-Thomas, the center's director, for permission to use the Randolph sermons, which are in her possession.

2. Charles V. Hamilton, *The Black Preacher in America* (New York: Morrow, 1972).

3. See William Andrews, ed., *Sisters of the Spirit: Three Black Women's Autobiographies of the Nineteenth Century* (Bloomington, Indiana University Press, 1986).

4. For a more detailed biography, see Bettye Collier-Thomas's *Daughters of Thunder: Black Women Preachers and Their Sermons, 1850–1979* (San Francisco: Jossey Bass, 1998), pp. 101–106.

5. For an understanding of the way that multiple affiliations are a part of black women's strategies for empowerment, see Cheryl Townsend Gilkes, "Building in Many Places: Multiple Commitments and Ideologies in Black Women's Community Work," in Ann Bookman and Sandra Morgan, eds., *Women and the Politics of Empowerment: Perspectives from Communities and Workplaces* (Philadelphia: Temple University Press, 1988), pp. 53–76.

6. W. E. B. DuBois, *The Gift of Black Folk* (1924; Millwood, NY: Kraus-Thompson Organization Limited, 1975).

7. Cheryl Townsend Gilkes, "Mother to the Motherless, Father to the Fatherless: Power, Gender, and Community in an Afrocentric Biblical Tradition," *Semeia: An Experimental Journal for Biblical Criticism* 47 (1989): 57–85.

8. Bettye Collier-Thomas, *Daughters of Thunder: Black Women Preachers and Their Sermons, 1850–1979* (San Francisco: Jossey Bass Publishers, 1998), pp. 128–129.

9. Florence Spearing Randolph, "Two American Gods: Money and Self," sermon no. 46, The Sermons of Florence Spearing Randolph (manuscript and typescript collection in the possession of Bettye Collier-Thomas). Used by permission.

10. Florence Spearing Randolph, "The Gracious Privilege of Knowing Jesus," sermon no. 56, The Sermons of Florence Spearing Randolph (manuscript and typescript collection in the possession of Bettye Collier-Thomas). Used by permission.

11. Florence Spearing Randolph, "The Punishment for Unused Talent or Opportunity," sermon no. 73, The Sermons of Florence Spearing Randolph (manuscript and typescript collection in the possession of Bettye Collier-Thomas). Used by permission.

12. The emendations of this sermon are based on the text to which Rev. Randolph alludes: "Ye are of God, little children, and have overcome them [spirits not of God]: because greater is he that is in you than he that is in the world," I John 4:4. Florence Spearing Randolph, "Freedom," sermon no. 133, The Sermons of Florence Spearing Randolph (manuscript and typescript collection in the possession of Bettye Collier-Thomas), p. 133. Used by permission.

13. Florence Spearing Randolph, "Every Christian A Missionary," sermon no. 75, The Sermons of Florence Spearing Randolph (manuscript and typescript collection in the possession of Bettye Collier-Thomas), p. 59. Used by permission.

14. Ibid., p. 160.

15. Ibid., p. 165.

16. Joseph M. Murphy, Working the Spirit: Ceremonies of the African Diaspora (Boston: Beacon Press, 1994), p. 1.

17. Ibid., p. 2.

18. Alice Walker, In Search of Our Mothers' Gardens: Womanist Prose (New York: Harcourt Brace Jovanovich, 1983).

10

A Time for Honor:

A Portrait of African American Clergywomen

Delores C. Carpenter

Introduction

This chapter highlights some of the findings of a 1999 national study of 324 black female and 448 black male Master of Divinity graduates, with special attention given to the status of women in ministry.[1] How well are black women advancing as professionals within the ministerial ranks? In the face of sexism, there are clearly a few important factors that enhance the advancement of clergywomen. Among these are hard work and an understanding that the Scriptures, which on the surface appear prohibitive, were written for particular situations and not intended for universal application against all women for all time, everywhere. Another asset for female clergy is the acquisition of a graduate theological education. It better prepares them to serve God's people. It helps women to see themselves in ways that the churches, which birthed their calls to ministry, often cannot. Further, it is clear that the Black Church needs affirmative action–type programs to open more doors for qualified female ministers. It will take time and resolve to deprogram the negative ideas that so many persons systematically have been taught about women in the pulpit. Sadly, such prohibitive teaching and preaching is still believed to be sacred truth in many places.

To pursue a professional career in any field, one needs to know how many jobs are available to him or her. From my studies of black female Master of Divinity graduates in 1985, 1992, and 1999, it is clear that most of the ministerial positions available in the profession are in pastorate and assistant pastorate positions. In the 1999 sample of 324 clergywomen, 69 were paid, full-time pastors and 32 were paid, part-time pastors. This is a combined total of 101 women pastors. Thirty-nine were paid, full-time assistant pastors and 62 were paid, part-time assistant pastors. This makes for an additional total of 101 women assistant pastors. Together, in my study, women as pastor and assistant pastor comprise an opportunity structure of 202 positions. This one pastoral category includes the lion's share of ministerial jobs. For this basic reason, the focus of this essay is upon ministry within the institutional church. I am well aware of the brilliant parachurch ministries that black women are leading. Opposition to women securing paid employment in the church has forced them into significant nontraditional ministries that have also added to the witness of the Body of Christ. For example, black clergywomen are making major contributions in the areas of counseling and global missions. It is hoped that they can continue to build upon these inroads at the same time more doors are being opened for women in the church.

In 1985, only 11 percent of the total 120 women considered were full-time pastors. In 1992 36 percent were full-time pastors. While there had been an increase in the percentage of women who had pastored in the first two studies, there was a decline in 1999. In numerical terms, the number of paid, full-time women pastors in the study rose from 13 in 1985 to 73 in 1992; it declined to 69 in 1999. Although the most recent seven-year decline is much smaller than the previous seven-year increase, this finding substantiates the need for a more concerted advocacy to produce a positive, progressive advancement of black clergywomen.

Another important factor is salary. Overall, the salaries for ministry-related jobs are quite low for black men and women. However, they are even lower for women. While the mean for men falls within the $30,000 range, the mean for women falls within the $25,000 range. This is a salary gap of $5,000. This is especially limiting for the 71 percent of the single women in the 1999 study who have primary responsibility for raising children.

Some black women say, "I can be an assistant, but I don't want to be a pastor." Speculation is that some of the women who say this are fearful of rejection, are lacking same-sex mentoring, or perhaps are fearful of success itself. Some are entrenched in the traditional teachings of men being the head of the home and the church, in the imaging of God as an anthropomorphic father. Such perceptions limit women and render them incapable of fully utilizing their gifts and talents in church and society.

While much has been written about social change, not much has been written about social change within African American religious institutions. The needed change spoken of here is gender equality. For gender equality to take place it has to be undergirded by two important pillars—one is the acceptance of the historical critical method of biblical interpretation and the other the meanings of womanist theology. The former deals with the sacred texts that are the authoritative foundations of the community. The other deals with how people think about God-ordained systems, in this case, the church. What people have been taught and are learning shape the structure and content of their beliefs and self-actualization. At the Hampton Ministers' Conference in 2000, with a gathering of more than 5,600 African American clergy, black women ministers defended their right to serve the church as pastors. Bishop Barbara Amos, founder of Faith Deliverance Christian Center in Norfolk, Virginia said, "We all know that evil thrives in institutions. But anything systematically taught in us has to be systematically taught out of us."[2] Both the scholarly interpretation of the Scriptures and womanist theology are firmly established within the curricula of graduate theological education. Thus, seminaries are the major centers of ferment for social change regarding the empowerment of women ministers. Laywomen and clergywomen are studying side by side, forging a new partnership. Male allies are also won both within the student body and the ranks of the faculty and staff. These persons can recommend female students and graduates to those looking to fill various positions.

There is another countervailing authority within the black religious community. It is Spirit—the animating connection in the divine-human encounter. The Spirit is neither male nor female. It cannot be contained by human gender categorizations. It is this authority that has rooted and grounded the calling and anointing of black women for ministry over hundreds of years. It has been personal and corporate in its manifestation, but how it intersects with ecclesiastical life is of great interest to the subject at hand. A reconceptualization of the Spirit's movement within institutional life is warranted at this time. Men and women alike must feel the Spirit moving them to transcend the social and psychological obstacles to full acceptance and enhancement of African American clergywomen. This Spirit-led movement may be called "transgender freedom within a religious liberation movement." Although black theology addressed liberation well, it has only in more recent years recognized the need for liberation from the sexism of the church. Now is the time to apply the liberation paradigm to gender.

There are four essential building blocks for change in the black church. First, there is Spirit and the black woman's call to preach. Second, there is the historical critical method of interpreting the Bible that throws off the bondage of restrictive texts against women. Third, there is the formulation of womanist theology within the construction of liberationist theologies. The fourth will be the socio-psychological freedom of black women and men that may remove gender as a defining factor in institutional leadership. As the fourth step is being accomplished, talented, well-equipped and trained women will overcome their hesitancy to move forward as a professional group. In this process, larger numbers of women will see the position of assistant pastor as a constructive step toward the pastorate. Concurrently, this will propel a growing number of laywomen into other leadership positions in the church which have traditionally been filled by men, including financial officers, property care officers, deacons, and trustees. At that point gender equality as a contemporary movement within the church will be increasingly obvious. Happily, it has already begun.

Based upon demographic data collected from black women ministers around the country, a composite profile can be derived that embodies the typical black woman pastor. Let us call her Mary. She embodies the average or most common traits found in the women pastors who responded to the 1999 study. Pastor Mary is a single mom in her forties who lives in Maryland and serves a United Methodist Church. Her salary is in the $25,000 range. She is divorced and has two children. Mary was 39 years old when she entered seminary and graduated in 1992. She is now in her forties. She has had two male mentors, one was her pastor and the other was a friend. She feels accepted as a minister.

Two items are particularly troubling in this profile. The first are Mary's low wages. Given her three years of graduate education and their cost to her, this seems to be a small return on her investment. One would conclude that she does not have monetary gain as an objective. In addition, there are probably huge responsibilities placed upon her as a single mother who is a primary caregiver and provider. Like most of the women in the study, it is only her faith that sustains her as she believes that God is with her to strengthen her. She has been highly educated but receives little fiscal compensation. However, she values the sense of peace and purpose that springs from her spirituality. American society has been described as narcissistic and materialistic, but her focus is upon spreading the Gospel of Jesus Christ and upon serving others.

Although there are certain clergy tax advantages that may help Mary financially, these advantages are offset by the probability that she does not receive the customary benefit package. In most cases, companies or institutions offer some kind of benefits on top of the designated salary, including contributions to pension and health insurance plans. Because ministers are self-employed, such items as health insurance, pension, and annuity must be subtracted from their salary package, thereby reducing their consumable income. For example, if a clergyperson earns $30,000, he or she may have to subtract 14 percent for pension ($4,200) plus another $4,500 for family health insurance. In this manner, the $30,000 is reduced to $21,300. If an annuity plan or dental plan is added, the salary becomes even lower. This explains why so many black ministers are bivocational.

How well are seminary-trained black women doing as a professional group? The 1999 survey disclosed some important indicators of their success in the ministry. Ninety-four percent of the women felt accepted, liked, and appreciated in their ministry positions. Comparing where the congregation was when they arrived with where the congregation was in 1999, there is an increase in the number of women who indicated growth and development—from 40 percent when they arrived to 64 percent, or nearly two-thirds, in 1999. Respondents reporting declining churches fell from 28 percent when they arrived to 13 percent in 1999, lower than a quarter. It is healthy that most of these women perceive that the congregations they serve have improved since they arrived. This is also an excellent point for those who disparage or are skeptical of the ability of women to lead churches toward vitality and renewal. A male executive expressed the risk in hiring a woman pastor in this way, "I don't blame the churches for not wanting to hire a woman. They know what a man can do in the job, but they are not sure of what a woman can do."[3] At least according to the women themselves, their leadership is resulting in churches that are growing and developing. This explains why 90 percent felt that they were accomplishing things.

Ninety-five percent of the women experienced joy in their work. Eighty-nine percent were successful in overcoming difficulties in their ministry. Eighty-seven percent were able to maintain separation between their ministerial duties and their family duties. Ninety-two percent expressed spiritual well-being and a sense of growth in spiritual depth. Nine-four percent felt physically healthy and energetic. Ninety-six percent were assertive on issues of justice for others. Eighty-nine percent were assertive in obtaining justice for themselves.

Overall, therefore, these women are faring well in the areas mentioned thus far. However, their portrait is not without some formidable problems and struggles. The women themselves attest to sizeable dissatisfaction. When asked the overall level of satisfaction which they experience in their ministerial career, only 44 percent indicated excellent or good; 56 percent, or more than half, expressed fair or poor satisfaction. In the next section I will try to give a balanced view of life among contemporary black clergywomen relative to their black male counterparts.

Problems within the Opportunity Structure

To assess the opportunities available to these women, we can examine the number of inquiries that these women receive from local congregations to become pastoral candidates. Over one-half of the women (59 percent) compared to one-third (34 percent) of the men indicated that they have received no letters of personal invitation to be candidates for pastoral positions. More often than not, black churches who are seeking a new pastor will invite recommended ministers to apply and preach as part of the search process. One Baptist church, after reviewing the applications that they received, invited 12 candidates to come and preach in their pulpit. The number of persons who are allowed to preach and be interviewed varies greatly. Being the finalist can mean that a church considers one candidate at a time. In other words, the favored candidate will be carried through the entire process without comparison. If he or she is blessed to emerge from the screening process as the top candidate, no competition will be necessary as that candidate is affirmed each step along the way. On the other hand, a church may settle on three or more finalists and want to interview each of them and hear all of them preach. Sometimes this preaching is done in a neutral pulpit. Sometimes such preaching is done in the church that is searching for the new minister. When preaching in a neutral pulpit, usually members of the search committee attend and report back to the larger committee and to the congregation.

A mere 13 percent of the women have received one such request to be a pastoral candidate; 15 percent two requests, 5 percent three requests; and 9 percent four or more requests. Once placed, the struggle is extended to the issue of career mobility. According to these women, once one church hires them, it is admittedly difficult to get another church position. Only 33 percent said it was easy; twice as many (67 percent) said it was difficult. Fourteen percent of the men compared to

30 percent of the women indicated very great difficulty in getting another church position. Conversely, 18 percent of the men and 8 percent of the women said it was very easy.

The women reported additional difficulties. Fifty-three percent reported having trouble with one or more lay leaders in the church they pastor/attend. Over half (53 percent) felt bored and constrained by the limits of their church position, resources or people. More than half (51 percent) did not feel sufficiently compensated for their ministerial work. Fifty-five percent felt lonely and isolated. Thirty-one percent thought seriously about leaving church-related ministry for some other kind of work. Fifty-seven percent felt the need for confidential counseling. Fifty-nine percent felt that they did not have enough time to do what was expected of them by family or spouse/partner. Seventy-two percent felt that they imposed unrealistic expectations on themselves. Factors such as these are real stressors that may contribute to the dissatisfaction that a good number of the women expressed about the ministry.

Let us now take a closer look at a few of the interesting findings in the 1999 study.

The single denomination in which the most black women grew up was the United Methodist Church (22 percent). United Methodists are a predominantly white mainline denomination. Almost one-third of the black men grew up in one of the three historically black Baptist denominations—Missionary, National, or Progressive National (30 percent). The next highest percentages of black women grew up in one of the three historically black Methodist denominations—African Methodist Episcopal, African Methodist Episcopal Zion, and Christian Methodist Episcopal (16 percent). The next highest percentage of black men grew up in the United Methodist Church. Unlike the black men, a significant number of black women grew up in mainline white denominations. Looking at men and women combined in their present denominational affiliations, the United Methodists account for 18 percent; the National Baptists account for 12 percent; the African Methodist Episcopal account for 10 percent; the American Baptists account for 8 percent; and the Missionary Baptists account for 7 percent. These five groups represent over half of the respondents. It is safe to say that black seminary graduates in 1999 were almost equally divided between the historically black denominations and the mainline, predominantly white denominations. Again, this is due to large numbers within United Methodism but also the American Baptist Convention. The latter affiliation is tricky because many black congregations are duly aligned

Table 10.1
Present and Formative Denominations for Men and Women

Present Denominations		Religious Upbringing	
Historic Black	Men and Women	Men	Women
African Methodist Episcopal	10%	9%	11%
African Methodist Episcopal Zion	2%	1%	3%
Christian Methodist Episcopal	2%	3%	2%
Church of God in Christ	1%	2%	2%
Missionary Baptist	7%	8%	5%
National Baptist	12%	14%	8%
Progressive National Baptist	7%	8%	5%
Total	41%	45%	36%
Mainline White			
American Baptist	8%	6%	12%
Disciples of Christ	4%	4%	3%
Episcopal	3%	4%	1%
Lutheran	4%	4%	3%
Presbyterian	5%	4%	6%
United Church of Christ	4%	3%	4%
United Methodist	18%	16%	22%
Southern Baptist	4%	5%	2%
Total	50%	46%	53%
Other	9%	8%	11%

Source: 1999 study

with American Baptists and one of the historically black Baptist traditions. For our purposes the respondents were asked to check only one designation. Eight percent checked American Baptist.

Switching Denominations

In the 1985 study, 51 percent of the women had switched from their denominations of origin during and after seminary. In 1992, 52 percent had switched denominations. In 1999, 45 percent reported that they had switched denominations. This is a slight decrease but still represents a significant finding, which is that nearly half of the participants have switched denominations. Such switches reinforce the observation that churchgoers in general lack denominational loyalty. Among those who changed denominations, 24 percent indicated that the change was ordination related. This usually means that they left their denomination of origin for another in order to become an ordained minister. Fifteen percent indicated that it was employment related. Among the factors listed as reasons for changing denominations, other than ordination and employment, marriage-related matters accounted for 22 percent of the other category.

It is interesting to note that men switch denominations in nearly the same proportion as women. More research needs to be done to ascertain the reasons why male clergy switch denominations.

Those who switched denominations experience lower salaries. Eighty-one percent of those who switched earned under $40,000, while 68 percent of those who did not switch earned under $40,000. Among those who earn over $40,000, only 19 percent switched as compared with 31 percent who did not switch denominations. This seems to be an economic argument for not switching; that is, of course, if one can find paid ministerial employment in one's denomination of origin.[4]

Paid Professional Ministry

Turning now to paid employment, the vast majority of the women studied in 1992 worked in ten areas of ministry, with guest-speaking being the most common job at 55 percent and pastor second at 48 percent. Thirty-six percent pastored full-time. This was more than triple the 11 percent who pastored full-time in 1985. Thirty-six percent of women were also associate pastors in 1992. Counseling came in third at 25 percent in 1992. This was a healthy increase over the 14 percent who were working in counseling in the 1985 study.

The 1999 data, which includes a larger sample, paints a less optimistic picture regarding women in these same positions. Looking only at full-time employment, 21 percent were pastors (69 women—a decrease of 15 percent from 1992), 12 percent assistant pastors, 11 percent guest speakers, and 7 percent counselors.

One way that we assess the size of the churches which these women serve is to look at their weekly attendance. The median attendance in 1999 was 100. This means that half of the women served churches with an attendance of over 100 and half served in churches where the attendance was less. Another important indicator of congregational

Table 10.2
Salaries and Denominational Switching

Salary Range	Percentage of Clergy who Switched Churches	Percentage of Clergy who Did Not Switch
Under $10,000	16%	16%
10,000 – 19,999	16%	12%
20,000 – 29,999	26%	23%
30,000 – 39,999	23%	17%
40,000 and Over	19%	31%

Source: 1999 study

vitality is the annual budget of the congregation. The median budget of the churches where these women served was $113,000.

When part-time positions are added to full-time positions, the percentages change. In 1999, 41 percent of the women served as guest speakers (down from 55 percent in 1992), 31 percent as pastors (down from 48 percent in 1992), 12 percent as assistant pastors (down from 36 percent in 1992), and 15 percent as counselors (down from 25 percent in 1992). Reviewing the lists of job designations, it becomes clear that primary jobs for most of the women are not church related and their second jobs are church related. This raises the issue of health concerns for black women in ministry, many of whom are overextended from working two jobs and bearing chief responsibility for child rearing. They are working one paid "day" job, volunteering in nonpaid positions of major responsibility and leadership in the church, and fulfilling nonremunerative family duties. The National Council of Churches' Committee on Women in Ministry has targeted health concerns as a major problem for women ministers. Some health problems are stress related while others are due to a lack of adequate self-care. Many black women ministers need a health sabbatical or medical leave and biofeedback to realign the priority of balancing their lifestyles with behavior that promotes good health.

In addition, some black women ministers were working in other ministerial positions as consultants (15 percent), professors (8 percent) hospital chaplains (11 percent), church administrators (12 percent), campus ministers (5 percent), and youth ministers (6 percent). In all areas these figures represent a decline in paid positions. There has been a slowing down in the advancement of black women ministers. The gains that were made in the seven-year period between 1985 and 1992 have seen a reversal between 1992 and 1999.

The most obvious explanation for this reversal would be that employment opportunities for black women in ministry are not keeping pace with the growing numbers of women now completing graduate theological education. One-third of those surveyed in 1999 were new seminary graduates between 1997–1999. The three most recent graduating classes composed one-third of the female graduates over a 27-year period. The first third finished between 1972 and 1991—a twenty-year span; the second third finished between 1992 and 1996—a five-year span; and the final third in the next three-year span. The accelerated growth in the numbers of black women finishing seminary with an ordination degree is phenomenal. But there is a deeper and less quantifiable issue also at work here, namely, a resistance to gender equality that is perpetuated by an environment unwilling to seriously advocate career opportunities or job placement or equitable pay for black clergywomen. Since this environment is the domain of the church, it is impossible to bring the power or scrutiny of governmental agencies to bear. The constitutional tradition of separation of church and state is the keystone that prevents this from ever becoming a public policy issue.

Lay members could initiate change in church policy with regards to equity and parity considerations. The greatest hope for advocacy is among black lay women, because they are by far the largest constituency in the black church. They could, if they ever elect to do so, control most of the budget since they give the majority of the money to the church. The second great hope is among sympathetic black men who are committed to going beyond just speaking out about the problem. Thanks be to God for those who have already spoken out. Without their voices, clergywomen would not be as far along as they are. There is no doubt that a more proactive male group is emerging, seeking to be of assistance in the cause because they recognize that sexism in the black church is wrongfully present. Unfortunately, this group does not yet appear to have enough leadership power in the black church to influence radical change in this situation. However, they are a hopeful sign that the future well-being of the church is linked to equity, equality, and justice for black women.

The fact that these women are still having difficulty being placed after seminary was illuminated by some of the nonchurch jobs which they held. Some of the professionally trained and ordained women in the study were working as secretaries and office managers. Many women worked in nonchurch educational settings and some worked for government agencies. Some women returned to their first career occupation after investing in three years of full-time study only to receive low wages in a rather uneven ministerial career. Some never left their preseminary job. They worked their way through school, taking classes in the evening.

The single biggest difference between men and women in full-time paid employment is in the category of full-time pastors. In the 1999 study, the men dominated by a more than two-to-one margin (49 percent of the men compared to 21 percent of the women were full-time pastors). With the two exceptions of director of Christian education and counseling positions, men held full-time ministry jobs to a larger extent than women. In full-time employment among men, there was a 3 percent or more lead in the job of church administrator, pastor, military chaplain, and youth minister. Turning to part-time employment, women led the men in every category except pastor, military chaplain, professor, and youth minister. Again, some of the difference can be accounted for by the fact that women take major responsibility for child-rearing and family cohesion. Juggling family life and full-time ministry is a concern for women ministers. Part-time ministry, especially assistant pastor, is attractive to married women. It is interesting that 30 percent of women are paid guest speakers compared to only 20 percent of the men. Two explanations may be offered. First, more speakers are needed for women's day and women's retreat events. Second, it may be the case that men who are more heavily subscribed in full-time paid ministries are less available for part-time guest speaking. The major exceptions would be revivals and services of fellowship where male pastors do pulpit exchange. In any event, this finding invites further research. The opportunity for women to speak in black churches may constitute a parallel organization within the institution that gives the illusion of empowerment. Certainly preaching and speaking have the benefits of visibility, status, and moral persuasion. However, when it comes to governance and decision making, these same women can be voiceless and serve only as advisors without a vote. Consequently, their well-being is in the hands of male clergy, male laity, and female laity. Often the "lady preacher" does not hold a formal office or position. This form of co-optation has been well documented in Rosabeth Kanter's classic study *Men and Women of the Corporation*.[5] Creating a parallel mechanism can be a way that an institution responds to complaints about sexism without allowing women to hold the same offices as men. Women may therefore speak in the church without holding the same offices as men.

Looking at table 10.5, additional part-time denominational positions and hospital chaplaincy appear as viable jobs for ministers. The part-time counseling area seems particularly fruitful for women (59 percent).

Salaries

In 1992, 10 percent of the women were earning $10,000 or less, while 42 percent were earning $30,000 or more. When looking only at the primary job in 1999, 16 percent earned under $10,000 and 45 percent earned $30,000 or more, with the median salary being between $30,000 and $35,000. Of course, when the family income of the married women is included, the figures improve. The median family income for this group is between $50,000 and $60,000. The family income ranges from under $30,000 for 15 percent of them to $80,000 or more for the upper 15 percent.

A recent *Washington Post* article entitled "Clergy Pay Varies Widely, Survey Says" notes the following national averages for clergy salaries: The senior pastor's salary, $63,940; the associate/executive pastor's salary, $48,061; the religious education minister's salary, $48,338; the minister of music's salary, $50,824; the youth pastor's salary, $39,406; and the pastoral care minister's salary, $47,074.[6] These findings are based upon information collected and published by the National Association of Church Business Administration in Richardson, Texas. The figures only include salary and housing, excluding retirement, automobile expenses, insurance, convention expenses, and continuing education expenses. There are also discernable regional and denominational differences. It is clear that both black women and men in this study, based upon the national norms cited above, are poorly paid.

The Black Church has been notorious for not paying an adequate pension for its clergy. The author has personal knowledge of a pastor of a large Missionary Baptist Church who was retired without a pension and consequently was forced to live in subsidized housing for the elderly. Although he had been the pastor of this congregation for over 40 years his successor was moved into the parsonage and he was moved out. He was well over 70 years old and one of the first black graduates of Oberlin College in Ohio.

Table 10.3
1999 Full-Time Paid Employment

Position	Male	Female
Church Administrator	13%	6%
Director of Christian Education	2%	4%
Military Chaplain	5%	1%
Pastor	49%	21%
Assistant Pastor	14%	12%
Guest Speaker	12%	11%
Counselor	7%	7%
Professor	4%	3%
Youth Minister	4%	1%

Source: 1999 study

Looking at gender comparisons, the largest differences in salary in 1999 were at the $40,000 and over level. While 36 percent of men earned at this level, only 21 percent of women earned in this range. This is a salary gap of 15 percent in the highest range. Salaries for secondary jobs are lower and do not show any significant salary gap between men and women (see also below). This category contains many of the ministry-related jobs.

Ministry-Related Salaries

The salaries reported here come from a mixture of ministry-related types of jobs and nonministry-related types of jobs. Only 52 percent of the women were employed in ministry-related positions. Looking only at income from ministry-related employment, and excluding nonministry related positions in the 1999 study, 18 percent of the women earned under $10,000 and 42 percent earned $40,000 or more. The high percentage of women with very low wages reflects the lower salaries paid for part-time ministerial work. Much of the under-$10,000 income is from second jobs that are ministerial. The majority of the women acquire their primary salary from secular jobs. The average salary earned by women from ministry-related jobs within the Job 1 or primary career response was between $25,000 and $29,999. The average salary for men in ministry-related Job 1 was between $30,000 and $35,000. This is a gender difference of $5,000. Further analysis is

Table 10.4
1999 Part-Time Paid Employment

Position	Male	Female
Church Administrator	2%	6%
Director of Christian Education	3%	10%
Military Chaplain	3%	2%
Pastor	13%	10%
Assistant Pastor	14%	19%
Guest Speaker	20%	30%
Counselor	7%	8%
Professor	11%	6%
Youth Minister	5%	5%

Source: 1999 study

needed to determine how much of this difference is due to job-related experience.

The ministry pays far less than other professional groups. This may be one of the reasons that some denominations are having difficulty attracting ministers, particularly younger ones, and particularly males, who usually strive to be trained in areas that can support their families. This has become more of an issue now that spouses and potential spouses are more likely to be well educated and to have their own careers and sources of income. Most men prefer to at least match the income of their spouse. When the wife earns more than the husband, the husband can feel that he is not carrying his weight or fulfilling an equal share of the family's financial responsibility. In some cases marital strain results when the husband cannot compete with the wife's salary. The black church as a whole needs to explore this phenomenon further and develop new strategies for educating congregations about the cost of leadership in the twenty-first century. Small-sized congregations need to understand when they cannot afford a full-time minister. Some ministers need to be trained to be bivocational, that is, willing to work another job alongside pastoring a church. In the past, most black ministers have been bivocational. The acquisition of the Master of Divinity degree has traditionally brought with it the hope that the graduate would be called to larger churches that can afford an adequate salary so that he or she would not have to work in secular employment. But unless the salaries offered keep pace with the rising cost of living, this will be less and less true. The ministry-related salaries reported in

Table 10.5
1999 Paid Positions Compared by Gender

	Full-Time		Part-Time	
Additional Position	Male	Female	Male	Female
Minister of Music	.4%	0%	2%	1%
Global Missionary	.6%	.6%	.4%	.3%
Denominational Staff	6%	6%	41%	59%
Campus Minister	3%	2%	4%	3%
Hospital Chaplain	8%	7%	56%	44%
Prison Chaplain	4%	2%	2%	.6%
Founder of Own Church/Ministry	5%	6%	3%	3%
Missions Worker	.8%	.9%	.2%	.6%
Evangelist	3%	.6%	6%	4%
Consultant	5%	4%	7%	11%
Teacher in Church-Related School	6%	4%	6%	4%

Source: 1999 study

this study appear to be alarmingly low. Divinity students for whom the ministry is a second career frequently keep their secular jobs until retirement. Most graduates need to have a living income of $60,000. But there are few churches that can pay this amount to a recent graduate. It helps the second career minister to have a pension or some other form of savings in place.

Conclusion

Black women are touching many lives with the life-giving message of the gospel of Jesus Christ. Now is their hour of opportunity. This is the time to give them honor. Many unnamed biblical women have in the past received little or no recognition, but they are increasingly being remembered and honored. The same is no less true for the women of today; no longer will a token few circumscribe their opportunity. Everyday, women are walking into arenas that were considered off limits or unknown. They are rightly and confidently taking their places at the table of recognized influence. More and more the whole world wants to hear what black women ministers have to say. The whole world is receiving the hope that they dispense. The world wants their care and touch. Their service can no longer go unrecognized. It is the time for honor. In the Holy Scriptures glory and honor go together. As the glory of God is revealed to rest upon them, the elevation of honor should be bestowed.

It is refreshing to discover that there is new revelation from God to this generation. Bishop C. L. Long's *What About the Woman: God's Revelation Concerning Women* is a liberative account by a prominent pastor and Apostolic bishop who has changed his teaching about women in the church.[7] The biblical treatment is sound and very helpful for use with the laity. Another excellent biblical treatment, which answers the prohibitive interpretation of 1 Timothy 2:11–15 is Richard and Katherine Kroger's *I Suffer Not a Woman.*[8] Minister Louis Farrakhan has also called for the elevation of women into the Christian pulpit and out of the clutches of sexism. Many women of all faiths rose to their feet at his Million Family March, held at the steps of the nation's capital on October 16, 2000. One week later former President Jimmy Carter held a news conference that received national television coverage. He announced that his 155-year-old congregation, one of the founding churches of America's largest protestant body, the Southern Baptist Convention (SBC), was withdrawing from the SBC because of their mandate to refuse the ordination of women pastors. These are signs of hopefulness and progress for women amid continuing discrimination.

Honor is not just a feeling of respect but an outward expression of that feeling. Romans 12:9–10, according to the New Revised Standard Version, says, "Let love be genuine; hate what is evil, hold fast to what is good; love one another with mutual affection; outdo one another in showing honor." Romans 13:7 further reads "Pay to all what is due them—taxes to whom taxes are due, revenue to whom revenue is due, honor to whom honor is due." Finally we must stop by 1 Timothy 5:17–18, "Let the elders who rule well be considered worthy of double honor, especially those who labor in preaching and teaching," for the scripture says, "You shall not muzzle an ox while it is treading out the grain," and, "The laborer deserves to be paid." Double honor means respect plus remuneration, a salary that is equitable and just.

Because of the faithfulness, fruitfulness, and accomplishments of clergywomen, it is a time for honor and double honor. Double honor is due all ministers, male and female. But we must commit to closing the salary gap between female preachers and pastors and male preachers and pastors. For when we lift the women we also lift the children and the men, the family and the community.

May the Christian service of black women no longer be suppressed. The honor due them is not theirs alone or for the sake of themselves. Their ultimate honor will come when they join with the elect to crown

Christ Lord of Lords and King of Kings. Their royal entourage will be the souls that they lead to salvation, healing, and wholeness. When we honor them, we honor the Creator who placed the gifts and graces within them. When we dishonor them, we dishonor the One who called them and sent them to minister in our midst.

For every woman preacher who has attained the status of senior pastor, solo pastor, copastor, bishop, regional minister, associate regional minister, district superintendent, or president of a ministerial conference, we give thanks. They are a strong group of pioneer leaders. May God continue to strengthen them to pull down the strongholds of sexism. And God bless those who have promoted, advocated, supported, and followed their leadership. May their numbers continue to increase.

Black women are rooted and grounded in preaching the gospel and providing leadership in the church. The last decades of the twentieth century and the beginnings of the twenty-first have brought progress in the status of black women clergy. The resilience and strength of black women in the face of many challenges leads one to embrace the notion that they will continue to persevere at whatever level possible. It will be a great and glorious day when the evil of sexism will have been abolished from our churches.

Notes

This speech was first presented at the C. Eric Lincoln Lectureship Series, Clark Atlanta University, Atlanta, GA, 1996.

1. Unless noted otherwise, the results reported here come from an analysis of the 1999 returned questionnaires. Methods used to collect data include a 15-page questionnaire mailed in 1982 and a 16-page questionnaire mailed in 1985 to female Master of Divinity graduates. The data in the 1985 study was collected as part of my doctoral dissertation at Rutgers University in 1986: Delores Carpenter, "The Effects of Sect-typeness upon the Professionalization of Black Female Master of Divinity Graduates 1972–1984." Telephone calls were made to some of the participants. The 1992 study was an update of the 1985 study and included five additional graduating classes (1972–1989). Although seven years apart, the two surveys sought to measure similar information about black female Master of Divinity graduates.

   The data for the 1999 study was collected in the summer and fall of 1999. The participants included both male and female Master of Divinity graduates. Potential respondents were identified by the Association of Theological Schools (ATS). ATS provided the names of member schools that had enrolled African American M.Div. students between 1972 and 1998.

A total of 3,119 questionnaires were mailed and 753 were completed and analyzed. The sample includes 448 males (60 percent) and 301 females (40 percent), and 4 persons who did not indicate their gender. The return rate of 24 percent is lower than the 1985 study return rate of 39 percent and the 1992 study return rate of 34 percent.

The study remains national and ecumenical. The respondents are from 18 denominations and from 61 seminaries across the country. The results published at this time only report on 15 of the 18 denominations, because 3 denominations had only 5 or less graduates represented.

2. Liz Szabo, "Women Defend Call to Church in Hampton, Female Pastors Denounce 'Minefield of Sexism,'" *The Virginian-Pilot,* 8 June 2000.

3. From an exchange the author had with a postal executive in Largo, Maryland, 1999.

4. A fuller treatment of this subject may be found in my book of the same title as this essay, *A Time for Honor: A Portrait of African American Clergywomen* (St. Louis, MO: Chalice Press, 2001).

5. Rosabeth Moss Kanter, *Men and Women of the Corporation* (New York: Basic Books, 1993).

6. Bill Broadway, "Clergy Pay Varies Widely, Survey Says," *Washington Post,* 16 September 2000.

7. C. L. Long, *What About the Woman: God's Revelation Concerning Women* (Shippensburg, PA: Destiny Image Publishers, 1998).

8. Richard and Catherine Kroger, *I Suffer Not a Woman* (Grand Rapids, MI: Baker Book House, 1992).

III

The Religious Community Bears Witness

11

Freedom's Song

To be associated with my good friend C. Eric Lincoln, for whom this distinguished lecture series is named, is a great and memorable honor. I sat with Eric in a Ford Foundation meeting some time ago, and he had lost all of his books and manuscripts by fire. I was commiserating with him, and he said, "Well, I feel relieved that I don't have to carry that burden of all those books and manuscripts." I said to myself, "this man must be crazy," but I found out as I reflected upon it that attachment to this world's goods is a dangerous attraction, and I learned a great lesson, Eric, from that, though I want you to know I don't want to lose my books. I learned a great lesson from that, and I do not know anybody in this country to whom the religious community is indebted as much as it is to Eric Lincoln for his research into our religious background, and for his assessment of who we are, and for his tremendous work on African American Islam, which stands as, I think, the high water mark of a movement which was little understood by Americans.

I remember participating with Mike Wallace and the late Jackie Robinson, and one or two others in a program about Islam in the African American community. And it was Eric Lincoln who finally delineated for America the importance of African American Islam, which has had more success with the most downtrodden of our people and the incarcerated of our people, of whom there are so many, than any of us have had. I salute him for documenting the significance of Islam for black Americans and for the entire nation.

Now I am in a quandary this morning. I was informed that I was to preach but I see printed in the program "a lecture." President Cole,[1] I must say to you that I knew Matthew Dawage, and to come to this chapel that is named for him is a great honor, and to Clark University, which has such a distinguished history. Now I have asked people what is the difference between a lecture and a sermon. Some people have said it is a difference of temperature. I never did understand that. So I asked a woman, a very astute woman, who listened to me for 20-odd years, preaching in the Concord pulpit, and I said to her, "What do you think is the difference between a lecture and a sermon?" She said, "I think a lecture has more information in it than a sermon." Well, I didn't quite understand what she meant by that, either, but I let it go by the board. Nevertheless, I am delighted to come among you today. I do want to read a passage of Scripture which I think supports the Scripture already read in our hearing. It comes from the Book of Revelation, and it comes from what I believe is the shortest chapter in that book, the fifteenth chapter. Let me read the second and third verses:

> And I saw, as it were, a sea of glass, mingled with fire, and them that had gotten the victory over the beast and over his image and over his marks, and over the number of his name, stand on the sea of glass having the harps of God, they sing the song of Moses the servant of God, and the song of the Lamb saying, "Great and marvelous are thy works, Lord God Almighty."

There is a story told about a man who went to the English Midlands. This prelate went to the English Midlands to hear one of his ministers. And at the end of the service the bishop said to the minister, "Sir, I thought that was a very brief word which you gave to the people today." The vicar replied, "Your grace, better to be brief than boring." The bishop said, "Ah, but sir, you were both."

Today, I wanted to talk about something that had a song in it because of Eric Lincoln's gifts. Here is a man who is a playwright, distinguished theologian, and sociologist of religion, but who is also a songwriter, and composed the school song for his alma mater.[2] Clark University, what a variety of talents! You can't tell how and where God is going to do something. This man was born in Athens, Alabama, with all of these talents. God keeps surprising us by bringing gifts out of the most unlikely places. No wonder the people said about Jesus "can any good thing come out of Nazareth?" And here God has produced Eric Lincoln. Out of Athens, Alabama. God keeps surprising us.

But I wanted to talk about this song business because music has been the drumbeat by which we have moved. Take, for instance, the spirituals we would sing on Sunday morning, and then on Monday we would look at each other, men looked at women and women looked at men, and we would sing the blues, and then finally we got them together. But here I read in Revelation of "the song of Moses, and the song of the Lamb." Both of these pieces of music grow out of great struggle. There is a notion abroad about success through effortlessness. Thank God Eric Lincoln epitomizes it in his life as many of you do—that there is no victory without great struggle. It is perhaps, students, one of the crowning heresies of our time that so many believe you can get something for nothing, and that you don't have to put in to get out.

No student ever excelled in class without application. That marvelous preacher, Paul Scherer, who greatly enriched New York during my time, used to say that inspiration in preaching, in literature, and whatever else consists of the firm application of the seat of the pants to a chair. There is no other way. When a baseball player drives in the run home that wins the World Series, he doesn't just happen to be able to hit a ball that well. He has worked at it a long time. Many of you don't know that Eric Lincoln is a masterful cook. How many things can this man do? He cooks, he writes music, he writes poetry, and he is a scholar of religion, all of these different things. He cooks, but his cooking comes by practice. Nobody gets to be anything without effort. This is one of the crowning heresies of our time: that you can get something for nothing. It cannot be done. Both of these great hymns come out of great struggles.

Now the first hymn: the song of Moses. Moses came out of a great struggle. Israel left Egypt one night. They hardly had time to gather their possessions. They flung across their shoulders what few things they could carry, and even the bread that they had baked they had no time for it to rise, so they carried it out with them on their long trek toward freedom, toward liberation. And we ought never to forget that Israel's exodus, its journey toward liberation, forms a paradigm for our own struggle, so that our own foremothers and forefathers sang, "Go down Moses way down in Egypt's land, and tell old Pharaoh, let my people go." They struck out by night, and they came at last to a place of camping.

Some of the biblical experts say there were walls on both sides of the Israelites, that there before them lay the Red Sea, and those who made up the farthermost ranks in the rear heard the faint murmur of what sounded like a strange noise in the desert, because a desert is supposed to be a silent place, and any noise in a desert is bound to be upsetting. They discovered that it was the ringing of the wheels of the armies of

Pharaoh against the rocks. It has often puzzled me why Pharaoh—having said to these people, under great pressure, to leave, to get out—decided to pursue them. And I decided there are two reasons: First, I think the economists of Egypt must have met and decided that the Egyptian economy could not well stand to have this whole free labor market drop out, because the most demanding work would have to be done by the Egyptians themselves. So they counseled the Pharaoh that "we better get them back because we're losing a free labor market that will upset the Egyptian economy." And there was a second reason why Pharaoh pursued these Israelites. Evil does not know when to stop. This is its fatal mistake. It does not know when to quit.

Someone was talking last night at dinner about some people who had been out to Las Vegas and won some money, but before they left every bit of the money that they had won was lost because it is hard to stop when you look like you're getting ahead. Evil doesn't know when to quit. The Egyptians had suffered all manner of plagues, but they could not stop; they kept on going. You know, if Governor George Wallace had had sense enough during the march from Selma to Montgomery to say to the marchers, "twenty miles after you cross the Edmund Pettus Bridge we'll have lemonade waiting for you, and we'll have a welcoming committee," it probably would have broken up the march before it got started. But evil does not know when to quit. The bad problem is it keeps on and it feeds on its own vanities, and it feeds on its own failures, and it feeds on its own pride.

And so the Pharaoh pursued these Israelites, then in the rear ranks of the Israelites they heard the clatter of the sound of the wheels of the chariots of Egypt ringing against the rocks. It became clearer to those in the rear ranks, as they listened, that something ominous was happening. Then they saw these chariots moving forward, 600 of them I think the Old Testament says, moving forward, and a cry, a terrible cry, ran through the ranks. Egyptians! The Egyptians are coming! Water was on both sides, a great sea lay ahead of them, and behind them thundered the pursuing army of Egypt. Moses doesn't know what to do. He cries out to God, and he is told, so to speak, "What is that in your hand?" Moses says, "It's nothing but a shepherd's staff." "Well, use that because anything and God are enough." A walking stick and God are enough.

A poor student unable to pay tuition and God are enough to bring graduation day. I am a living witness. Take God and anything—a crutch—and God are enough. So Moses was told to stretch out that staff, and he did, and the biblical record says that the waters parted, water to one side and water to the other. So not only did the Israelites cross over, but they went over on dry land. As they stood on the far side of their deliverance and watched those Egyptians with their wheels spinning disappear in the waters they sang the song of Moses, they sang that the Lord is a God of war. The Lord God is God's name. The Egyptian and their chariots had disappeared. Israel sang the song of Moses. It is the declaration that belongs to all of the great deliverances that come out of the Abrahamic tradition that God does act in human affairs. It is a false notion that to serve God is to serve some far-off deity that has nothing to do with human affairs. God moves in human affairs. God straightens out crooked roads. God fixes things for people who cannot fix it for themselves.

Here we are today in Atlanta. Surely you know that the best minds of America tried to preserve slavery: Henry Clay, John Calhoun, and, to his shame a recreant and a betrayer, Daniel Webster up in Massachusetts, and in St. Louis, Judge Roger Brooke Taney, who wrote the Dred Scott decision. They all tried their best to stop freedom. People North and South were intermarried on this issue. Many were against the idea of freedom, but it happened. At Spotsylvania and Gettysburg and across the land, including down in my native state of Louisiana, they fought; the best blood of the nation went to war. They tried to say the Civil War wasn't about human freedom, but God said "no freedom, no peace; no freedom, no nation; no freedom, no republic"; and the more they tried to separate the war from the demands of freedom, the more things got tied up until there was but one result to come out of it all. In 1866, one-fifth of the whole budget of the state of Mississippi was spent for artificial limbs, for the best blood of the South lost their limbs. Think about the women, whose loved ones did not return to them, and the battlefields filled with blood, the five or six hundred thousand people who perished in the Civil War. All this because there existed a people who had been much maligned, who were enslaved, deemed inferior, and declared incapable of doing anything for themselves. Free because God moves in human affairs. Yes, God moves.

History, young people, is clear on this point. Yes, I know all of the economic theories, all the political reasons, but underneath it all you will see the word "God" every time. God moves in human affairs, make no mistake about it, and God is still moving. We're not going to get this nation straight until we get this problem of race straight. I read in this morning's paper where a woman said, "God help America," because she figured that the Rodney King trial in Los Angeles was influenced by race. Well, my God, what in this country is not influenced by race?

Last night a group of doctors were talking about the baseball game in Toronto. They were all Toronto Blue Jays fans, and I am, too. Now I live nearer to Philadelphia than I do to Toronto. I don't need to explain to you why I am rooting for Toronto in the World Series, even though I live 90 miles from Philadelphia; it is self-evident. Toronto has a black manager. Everything in America is influenced by race, to the point where even white people are afraid of a jury trial. First, you can't exclude blacks, and then blacks are going to have an influence on the outcome of the vote—everything. If you poison the well, you cannot draw pure water out of the well. You can get the water from the bottom, you can dip it from the middle, you can dip it from the side, but if the well is poisoned you are going to draw poisoned water. Some day we as a nation will understand.

I preached in my hometown of Baton Rouge the other day. Back when I was growing up there were open ditches in both the white and black sections of town, and the municipality would be out and around spraying, spraying to control the mosquito population. They sprayed all the white sections as if the mosquitoes knew where the white sections ended. God moves in human affairs. Those mosquitoes moved across Reddy Street where the black people live into East Boulevard and Convention street where the white people lived, they gave them the same malaria that people on the other side of Reddy Street had because God has a way of fixing up things, and God will take wrong and make right. God will fix things up for you and God will straighten out crooked paths. That was why Israel sang the song of Moses, about a God who moves in human affairs. But then I also read about the song of the Lamb.

There are great evils in the world that go on, and some of us have come to the place in life where we know we will never see righted all of the wrongs. Many of our foremothers and forefathers perished, died, without ever seeing even a semblance of justice come to them. But the song of the Lamb tells of another victory. It tells of a victory where in one awful event the powers of darkness met God. It was so awful it was the only day in history that saw night twice because the daylight refused to watch what was going on, and the sun hid its face from view. Daylight pulled the curtains of darkness in order not to watch it. It was a great contest, and it looked like the powers of darkness were going to win. An awful cry came shivering up from that hill, from out of the darkness, "My God, my God, why has thou forsaken me?" They wrestled on that hill until the power of hell's grip loosened, and the power of God's grip held, and at last Jesus was heard to say, "Into thy hands, I give my spirit." He held captivity captive (Ephesians 4:8). It is the promise that at last every wrong will be made right. It is the promise, at last, that the will of God will be done on earth as it is in heaven. It is the promise, at last, that God will stand triumphant over all the powers of darkness; that life will, at last, triumph over death; that health will, at last, put sickness down; that peace will, at last, conquer confusion; that prejudice will, at last, be behind us. That somewhere in God's own time, and in God's own day, the things that plague us will be no more, and we shall walk in the glorious freedom as the daughters and sons of God.

I look for that day. I look for that day when sickness and sorrow and pain and death will be felt and feared no more. I look for that day when evil will be put down forever. I look for that day when humanity's dislikes for one another will be behind them. I look for that day when all of God's children will walk together. I look for that day when God will be all in all. I look for that day when peace will cover the earth, as the waters cover the sea. I look for that day when everywhere we look there will be peace. I look for that day when every mountain will be brought down, and when every crooked place will be made plain. I look for that day when every valley will be lifted up. I look for that day when all flesh will see it together. I look for that day.

Notes

This speech was first presented at The C. Eric Lincoln Lectureship Series, Clark Atlanta University, Atlanta, GA, 1993.

1. Thomas W. Cole, Jr. was the first president of Clark Atlanta University from 1988–2002.
2. C. Eric Lincoln, "Reign Clark Atlanta!" 1995.

12

Turning Burdens into Blessings

Floyd H. Flake

Over the last 23 years I assumed that I was on the road to becoming a college president but instead ended up on a very different route laid out for me, I believe, by the Lord. When asked by my presiding bishop if I would be willing to leave my university post and come to New York to pastor a church I did not want to go. Furthermore, I did not want to be a full-time pastor in the African Methodist Episcopal (AME) Church because I did not want to risk the possibility of having to uproot my family. However, the reality was that I had ideas I could not explore within the academy, and now I was being presented with an opportunity to fulfill my ministry.

From the onset, I asked the members of Allen AME if they would be willing to participate in community development, in building a school and doing economic development through the purchase of buildings, vacant buildings, boarded up buildings, and property—I don't think they knew what they were in for—and today we are the largest AME congregation in the city and the state of New York. We have worked diligently to be responsive to the needs of the entire community, opening a church-related school and clinic and many of the stores that had been vacant and boarded up. We are also blessed with a strong youth church, some fifteen hundred strong, seven or eight hundred of which come together every Sunday morning. I know that Allen is moving in the right direction and my prayer today, as I unveil certain portions of our church model, is that you will be inspired to return to your own places of worship and help set them on Holy Ghost fire, understanding that it is not the will of the Lord that we live in paradise and not do everything we can to dress it and to keep it. Indeed, the scriptures in Genesis 2:17 says that the Lord made Adam in his own image and then put him in the garden and gave him vegetation and herbs and the rivers to be able to water them and then he gave him the challenge of dressing it and keeping it—and all of us would have to agree that as we travel through most of the urban communities of this nation we have not done a good job of dressing and keeping. So hopefully the paradigm we have built is one that you will find edifying and useful as a model for the church.

This morning I would like to focus on the eleventh chapter of Numbers and especially verses 23–25, and they read as follows: "The Lord answered Moses, 'is the Lord's arm too short? You will now see whether or not what I say will come true for you.' So Moses went out and told the people what the Lord had said. God brought together 70 of their elders and had them stand around the tent. Then the Lord came down in the cloud and spoke with them, and God took of the Spirit and put the Spirit on the 70 elders. When the Spirit rested on them, they prophesied, but they did not do so again."

I would like to use as my topic for this lecture, sermon, address, you name it, "Turning burdens into blessings." The book of Numbers, whose authorship is commonly attributed to Moses, presents to us a people who are making their march from lives of slavery to the place they called their holy promised land—the land of freedom, the place which they ultimately hope to occupy, and, on the basis of that hope, receive the fullness of the blessings of the covenant that God had promised to them. We find them at a point where a controversial census has been taken, and it seems to me wherever there is a census involving people who are on their way from slavery to freedom there is always controversy. You know that in Congress there are discussions today about whether to use samplings or to count every individual, because the count is so important. In a census the influence a people wields is determined by their numbers. In the United States, the census makes the difference between what a community receives and does not receive in terms of political representation.

So the Israelites receive their instructions, they are assigned a certain responsibility; every tribe knows what they are supposed to do, including the tribe of the Levites, who have the sacred task of taking care of the sanctuary. One of the responsibilities of Aaron and the other Levite priests was to help the people sustain their strength and power during the sojourn, to prepare for the burdens they would have to endure along the way. So Moses, with an army of over 600,000 people, led them toward the Promised Land. One would think that now that the people had received their freedom, now that they were on their way to the land of promise and opportunity, they would be a joyful throng in anticipation of that which awaited them. They would be filled with hope and possibility because they had been set free; Moses had made his declaration before Pharaoh, and he had been able to safely guide the people who have followed him.

The unfortunate reality is that the Israelites were not a happy people; they were not grateful, nor were they rejoicing. Instead, they looked back on their slave experiences and wondered if perhaps they would have not been better off staying under the hand of Pharaoh. The children of Israel complain to Moses about every kind of hardship; they are tired of marching, they are suffering from fatigue, they are anxious about their future, they are fearful of the unknown and the unexpected, their nerves are shaken, and their minds are upset, because while they knew what hardships to expect when they were in slavery, now they are faced with new difficulties and an uncertain future.

I tell you it is a terrible thing when people spend their time in the sojourn from slavery to freedom doing nothing but complaining. The best way not to get anything done is to complain. This is the well-known attitude of many liberated slaves even toward their benefactors and their liberators. The price of emancipation and liberation is often burdensome for those who have been set free. Had the Israelites forgotten that it was the Lord who had brought them through the Red Sea? Did they not remember that God had provided for them clouds by day and fire by night so that their journey would not be impeded? Were they not aware that even when they were hungry God had provided them with manna from on high that they might be fed? Had they forgotten that in the worst of times God had seen to their needs with one miracle after another? Yet and still, after the blessing of emancipation they complain about hardships and disappointments and their discontent is heard by God.

The divine disapproval descends swiftly in the form of fire that consumes a portion of the believers. And as I have studied this text and looked at the history of African people on the shores of America I find similar comparisons in terms of our complaints, dissatisfaction, and displeasure, which suggests that we have not learned the lessons of history. We have forgotten from how far the Lord has brought us. We do not seem to appreciate the fact that we have been emancipated, we are enfranchised, even as we are still a long way from enjoying the fullness of the fruit of the Promised Land. So rather than work to build on the successes that have been ours we spend too much of our time complaining.

I would agree that there are good reasons for our complaints, given the pain we have suffered, the grief we have born, the lack of respect we have endured, the accusations we have received, and the uneasiness we feel as it appears that the rest of the world is rapidly moving toward the turn of the century without having to endure the struggles that are yet ours. All too often, we find ourselves concentrating on the issues of the past without looking carefully at the prospects and the possibilities for our future. Yes, we have reason to complain, but I believe that it is time we put our complaints into proper perspective, for murmurs and complaints will not solve our problems.

As a people, we are experiencing fatigue and anxiety as we move toward the twenty-first century. Most of us who are from the civil rights generation could not have imagined that our people's plight is not better today than it is. We could not have dreamed of the day after marches and legislation and equal access to education when our young people would not be standing firm and tall and at the head of the class, competing with the best who have immigrated to these shores since then. Those who have arrived over the last 20 years have not spent their time complaining about the past but have come to the land of opportunity and decided that this is their paradise. My young African American brothers and sisters, it is time for us to understand that this is not a perfect place, but it is our paradise and land of opportunity. If we merely spend our time complaining about what is wrong with it we will never be full citizens helping to make it right. Nor will we be able to declare ourselves a fully free people. The road from emancipation to enfranchisement has been long and arduous, and it seems to me that the road from enfranchisement to empowerment will be even longer.

There are three phases to liberation: emancipation, enfranchisement, and empowerment. Empowerment is the third phase of liberation that we have not fully embraced because we spend too much of our time and energy resenting, fault finding, and even expressing hatred for those who are not fully responsible for all of the problems we have encountered. Yes there are problems of oppression and vestiges from the segregated era that have not been completely removed, but enfranchisement by virtue of laws that were passed, inclusive of the voter rights act, affirmative action and changes that invite our full participation in the educational process have occurred—that is what we call enfranchisement.

If we merely sit at the door of enfranchisement and not understand that our next responsibility is to deal with the reality that we are not a fully empowered people, we will never be able to enjoy the fruits of this land of promise. Enfranchisement has opened the door for us to live in neighborhoods of our own choosing, yet our historic urban communities are totally devastated. We now have integrated schools, but the urban schools of this land are committing educational genocide, paralyzing our children and depriving them of the opportunity to meaningfully compete in the future. I believe that if a police officer shot one black child we would have riots and protests moving through the streets. Yet everyday in our public education system our children are being killed and there are no voices speaking out. The challenge before us is to deal with the reality that children who are paralyzed by educational genocide early on in their lives will in all probability never recover. And if they never recover the gap between the haves and the have-nots will become even wider. We will continually be on the lower rung of the socio-economic ladder of America, and we will never be able to move beyond that which in the end is dysfunctional. Many of our families are dysfunctional. Our children are having babies before they are prepared to assume life's responsibilities. This places a great deal of social and economic stress on the black community when persons lack the ability to properly care for a child and where few prospects exist to assume full responsibility for raising a family. Tragically, too few such persons are ever able to recover economically.

As an aside in closing, I realize that as college students some of you have already fallen in love with each other. Those of us who have been where you are today will tell you that if you are involved with somebody who doesn't want to go anywhere in life, leave that person alone, leave them where they are so that you can move forward and succeed. And if that person says they really love you then let them prove it. Tell them if they are willing to join hands with you, regaled in their cap and gown on commencement day, then you can march through life and make significant contributions together rather than alone. Those of us who are over 50 like myself, will tell you that in the years between our college days and where we are today we have fallen in and out of love many times. Be patient. Love will find you. Love always finds a way.

This speech was first presented at The C. Eric Lincoln Lectureship Series, Clark Atlanta University, Atlanta, GA, 1998.

13

Can the Intellect Analyze the Spirit?

Ava Muhammad

In the name of Allah, the beneficent, the merciful, I bear witness there is no god but Allah, and Muhammad is His servant. I greet all of you in the words of peace, in the original language of As-salamu-alaykum. I am really honored to have been asked to take part in this forum, which is not only in the memory of but to make sure that we spread the work of a very great man, C. Eric Lincoln. I really have to give a special thanks to the many members of Muhammad mosque 15, which is our southern regional headquarters under Minister Ray Muhammad's direction, and I thank you for being out. And last but certainly not least, my best friend next to God, my husband, Darius.

We really need to realize that it is our duty to see to it that the great work of our scholars goes beyond the confines of the academic world. You know, Minister Farrakhan, for those of you that don't know, always held Dr. Lincoln in the highest esteem, and it was my privilege to be in the presence of these men, as well as Dr. Lawrence Mamiya. And the dialogue that would take place was so exalted that it just would fill you with the desire to know, the desire to learn, the desire to have and be anything that you can. And right now the American people in general, and black people in particular, are in danger of losing the critical tools of civilized nations: reading and writing. And right now our society is one where ignorance is often exalted, and many people are proud to be semiliterate, and we really fail to appreciate sometimes what God has given us and those among us who apply themselves to study. And we have no hope of knowing who this man, C. Eric Lincoln was, and what he gave us, if we do not read.

The first revelation of the Holy Qur'an, to Prophet Muhammad Ibn Abdullah, was to read. And though I didn't come here to lecture about reading, I have to say this before I move into my subject. Studies have proven what we already know. I have a sister who just completed her master's degree in education, and she does evaluations for preschool and elementary schools in Columbus, Ohio, and she was telling me the profound impact that reading to children has on their development, and how babies and toddlers who are read to, when they do go to school, they tend to have a higher level of self-esteem then those who have not been read to, and they learn more quickly, and ultimately have a much stronger command of the language. So, read to your children. Turn off the television and read to your children.

Now, my topic is "Can the Intellect Analyze the Spirit?" In the wake of the vicious and atrocious attack on the United States, and as we begin to recover from the initial shock and horror of the unthinkable, I, like most of you, watched the television news day and night, read the papers, listened to the radio, and still do as events and circumstances develop and change. And as the focus turned from the tragedy to an effort to understand the motive of the perpetrators, I noticed a lot of articles in the papers that were written by people who were characterized as experts in terrorist psychology, experts in Islam, experts in this, and experts in that, and this gave me pause. As a student and national spokesperson for the Honorable Minister Louis Farrakhan, I have been taught to strive to rise above emotion into the thinking of God, to try with my finite knowledge, knowledge so small in God's eyes that we could put it on the head of a pin and have room to walk around. And yet in that finite knowledge, and in my human tendency toward self-indulgence, I still must strive as a human being, as God's vice-regent, the highest form of life on this planet—the human being—I must try to see things the way God sees things. And, of course, that is like being in the valley and imagining what the view is from the mountaintop. But through prayer and study, you realize that God is more than willing to share with us his view. It is not that we possess that view, but if we can strive to submit to God in any way, God will confer upon us some divine knowledge and wisdom, even if it's only for a fleeting moment.

And so, I asked myself in reference to all of these experts: What makes someone an expert? And if becoming an expert is an intellectual endeavor (and we know it is), then can you effectively use the intellect to get to the root of what drives a person to do what he or she does? Now certainly it is useful to find the motive. In fact, I once served as an assistant district attorney in New York, and in fact, my first job coming out of law school was in the World Trade Center, in the Office of Child Support Enforcement. And our office was somewhere in the fifties (floors), and I couldn't handle it. I couldn't handle that height. One time our boss took us up on the 107th floor to the restaurant Windows on the World; I had to leave. I couldn't handle it. You could actually feel the building sway at that height. One day I looked out the office window and I said, "What's that gray stuff in the window?" They said, "Those are clouds." I began sending my resumé out! But that held great memories for me because being a hick from Ohio, coming to New York, being so fascinated by the awesome skyline, was a very memorable experience in my life.

I left there and went to Queens and served as assistant district attorney in homicide. The first thing we looked for was motive. You must, in order to convict someone of a homicide, prove not only the act, but you must prove the intent. There must be motive, there must be opportunity, and one detective used to say, "If you show me why it happened, I will tell you who did it." You see, once you know why, then it's just a matter of time before you arrive at who. Motive is susceptible to intellectual analysis in one sense because technically speaking, motive is simply what prompts you to do something. The word "motive" comes from motion. It's what moves you. Now here is where we have to be careful, because in order to get to what moves somebody, I have to guard against my own mind. My mind is not necessarily exquisitely balanced, and my mind may have issues that it is coping with, and, in fact, anybody that makes it to adulthood has issues. As I like to say, "All of us are ill, it's just that some of us are chronically ill and others are acutely ill." And to say someone is mentally imbalanced almost begs the question, because God's whole work with us is to bring us into exquisite balance. Balance is justice, and justice is peace, and when humanity becomes spiritually developed to the point where we can balance our spirit, mind, body, and emotions, there will be peace.

Now, if my own perception of reality, as I'm looking for motive, is damaged by my environment, and what I have been taught to think, then I might cut myself off from the answer that I need to protect myself from further assault at the hands of this perpetrator whose actions have mystified me. I really need to analyze this, then, not from the mind, which is ego driven, but from the spirit, which is God driven and through which I can avail myself of God's guidance in finding the answer. Can the intellect analyze the spirit? That's almost like asking, can your two-year-old figure you out? I don't know if I should use that example because there are some sharp two-year-olds today. And you know, each succeeding generation is brighter than the last. And so, I used to have a law professor who would say, "You may be more intelligent than I am, but I know more than you do." And we know more, oft-times, than our babies simply from having been around, but they are more intelligent than we are. The brain is constantly evolving, and each generation is born to solve the problems of its time. So to shut down and shut off young people is fatal.

But let me get back to my main point. The reason that the mind cannot analyze the spirit is because the mind is centered, it's ego-centered; it centers all action around itself. It's motivated, or it moves on logic, and logic and reason are only as good as our level of knowledge and wisdom, which by virtue of us being human beings is finite.

I heard Fred Price of Ever Increasing Faith Ministries say the other day in a lecture that you have to have knowledge in order to have faith, and I have to respectfully disagree with that. *Faith is the bridge that will carry you over the abyss of the unknown until you arrive at certainty.* We walk by faith, not by sight. Faith is the substance of things hoped for, the evidence of things not seen. It was faith that enabled Jesus to get out of the boat and walk on water. If Jesus had followed his intellect, or his logic, it would have told him you cannot do this because you weigh too much. You are heavier than this water, and you cannot walk on it. So logic will tell you: You cannot do what the spirit can appeal to God that will make the impossible, possible. Now, many have said of the Jekyll and Hyde in us, "they [the September 11 bombers] did this because they're envious." Well, we know envy is not a good thing to feel toward anyone, and it's not a good thing to have someone feel toward you. Envy has no redemptive quality. Envy is when you feel that someone else who receives a blessing received what you should have had. When you envy, you're angry at God because God gave somebody something and you want it. Envy is not where I see someone driving a nice car, and I say, "I would like a car like that." Envy is when I say, "I want *that* car. I want to drive *that* car," which means *that* person has to be removed. Envy is why Cain killed Abel.

So, we have to ask ourselves before we throw words around, do we mean "envy," or do we mean "jealousy," because they are two different things. Jealousy is a form of resentment, but it differs from envy in one critical way. Jealousy springs from being vigilant in guarding something. Therefore, in some circumstances, jealousy is justified. The Old Testament says, "The Lord, thy God, is a jealous God." Let's say, for example, that a man meets a woman and the two somehow end up in an intimate embrace. The brother is just standing somewhere out in the open, hugging and kissing the woman, for whatever reason. And as he is hugging and kissing her, another man rushes up from behind and grabs him, spins him around, punches him in his mouth with all of the force he has available, and knocks out all his teeth. Later on you learn that the second man is the woman's husband. I don't even want to get into what was going on, I'm just trying to use an illustration.

Well, was that envy or was it jealousy? Do you understand the difference? Because the first man might have been hugging or kissing the woman to congratulate her on some achievement, but he was also engaged in conduct that could lead to a major violation of the divine commandments. He was threatening the sanctity of another's marriage vows. Do you understand? So, we have to be spiritually developed as individuals, spiritually developed as a community, and spiritually developed and guided as a nation in order to properly evaluate any course of action, because we will not get to the origin of the thought that prompted the action unless we get into the spirit. The only real expert in spirit is the Creator. The mind has power over the body, and the spirit has power over the mind. Sometimes the mind allows the body to have its way, and sometimes the spirit lets the mind have its way. That does not change the chain of command.

If you look at actions only, you will stress yourself out, and you'll never solve the problem, and this problem that we have with what happened to us on September 11 is way beyond resolution strictly through military force. Now let's look at it. The mind rules over the flesh. Let's look at the incident on American Airlines two days ago, and Delta Airlines today.[1] One plane was headed away from and the other toward Los Angeles. They are large aircrafts. I believe the Delta was a 757, and the American was a 767, with lots of people, well over 150, close to 200 people. From Los Angeles back to Chicago, thirty minutes out, a passenger jumps up and rushes the cockpit, yelling, "Save the tower!" He is quickly subdued by the passengers, and two F-16 fighter planes are sent to escort the aircraft to a safe landing. The man is then characterized as mentally imbalanced, which as I have already said begs the question. All abhorrent behavior is the product of mental imbalance, whether it is criminal behavior, suicidal, or whatever. If you behave in a way that is harmful to yourself and society, that is the product of imbalance.

So we're talking in circles. There are metal detectors, explosive detectors, the National Guard is in the airport, carbon monoxide detectors, poison detectors, you are searching people and their luggage, confiscating plastic coat hangers and manicure sets, going through undergarments, having people take their shoes off; nevertheless, the man in question runs down the aisle into the cockpit. The aircraft is lurching, there could have very easily been another unspeakable disaster, because the plane was over the city. They were in a major metropolitan area. Can you imagine what would have happened if that plane had crashed in the Chicago area?

Same thing today. A Delta flight takes off from Atlanta on its way to Los Angeles. Air traffic gets a distress call from the pilot saying "we have to land in Shrevesport, Louisiana." It wasn't clear what had happened by the time I left home, except they arrested a man. He was mentally imbalanced, but if you ask the passengers on the plane, at the moment that the man ran screaming down the aisle, what they felt when the plane started banking on its left side, I guarantee they will tell you they were terrorized. One passenger thought "he bought the farm," which is a Mid-west expression for death. Terror is what they felt because the person who rushed the cockpit is what white, American males like to call "one of our own." So he was deluded, but his actions generated terror. Another, a woman who was on the plane said, "I thought about September 11 and I said to myself, 'Now, it's my turn.'"

Look at the aftereffects of September 11, 2001. I was vacuuming the carpet the other day and the thought crossed my mind of a nuclear missile just coming in and blowing me and everybody to smithereens. These are the kind of thoughts you entertain. You are out jogging in the park, a plane flies over, and you start looking around. Well, I'll dive under that bush. I don't know about you but my husband and I were watching before 9/11. My husband has always watched every single person that gets on the plane. You're not getting in the cockpit with him on the plane, because his posture is, "I'm not going out like that." Now people don't want to fly. Now you have to get to the airport four hours ahead for a 45-minute flight. You could drive in the time that you're sitting in the airport. This is rough and it is just beginning. It is just beginning.

My youngest sister, who works in the Ohio Court of Appeals, called me this afternoon. She said the FBI is all over the building. I said, "Well, what are you doing?" "Well, I'm just sitting here." I said, "What does it take for you to learn? Get out! They're not in there to say 'hi.' Why are you calling me? You call me from home." "Well, we're just trying to find . . . " I said, "Yeah, that's what people said on September 11." Because sometimes the mind just can't process what the Holy Qur'an calls the shock of the hour, the shock of the hour. Every time you see powder . . . is that Anthrax? People are running around, buying antibiotics, buying gas masks, wondering what's going on with my child at school. And by the way, somebody shot the perpetrator on the

American flight with Valium, according to the report on NBC Nightly News. The report said it was a nurse or some "medical person" on board who shot the perpetrator with Valium.[2] And I'm saying how did somebody get on the plane with a big hypodermic needle and a bag full of drugs and they are going through people's underwear? A pilot said he was walking through the search area in Miami's airport and the guy at the counter was just going through everything he owned, and he finally said, "What are you looking for?" after he had gone through his things for the fourth time. And the guy said, "I don't know, they just told me to do this. They just said go through everything." So, we can see, beloved, that analyzing action is not going to get us to the root of the problem, because you can detect metal, you can detect smoke, but can you detect thoughts? If you can detect thoughts you can do away with everything else, because there is no action taken by any human being that is not preceded by a thought. Because human beings are creatures of reason. We do not act unless we have a reason. Even if it seems instant, it is still of the cumulative thoughts over a period of time. So something may seem spontaneous, but if you ask a robber why he robbed the bank, he'll give you a reason, because we can't act unless we have rationalized the rightness of our action. And your power to read thoughts is not in your mind, it comes through your mind, but the origin of that power is your spirit.

If you remember, in the New Testament of the Bible, it says: "And Jesus, knowing their thoughts, did thus and so. And Jesus knowing their thoughts did thus and so."

Now, I have noted in previous books and research that scientists among us have shown us that thought is manufactured by the brain and it lives in the brain in liquid form, and thoughts are carried through the blood and nerves to every single cell in the body. You know when you're thinking something, it is not just your brain, but if you're angry your liver is upset, the kidneys are saying "what's up, what's up?" Your thoughts penetrate every cell, every one of six trillion tissue cells, and they penetrate the membrane of every cell and go into the nucleus of that cell, and in that nucleus is a chemistry lab. That is why you hear you should not eat a meal when you are upset, because the acid that you are producing in your stomach will ruin the benefits of any nutrition.

Scientists allegedly did a study a few years back and drew blood from an enraged "mentally imbalanced" patient, injected it into a laboratory rat, and the rat died. So while we're looking for Anthrax and all this stuff, we better look at what is already floating around inside our own blood stream.

During our life here on earth, we undergo a three-dimensional experience. The first dimension is length, the second dimension is width, the third dimension is depth, and these three dimensions are interdependent. These are the essential components of existence in this realm. There is a fourth dimension we know about, but we know it on a shallow level, and we lack comprehension of its effect on us, and that dimension is the one we need to comprehend so we can rise to the elevated places we are supposed to rise to as the human family. And that fourth dimension is time.

The fourth dimension—time—rules over the first three. It governs them because length, width, and depth concerns matter, but it takes time to measure motion. Motion is necessary to life. If there is no motion there is no life. Well, time measures motion. Time tells us how long it takes to get from one point to another, and time is the basis for the cycles that we grow and diminish in. So we need to be looking at what time we're in. If we look at the time that we are in, we will get a much deeper understanding of the events that are going on around us. You've heard people say "so and so is in a time warp." They're living in the sixties, they're living in the forties, they're living in the eighties, meaning that this person is locked in and living by the context of the way the earth and everybody was functioning however long ago, and time changes constantly. Tomorrow this day will be gone forever, so we have to comprehend the time in which we live.

Now in the wake of what has happened there have been a lot of terms used: Islamic radicals, Islamic extremists, Islamic fundamentalists, and yesterday or the day before I read in either the *Atlanta Journal-Constitution* or *USA Today* a letter that someone wrote talking about the Islamic terrorists. The word "Islam" means peace. There is no such thing as a peaceful terrorist. There's no such thing as a radical, peaceful person. The application of these adjectives negates the word. I do not, as a Muslim, feel obligated to explain the kind of conduct of aggression and terror that took place on September 11 because nowhere in the Holy Qur'an, from cover to cover, can you find a sentence, a single word, that would justify the actions that were taken on that day. So it is not that you're an extreme Muslim, you're not a Muslim at all, you're not a Muslim at all. Peacefulness is a complete state of being in and of itself. Peace is a condition.

You know, when nations talk about conditional peace and peace treaties that means they don't get it. Peace does not have conditions attached to it. Peace *is* the condition. Peace cannot exist in the absence of perfect balance, also known as justice. And when you apply any adjectives to peace then you upset the balance. Now I want to say this, and this is still related to what I said about mind analyzing spirit, because the Holy Qur'an says we should revere the womb of the female.

To disrespect the woman and practice Islam is not possible. You cannot disrespect the woman and be a Muslim. Allah has ordained that. You can call yourself whatever you want; it does not make you that. You can say "I'm a Muslim," but you are not that in the eyes of the God you say you worship. When I look, I see wrong everywhere. As we are taught in the Qur'an, when two of you quarrel, both of you are wrong, because whenever you find yourself in conflict, even if the person you are an adversary to is completely wrong in the immediate sense, you still must ask yourself, "What actions have I taken to get myself in the position where God would even allow this?" It is not about the Coast Guard and the Air Force and weapons and guns, it is about thought, it is about a spirit that projects the spirit of God and gives you an oracle field of protection. That is what we're moving toward. We have to move toward the elimination of all physical weapons. Now, whether it is the Taliban or whomever, all we know is we're receiving our information from television. None of us could testify to any of this in a court of law because we saw it on TV, just like we see Bugs Bunny. But all that aside, whoever it is that is treating women the way they are being treated in Afghanistan, and in many countries in the Middle East and Africa, whoever is doing that to them, they're not Muslims. I don't care what they call themselves. They are other than themselves.

Do you know that if we were under that law, everybody in this room would be stoned to death tonight? Dr. Pollard and my husband would be tortured, him for inviting a woman to speak and my husband for not checking me. That's right. And in Afghani society women are not allowed to speak in public; they are not allowed to have an opinion. The Holy Qur'an exalts the female. How do you revere the womb and cover a woman's mouth and nose with cloth so that she can barely breathe, let alone speak? Yet there is not a human being alive that was not carried in the womb of a female.

Now, your brain was formed in the womb of a woman, yet a woman cannot teach you anything. That is how you become a psychopath. Some idiot was on television recently claiming expertise in Islam. He said, "You cannot be converted to Islam. You have to be born a Muslim, and to be born a Muslim you have to be born in Saudi Arabia." That's an idiot. When the Holy Qur'an was revealed to Muhammad Ibn Abdullah, nobody was a Muslim. That is why the Qur'an was revealed, because Arabia was a bunch of savages. Tell me I'm wrong. Show me in the Qur'an. I will sit down. They treated women like dirt. Female babies were killed, slaughtered. Women were buried alive. Everybody had to be converted to Islam, and if you cannot convert to Islam, why is it the duty of the Muslim to propagate the faith? We are actually born Muslim. We are born Muslim and Christian in that we are born with the natural desire to submit to do the will of God, and it depends on how we are brought up and taught whether that human potential is developed, or, as Minister Farrakhan says, "Man can be an animal, or man can reflect God." Because we are at one time, before we're born (when we are in the fetal stage); nobody would have anything to do with us if we came out like that. In fact, we are fish swimming around in a bag of water; we're not a land mammal. We're swimming in a bag of water, and, in fact, we are a plant connected by a stalk known as the umbilical cord for our nourishment.

So we go through all of the stages of development and then the Holy Qur'an says, "I bring you forth complete yet incomplete." Complete, meaning that we possess all of the necessary components to evolve into what God wants us to be, which Jesus tried to show us how to be, who is God's vice-regent. Jesus said in those days, he didn't say "peace," because the English language did not even exist. Jesus said, "As-salamu-alaykum," or "shalom alay kum." There was no English then. So, if you cannot be converted to Islam, then why bother to teach? You know, when you say somebody has to be from a certain race to be something, they have to be from a certain place or they have to be a particular gender, you're not expressing God's will. You are impeding God's will. To say I have to be from some place is nationalism. To say I have to be of a certain ethnicity is racism. To say I have to be a certain gender is sexism. To say I have to occupy a certain place in society is classism, which is a product of materialism or the worship of matter. So, as Minister Farrakhan writes in his study guide, these are the four great impediments to self-development: racism, sexism, nationalism, and materialism.

Now, in this land called Afghanistan, they are reverting to the way of life they followed prior to revelation, and by the way, I still have something to say about the West. I'm just in the East right now. But they are reverting to a way of life that they followed prior to the revelation. Prophet Muhammad himself said, "Three generations after me, will not be of me." So, all of these self-appointed keepers of the faith have been off the mark more than a thousand years. How can you say you are enlightened, or endarkened (as Dr. Pollard would say), and your country is a wasteland? And it is not poor only because of Western aggression. The Western aggression played a great big role—we will get to that in a minute—but it is also the rejection of a lost commandment to revere the womb. Because I ask: What would you do with Maryam, that is, Mary the mother of Jesus after whom the nineteenth chapter of the Holy Qur'an is named? What would you do with A'ishah, scholar and soldier, wife of Prophet Muhammad Ibn Abdullah? What would you do to Fatima, the daughter of the Prophet, since women cannot learn or teach? I am just showing us there is wrong on all sides. That is why the whole world is in distress.

There are mixed feelings and controversy in this whole situation. The work of women in Afghanistan in education in schools was destroyed, and the consequence of that was the destruction of society. When you exclude women from society, when you shut the mind and the mouth of the female, then you have no exposure to the feminine expression of the attributes of Allah. You begin to value force and violence. The civilizing components of your life are devalued right along with the women. You have no culture. You have no refinement. You don't even have a kitchen. That's right. That's right. You don't sit down and eat a cooked meal; you're sitting in the desert, stuffing bread in your mouth, slurping out of dirty wells.

Now, what allegedly prompted this behavior—some say—is that the people of Afghanistan were trying to protect their society from the West, which is the other extreme of madness. The wild, wild Western hemisphere, where women run wild and naked. You see, as long as the woman is crazy, there's not going to be a heaven. That's all I'm saying, on either side. You cover her from head to toe behind something that makes her look like a beekeeper. You have nothing. But if you go crazy and have her running around butt-naked, I'm talking about our home-land now. . . . You want to defend the homeland, women should cover up, first and foremost. Women feeding families out of microwave ovens—hello! But in the Middle East, they say we have to cover them and paint the windows black so nobody can look in the window. But that is what you were doing when the Holy Qur'an was revealed to you, when there was no West. What was the reason then? Maybe, just maybe, the reason humanity has to keep starting all over is this issue with the female—locked into this fairy tale that we came from a rib rather than the mind of the Creator. And if Eve led you astray, well, what does that tell you?

But it was through the revelation of the Holy Qur'an that Islam civilized Europe. Europe was in the Dark Ages, and Islam brought Europe enlightenment: Art, literature, and a system of jurisprudence.

But sexism is not limited to Islam, and I haven't forgotten the question I asked myself . . . can the mind analyze the spirit? No! It cannot. The Honorable Elijah Muhammad taught that a nation can rise no higher than its women. The Holy Qur'an reveres the womb: Your brain is shaped in the womb by the blood of your mother and the thoughts that were traveling through her bloodstream. If mother is semiliterate, if mother has a low self-esteem, if mother thinks nothing of herself or the man who fathered you, then what state of mind are you when you come forth? But sexism isn't exclusively the property of Islam. Christianity and Judaism both suffer from this affliction—and it is an affliction. None of the major religions is very successful right now where sexism is concerned, even though all of us are the children of Abraham.

Christians, Jews, Muslims: All claim Abraham as our father. Why? Because Abraham worshiped one God. He was not an idol worshiper, not a polytheist, but some of the most virulent expressions of sexism that I have personally encountered since I have been in this position have been on the part of men who call themselves preachers of the gospel. I was on my way to speak at a church in Mississippi and had to turn around after being disinvited when the pastor of the church found out that Minister Farrakhan's then–southern regional representative was a woman. He said, "no way is a woman speaking from my pulpit." Another man that Minister Farrakhan met, a pastor, said "I don't believe in women preaching or teaching the word of God." I mean how can this be when we speak of Mary giving birth to Jesus? I don't understand this. So Minister Farrakhan looked at the man and said, "Well, what about your mother?" The man said, "My mother couldn't preach in here." So sexism is definitely in Islam, and it is found throughout the world on every level, but it is also in every religion, and the exclusion of the female from preaching and teaching in major religions, I submit to you this evening, is a primary component of the problem that we're looking at right now.

The level of education, refinement, and spiritual development of the female determines her capacity to enlighten the male, and without that you have a bunch of savages calling themselves ministers, imams, rabbis, reverends, pastors, and preachers.

But quickly, let us look at the West. Even Pat Buchanan has told the United States to stop being an empire. Why are Muslims called upon to denounce the terrorists as traitors? Was Timothy McVeigh branded a traitor? No. Was he? Timothy McVeigh was charged with homicide. Why wasn't he charged with treason? I'm not just speaking rhetorically, I'm saying honest to God, why was he not charged with treason, referring to the death of babies as "collateral damage?" You can kill somebody in a gas station, in a robbery. That's murder, that's a homicide. So are you telling me that blowing up the Federal building at Oklahoma and murdering 186 innocent people is just your run-of-the-mill, somebody snapped homicide, or was that not terrorism?

The entire institution of slavery was justified with the Bible. Where is the condemnation of that? Where is the apology? Where is the repair, meaning reparations? Is terrorism something that is subjective, and changes with one's perception of reality? I want to share with you, in closing, some things for you to mull over and ponder. I'm not here to try to persuade anyone to one way of thought or another, but you know a close family member said to me a couple of days after the attack, a close member of my family who is a Christian—and I'm not Minister Farrakhan—she asked me, "How did it feel when you gave up Christianity to be a Muslim?" I said, "I didn't give it up." If you study these religions and look at them, there is no difference. To be Christian, to enter into oneness with God through Christ Jesus, all of it is about one God, the Creator, and seeking and striving for a world of peace. But she said to me, "I'm confused." I said, "About what?" "Osama bin Laden, whatever his name is, he's a Muslim, and you're a Muslim, and what is that about? Can you explain what he was doing?" I said, "Can you explain the Ku Klux Klan to me? I don't remember any Christians being called out to explain these men in Texas, lynching and dragging James Byrd to his death. They were Christians. That is what they said they were. I don't see anybody calling up talk radio and cable news, 'How does it feel to be a Christian, and did you know that these were Christians who did this?' How does it feel to be a Christian, and know you live in a Christian nation which held millions of people in bondage for three hundred and ten years, under the cross? How does it feel?"

As I told you at the onset, whoever did this is not a Muslim. I don't have to explain their conduct. Terrorism is not a religion. Being an aggressor is not ordained by God anywhere. The Holy Qur'an says fight with those who fight with you. Those people in the planes weren't fighting with them. There were babies on those planes. Some of everybody was in the World Trade Center. It was a potpourri of humanity. There were Christians, Muslims, agnostics, probably a couple of atheists here and there, Hindus, Jews, you name it. It was the World, hello, World Trade Center. The ones who are to blame for this act didn't go up and down the aisles of the plane and say, "Are you a Muslim? We're going to let you off here."

I'm going to share with you, and close with this, excerpts from a press statement delivered by the Honorable Minister Farrakhan. You know it just angers me that to this day, this very day I heard it again, people keep calling in to radio talk shows asking and in one case specifically saying, "Where's Farrakhan? Why haven't we heard from Louis Farrakhan?" So you need to ask this of the media, because he gave a press statement, invited world press to this. It was on satellite. Look up finalcall.com on the Internet and you can get his statement in its entirety because I have to close, and I only have time to give a short excerpt. But I want to read this quote from Minister Farrakhan:

> I can speak on behalf of Muslims, and I must say that no Muslim hates a Christian because he's a Christian, and believes in Jesus Christ. This is a mosque, and there are thousands of mosques in America [because he was speaking from our headquarters' mosque, Maryam, named after the mother of Jesus]. There are 1,250,000,000 Muslims, and every one of us believe in Jesus. This book, Qur'an, refers to Jesus in the same language that Christians refer to him, as Jesus the son of Mary, the Messiah."[3]

Now you notice that not anywhere in the news, not even in any of the analysis given by Muslims, is it mentioned that we and the Christian people share this important belief which is at the core of the Christian faith and that could overcome so many myths that keep us divided. I don't think that is by accident. To say we hate Christians is wrong. Now back to Minister Farrakhan's response:

> Beloved people of America, there is nothing of consequence that is not attained by the shedding of blood. That same World Trade Center, many workmen died building it. Every bridge in New York that connects the boroughs to each other, someone died to build those bridges. Death must serve the cause of life, freedom, justice, equality and righteousness. Let this terrible tragedy lead to a rebuilding of spiritual value that connect the children of Abraham—Muslim, Christian, and Jew—in a rebirth of moral and spiritual value that could lead to the making of a new world. . . . May God bless the citizens of America.[4]

Now, Minister Farrakhan has given a fuller statement, and I would kindly suggest that all of us avail ourselves of it to see what his position is. And so, beloved, I say, as he says, that we would be making a serious mistake if we forget those who lost their lives so suddenly and so tragically, and so many families now are fatherless. So many families are torn to shreds, and because of the horrible way in which they lost their family members, most of them will never even get a body that they can bury and have closure.

You know, the horror of seeing people walking around in those days after the bombing, smoke still covering the city, asbestos flying everywhere, and people with t-shirts on with pictures of loved ones, in shock, and the mind not being able to process what it has experienced. And this is why only the spirit, only the spirit has the power to heal the suffering. And what Minister Farrakhan is saying is that God is showing all of us we are at the end of super powers and military might, because everybody has weapons, more than one country has nuclear power. Do we all want to fly tomorrow and become a guided missile? The only way that we're going to come up out of the fear that we have to live in now is to submit to the will of God, and follow these two golden rules: "Do unto others, as you would have others do unto you," and "want for your brother and sister what you want for yourself."

May Allah bless us all with the light of understanding. Thank you for your patience. As-salamu-alaykum.

Notes

This speech was first presented at the C. Eric Lincoln Forum, Candler School of Theology, Emory University, Atlanta, GA, 2001

1. In the wake of the September 11, 2001, bombings, two air incidents received intense media attention, reflecting the heightened focus surrounding air travel in the United States. On October 9, 2001, a passenger on an American flight from Los Angeles to Chicago became intoxicated and unruly, striking a flight attendant. The next day, a passenger handed a threatening note to a flight attendant on a Delta airlines flight bound from Atlanta to Los Angeles. Both episodes ended without major incident. See Bob Keefe Henry Unger, "Scary Incident Diverts Delta Jet," *Atlanta Journal-Constitution,* 11 October 2001.
2. Ibid.
3. Louis Farrakhan, "A View from Islam," *Final Call,* 16 September 2001.
4. Ibid.

IV

Lift Every Voice

14

The Teachers of the World

Asa G. Hilliard

I have a very short time to tell a very long story. When I went to high school and to college the things that I was taught about African people were mostly very negative. Without going into all those things, the worst part of it was that we had no history. In fact, what they told me was that our history began in slavery. And so all the books that I studied in history at college, if I picked up a book in philosophy or mathematics, or if I picked up a book in art or music, there were no African people there before slavery. And if you raised the question of Africa or African people, or, as we were called in the United States in those days, Negroes or colored people, if you raised that question people would immediately say that yes, slaves were brought over here around the time of Columbus. But there was nothing said about us before that time. I always wondered about that as a child. I always identified very strongly with Africa. In fact, my wife and I were in an African dance group when we were in junior high school. I just didn't know enough then to know why we were doing what we were doing. Happily, I have had the opportunity to learn to think about African people since then.

One of the most remarkable things about African people, of course, is that Africans not only had a history before the European slave trade, which began during the late 1400s with the Portuguese and thereafter much of the rest of the Western world around the time of Columbus in 1492. Not only did we have a history before that time but ours was a history that stretches all the way back to the very beginnings of human civilization. That blew me away. I began to study and to dig and to talk to other people who had studied and who had dug. And we began to find out some of the most remarkable things. For four out of the first five million years in the existence of planet earth, human beings have been here and for most of that time there were only African people. There were no people in America four million years ago. There were no people in Asia four million years ago, and there were none to be found in Europe or South America. Only in Africa. Now you could say are you really going to call a prehominid a person? You don't have to call the prehominid a person. If you want to wait until the arrival of *Homo sapiens,* you still have to go to Africa. They brought out a *Newsweek* magazine in January 1988, and on the cover of the magazine were pictures of what they envisioned the first *Homo sapiens* looked like.[1] And they called this ancestral woman, the direct foremother of every human being on the earth, African Eve. She is believed to bear some resemblance to the people residing in the Kalahari region of Southern Africa right now. That is what the mitochondrion DNA study shows. DNA is the chemical material that makes up a person's cells, and myocardial DNA, in particular, allows analysis to be performed. DNA shows that black women in Africa have gone through more cellular or molecular changes than women anywhere else in the world.[2] That is how the ages of people are calculated, by how many changes they have accumulated over time. The DNA in the cells of African women from the Kung people in the Kalahari Desert of southern Africa is the oldest DNA on record. How old? The best approximation is between 150,000 and 250,000 years ago. Just for the sake of argument, let us accept the more conservative estimate and say that humankind began in Africa 150,000 years ago. If you go to Europe, you will find that the best archaeological evidence available on human beings there would be around 40,000 B.C., the first time that *Homo sapiens* appear in that part of the world. You have to wait 100,000 years before you have Europeans, and even they were Africans who had traveled to Asia and over into Europe. So by every indication, 40–50,000 years ago Africans left Africa, moved into Europe, and populated Europe as the first people of Europe.

Now you may be wondering where the various races came from, because at that time there were no races. There was only one race. In fact, there is still only one race. That is to say, either you are an African who looks like the original Africans, or you are an African who has faded. So in Europe, Africans faded for the simple reason that it was more advantageous to have less pigment. Pigment in the tropical regions of Africa keeps ultraviolet rays from destroying your cells and creating skin cancer. But that same pigment filters out many of the sunrays that stimulate the production of vitamin B, which is less needed in the tropics. In the north, in the snow and ice, where the sun is less intense, the body needs vitamin B production in order to ward off rickets. On the other hand, if you are heavily pigmented, you usually need to take lime or vitamin B tablets in the far north. So, human beings adapt to where they are. Now we call those differences race, and make a big political deal out of it. Race has nothing to do with biology and everything to do with politics. So these are the African people. We could go into that in more detail but my topic is the African origin of civilization.

Now to talk about the Africanness of human beings is one thing. The Africanness of the great contributions of human beings is something else. Imagine a little boy in Denver, Colorado, or my hometown in Texas, every Friday night turning on the radio and essentially being told that African people are like Amos 'n Andy. That is what I had to listen to, just like some of you had to grow up watching *The Jeffersons* on television. These shows represented the views most Americans hold of African people. The first people in the world were Africans and were civilized, not caricatures as we were said to be. When I did hear about Africa as a child, Tarzan was swinging through the trees and, along with Jane and Cheetah, keeping the population of the continent in awe. The message was not at all subtle: Come to Africa and show African people what to do, which is exactly the reverse of what happened in history.

African people were the first people on the planet for whom there is a recorded civilization. Now let me be very clear about this: When you find out the truth and it differs so radically from what you find in a textbook, somebody's going to say, "if we did all of that, why isn't it in the textbooks?" You really need to have a map and a time chart of Africa to make sense of it all. You need to be able to visualize where African people were born, which means where the human race was born. The human race was born on the equator, somewhere near Mount Kilimanjaro, in and around the Rift valley and the regions of modern-day Uganda, Tanzania, Ethiopia, and Kenya. Ethiopia lies 4,000 miles south of the Mediterranean region. That is farther than the distance across the United States. That is how far inside the continent African people were born, and it is also how far civilization was from Egypt, itself a mere 100 miles from the Mediterranean Sea.

The Egyptians, who are the world's first well-recorded civilized people, never said they created their own civilization. They were very clear on the subject, in essence stating, "we have a home and we are the children of the people of inner Africa." We have come from the beginning of this long river with 4,000 tributaries, the Nile River or the

Hapi, if you want to call it by its African name. We come from the sources of the Hapi, at the foothills of the mountains of the moon where the god Hapi dwells. This is what the Kemetic historians wrote about where they came from (the people of Egypt originally called their land Kemet or Kemit). We did not have to turn to Germany or France to ask their historians where Kemetic people came from because the Kemetic people speak for themselves through their own writings. We still have on papyrus, on monuments, on temples, and on tombs incredible amounts of their writings, and they tell us about the origins of the Kemetic people in the interior of Africa.

To the best of our knowledge, the first civilization of Africa is pre-3000 B.C.E. How much earlier we cannot say with precision, but we know it begins somewhere around Cush, which is now called Ethiopia, its Greek name. We know the people were black because this is what "Ethiopian" means in Greek: "Burnt skin people." Not brown-skinned, not yellow-skinned, not red-skinned, but "burnt," ebony-skinned people. The Greeks also took note of the beauty, intelligence, and comportment of the Ethiopians. They envied their black skin, nappy hair, tall stature, and wisdom. This is what the historical record says about Africa according to Homer and the Greeks. Of course, African people had already said many of the same things about themselves.

So Ethiopia is first, but then as we come down the river we get all confused because the map is upside down to our conventional minds. Remember the Nile or Hapi River flows downhill; water runs downhill the same way everywhere in the world. The Hapi starts in the highlands of Kenya and Uganda and flows downward 4,000 miles to the north and into the land of Kemet. That was the natural cultural highway of Africa's people who first came to life in the Garden of Eden and over time navigated down the river. In the process, the first civilizations were created somewhere in the vicinity of Cush and Punt, or present-day Ethiopia and Somalia. So Cush and Punt, or Ethiopia and Somaliland, are the home base out of which arises the heralded civilization of Egypt long before Babylon, Mesopotamia, Sumer, and Elam.

The first nation in Africa had already been started somewhere around 3500 B.C.E. Not in Egypt but Ta-Seti (or Ta-Zeti) in the ancient Sudan, somewhere between 3500 and 3200 B.C.E. The graves of the African kings in the region were uncovered when the Aswan Dam was built on the Nile during the 1960s, which also created a nearly 450-mile-long lake in the process. Now when you engineer a lake that spans the distance from Atlanta to New York, you also wipe out 450 miles of land where people used to live. They wiped out Nubia when they built the Aswan Dam and covered over the history of the origin of civiliza-tion; Ta-Seti is now under water.[3] But before the floodwaters came, the last known archaeological site there was excavated. On that site were found cemeteries holding the remains of African kings and the earliest writings known to the world, MeduNeter, or hieroglyphics, as they are called in Greek. MeduNeter, whose root words are "Medu" (the word) and "Neter" (is God), was regarded by Africans as a sacred text.[4] The earliest part of the writings refer to Ta-Seti as the land of the people who were good with bows and arrows. Ta-Seti is the oldest recorded kingdom in the world. MeduNeter is the oldest writing system in human recorded history. That is why you have to have maps and time charts dealing with African people. African people already had nations 4,500 years ago. There was no Europe yet. In fact, there was no Europe until after the birth of Christ. Europe was not unified in any way; no nations existed other than Greece or Rome in Europe.

Here we are three millennia before the time of Christ and Africans have already created the first nation that is well recorded, and it was called Kemet, or Egypt. And in Kemet, not so long after they had established the first nation, they began to do astonishing things like build pyramids, many of which are still standing. The Great Pyramid, or Step Pyramid, as it is also known, was built around 2500 B.C.E. Its principle architect was an African genius, an engineer, preacher, and medical doctor whom the Greeks called the father of medicine, and his name was Imhotep. This is the beauty of African history. Our writings, pictures, and paintings are still there, preserved in stone for all time. Our bodies are still there, preserved in the forms we today call mum-mies. You can look at the face of an African woman who died 3,500 years ago but who looks like she just died yesterday because of the level of medical knowledge about embalming, also indigenous to Africa. People in Europe, India, and elsewhere cremated their bodies until Europe tried to emulate Africa and embalm. Today, we still have not learned how to make bodies last 3,000 years like in Africa.

There was a professor of English at the University of Virginia named E. D. Hirsch who wrote a best-selling book not too long ago called *Cultural Literacy*.[5] Ironically, the book itself was not very culturally literate. Hirsch listed 5,000 things that every American needs to know to be literate, that is, what we are supposed to know in order to be able to function and prosper in this society. Psychologist Wade Nobles has said if you let somebody else define your reality they have power over you. So, if you allow Professor Hirsch to tell you what a literate person is, he has the power over you.

It is bad not to be in possession of your own record, because when you meet yourself in the pages of the Bible, when you meet yourself in history, you won't even know yourself. I am not talking about something obscure but something that is written in rock that has been there for thousands of years; I am talking about the African origin of civilization. Don't you think that if you originated religion you originated civilization? Don't you think that if you originated architecture and made the first stone buildings, that that speaks to the origin of civilization? If you originated the mathematics necessary to compute, calculate, and construct pyramids that cannot be duplicated even today, wouldn't you say that you created civilization? We have the textbook that African mathematics scholars used in 2000 B.C.E. called the Moscow Papyrus, and another from 1500 B.C.E. called the Rhine Mathematics on Papyrus.[6] In those books are contained problems of algebra, geometry, and trigonometry. Would you not say that people who had trigonometry in 2000 B.C.E., when nobody else had it, created civilization? The Greeks, who are revered as the founders of Western civilization, were so awestruck when they looked across the Mediterranean and saw these African people that they decided it was time to integrate the schools. They had no buses. They used shipping for integration. They left their homes and traveled across the miles and waters to Africa just so they could sit at the feet of African scholars.

I was talking to someone the other day who asked me, "how do we know that what you are saying is true?" Only when black people are portrayed in a positive light, returned to their right position, do we ask "is it true?" All you have to do is read some of the ancient Kemetic literature, like the *Husia* or *Book of the Dead* to see what we are talking about.[7] You will understand how Pythagoras came to Africa for 22 years to learn and returned as the father of mathematics in Greece. Plato also went to Africa, studying there for 12 years and returning to his home to write *The Republic*. All Plato did was describe the African political and educational system he had witnessed in Africa. Aristotle was impressed with the literature of Africa, which was so expansive that after Alexander the Great's conquest of Egypt, the world's largest library was housed at Alexandria. But this was not the first library. As early as the fourth dynasty in Kemet there was a presidential appointee, a cabinet member if you will, placed in charge of books for the land. The religious institutions of ancient Kemet were repositories of learning, which is what they ought to be today but all too often are not. Now we teach catechism rather than history in churches, we memorize stories rather than glean profound insights.

So Aristotle sets up a school, not just a library. As far as we know, Aristotle had not written any books previously; suddenly there are thousands of books on any number of subjects coming out in Aristotle's name. He never personally claimed authorship for what he had gained from Kemetic wisdom, but his students claimed the authority for him, which in turn became the foundation for Greek higher education. We follow a fouled-up curriculum of study today. At one point Kemet had a clear and coherent curriculum. There were seven subjects to study and you had to major in all seven. Today, our academic system of selecting a major and a minor means that something is left out. In the African system, you had to major in everything—grammar, rhetoric, logic, arithmetic, astronomy, geometry, and music. If you studied these seven things you would be free to think like a human being. You studied to become a virtuous person; that was the goal of their system. Our goal today is to get a job. We've drifted from the African ideal. If African people taught the Greeks, Romans, and other people over time it doesn't mean they were any better than anybody else. It just means that at one time it was Africa's turn. In fact, it is the turn of the United States right now, isn't it? If you want to study physics at its best you have to come here. That does not make the United States superior to the rest of the world. It just makes America more fortunate. We have more education, transportation, and armament. At that time, Africans did.

At one time Africans ruled the world and spread their civilization to the corners of the world. They did not copy anybody. Their culture stayed the same for 3,000 years. The Kemetic structure remained basically the same until the Christians invaded, followed by new conquest at the hands of the Arab Muslim world.

I do not have time to go through the whole of African civilization. I have only spent this little amount of time in the northeast corner of Africa. I did not say anything about the ancient kingdoms of Songhai, Ghana, Mali, or the numerous other civilizations spread across the continent of Africa. We did not have to wait for someone to come and teach us how to be civilized people. Tragically, some Africans now come here believing that their own people were uncivilized and have the foolish notion that they are going to go back and civilize somebody.

If you are able, go and spend some time in Mali with the Dogon people. You will be close to the spiritual source of the ancient religions. The Dogon people are in many respects like the ancient Kemets, who themselves acted like the ancient Cushites. They have the same religious system. Whatever your religion happens to be it may suddenly begin to make more sense to you in Mali. You will understand, perhaps for the first time, what you have been up to all this time. It all comes out of Africa. You owe it to yourself to know how and where African people are in the world. It is a shame to have an education and not know that African people are not a minority in the world. Most people think that there are only about 30 million of us, but as the eminent scholar John Henrik Clarke and others have noted, we are almost one billion strong. You just don't know where the others are because we lost our names and theirs. A people who went out and civilized the world now have new names. There are almost 90 million people of African descent in Brazil, nearly three times the number of Africans found in the United States. I have not even counted the Caribbean, Europe, Asia, and the Pacific Rim.

Three thousand and more years before the birth of Christ, African people were not savages. African people were not uncivilized. We became the teachers of the world. It is time that we become the teachers of the world again.

Notes

This speech was first presented at The C. Eric Lincoln Lectureship Series, Clark Atlanta University, Atlanta, GA, 1989.

1. John Tierney, Lynda Wright, and Karen Springen, "The Search for Adam and Eve," *Newsweek* (January 11, 1988): 46–52.
2. Ibid.
3. The construction of the Aswan High Dam flooded a large part of the Nubian region and forced 100,000 latter-day Nubians to relocate, mainly to Arabic-speaking regions.
4. See, for instance, Ivan Van Sertima, *Nile Valley Civilizations* (New Brunswick, NJ: Transaction Books, 1989), pp. 171–72.
5. E. D. Hirsch, *Cultural Literacy: What Every American Needs to Know* (New York: Vintage Books, 1988).
6. See Chiekh Anta Diop, *The African Origin of Civilization: Myth or Reality* (Westport, CT: Lawrence Hill & Co., 1974), and George G. M. James, *Stolen Legacy* (Chicago: African American Images, 2002).
7. Maulana Karenga, *Selections from the Husia: Sacred Wisdom of Ancient Egypt* (Los Angeles: University of Sankore Press, 1989); T. G. Allen, trans., *The Book of the Dead or Going Forth by Day: Ideas of the Ancient Egyptians Concerning the Hereafter as Expressed In Their Own Terms* (Chicago: Oriental Institute of the University of Chicago, Studies in Ancient Oriental Civilization no. 37, 1974).

15

"My Chains Fell Off":

Heart Religion in the African American Methodist Tradition

Love Henry Whelchel, Jr.

When I alone thought myself lost,
my dungeon shook, my chains fell off.

—Negro spiritual

One of the first tasks that faced white American slaveholders was to break the spirit of resistance among their black captives, and one of the chief means to that end, they realized, was to suppress every element of traditional West African religion and culture.[1] Whites regarded African beliefs and practices, such as the veneration of ancestors, drumming, ceremonial dancing, spirit possession, and "shouting," not only as expressions of the kind of "paganism" they claimed to deplore but also as vestiges of an identity they felt the need to destroy. For more than three centuries African American slaves were not only denied the freedom of their bodies but were also robbed of their heritage and their humanity. Yet Africans clung tenaciously to their traditions, and often practiced these forbidden things in secret or adapted them in surprising and creative ways whenever their captors tried to share their own faith with them or impose it upon them. The first whites to offer instruction in the Christian religion to African Americans were Anglicans. Their aim was to eradicate traditional African religion and culture. But they never completely succeeded. In 1709, an Anglican missionary lamented that he had not fully suppressed the African "feasts, dances, and merry meetings, upon the Lord's day." These, he reported, were "pretty well over in his parish, but not absolutely."[2]

The "rite of separation" denied slaves all rights of birth, which meant they ceased to belong to any legitimate social order. After being uprooted from Africa and reduced to chattel slavery in America, African Americans were separated from their past and their ancestry. According to Melville Herskovits, one of the myths commonly held by whites to legitimize their social, political, and economic subjugation of blacks is that blacks have no past worth remembering.[3] Unlike other ethnic groups in America, African Americans were not allowed to integrate the memory of their ancestors into their own lives. Stripped of their heritage, they were nearly dissolved as a people, and lost almost all sense of identity, purpose, and calling. Forbidden to speak their own languages, to practice their own customs and traditions, and to preserve their native beliefs and values, African Americans were scarcely able to give meaning to the humiliations and brutalities they endured daily. Slavery and the African spiritual holocaust were an attempt to erase the African's past and deny him his sense of self. This contrasted sharply with the treatment that other immigrant peoples received as they entered the great American "melting pot." As one scholar has noted:

> Whatever the difficulties and anomalies of colonization, a broad range of religiously inclined Europeans—Puritans, Scottish Presbyterians, German Lutherans, Dutch Reformed, Quakers and Jews—not only survived in America but often eventually prospered both individually and spiritually. But the rich religious systems of Akan, Ashanti, Dahoman, Ibo, and Yoruba societies—to name only some of the major sources of African religion in America—collapsed in the shattering cultural destructiveness of British slaveholding.[4]

Although Africans were some of the earliest people from the "Old World" to arrive in America, the great promise of freedom and new opportunities anticipated by European immigrants was not accorded them.

Not only were Africans denied the religion of their motherland, but many white slaveholders were reluctant for them to be converted to Christianity. And for the first 150 years of slavery, few were. Among the noteworthy barriers to conversion are the following factors: 1) Many slaveholders themselves had little interest in religion, much less in promoting it among their slaves—unless the *kind* of religion the slaves could be made to adopt would make them at once industrious and docile. 2) Many slaveholders resented the loss of productivity that would result if slaves spent too much time in religious activities. 3) European methods of evangelism and religious instruction were time consuming and labor intensive. 4) Recently "imported" slaves had difficulty understanding (to say nothing of adapting to) the language and culture of their captors. 5) Even after the linguistic and cultural barriers had been overcome, many African Americans found the religion of whites dull and unappealing.

Thus, not only were deliberate attempts made to purge slaves of their Africanisms, but there were serious obstacles to converting them to Christianity. Nevertheless, a distinctive brand of African American Christianity—rooted both in the African heritage (which was never entirely suppressed) and in the biblical narratives of liberation from bondage—emerged during the centuries of slavery. This religion has remained one of the strongest forces in African American culture. At the Third Atlanta Conference, held in 1898, W. E. B. DuBois reported:

> The Negro Church is the only social institution of Negroes which started in the African forest and survived slavery; under the leadership of priest or medicine man, afterward of the Christian pastor, the church preserved in itself the remnants of African tribal life and became after emancipation the center of Negro social life. So that today the Negro population of the United States is virtually divided into church congregations which are the real units of race life.[5]

One of the most popular brands of Christianity among African Americans has been Methodism, precisely because its emphasis on "the religion of the heart" allowed blacks to incorporate many cherished elements of their religious and cultural heritage, to resist the dehumanizing forces of slavery and then "Jim Crow" legislation, and to know the crucified and risen Savior in a personal way. This chapter will outline the history of African American Methodism, from the early eighteenth century to the present time, and analyze the distinctive brand of "heart religion" that it developed.

The Dawn of a New Day

African Americans did not become excited about Christianity in large numbers until the First Great Awakening (1738–1746), a period that the eminent black historian Carter G. Woodson labeled the "Dawn of a New Day." New forms of Evangelical Protestantism emerged during or in the wake of this great upsurge of religious enthusiasm, forms that proved far better suited to the spiritual needs of black people than colonial Puritanism or Anglicanism had ever been. One of these was Methodism, and although the roots of what was to become the first organized American Methodist church go back only as far as the 1760s, the founder of Methodism, John Wesley, had been a missionary in the colony of Georgia 30 years before. As is well known, Wesley seems to have regarded his brief ministry in Georgia (1735–1737) as a general failure. Yet it was this very failure that created an opportunity for Wesley's former Oxford protege, George Whitefield, to make the first of his famous missionary tours to America, a tour which helped to launch the First Great Awakening. Moreover, it is noteworthy that several of Wesley's few evangelical successes from that period were with blacks. As I shall try to show, the attraction that blacks feel toward Methodism goes back to that time. Moreover, when the Methodist Episcopal Church was formally organized at the famous Christmas Conference of 1784, two African Americans, Richard Allen and Harry Hosier, were in attendance. True, Allen later experienced racial prejudice in that denomination and left it in order to found the African Methodist Episcopal Church. But he was convinced that Methodism, with its message of personal holiness and its concern not only for doctrinal truth but also for practical action and fervent devotion, was the brand of Christianity best suited to African Americans. This conviction has been widely shared among African Americans ever since.

Wesley did not come to America as a proponent of "heart religion" but was introduced to it here by a group of German Pietists known as the Moravians. According to the famous story, it was during his voyage from England to Georgia that he first encountered these folk. A furious storm arose, which struck fear into the hearts of many on board, including the young missionary. But the small contingent of Moravian passengers displayed a serenity that both impressed and shamed Wesley, caused him to doubt the adequacy of his own faith, and ultimately revealed his need for a closer and more personal walk with God.[6]

Although the Moravians did not renounce the institution of slavery, they welcomed slaves into their fellowship and were not above visiting them in their cabins, sharing food and clothing with them, and greeting them with a warm handshake.[7] Moravians not only nurtured the spiritual and physical welfare of the slaves but also demonstrated concern for their mental welfare. They pioneered in teaching slaves to read the Bible. This literary opportunity enhanced religion's appeal to African Americans. Many slaves were as eager to learn to read as they were to get converted. A Moravian missionary reported, "Every one wanted to have a textbook. Whoever was lucky enough to have one carried it with him everywhere and devoted every moment to studying it."[8]

Wesley adopted many of the evangelistic methods of the Moravians, which helped to endear Methodism to African Americans. Wesley devised the most comprehensive network for spreading the gospel among a scattered and widely dispersed population in colonial America. Since slavery was not permitted in Georgia until 1750, Wesley's initial contact with blacks on his missionary journey to America in 1736 was in Charleston, South Carolina. Alexander Gardner, a well-established Anglican Missionary in South Carolina, invited Wesley to deliver his first sermon in Charleston. Wesley reported with joy in his journal, "I was glad to see several Negroes at church."[9] Following the service, Wesley had an extended conversation with an African woman who had allegedly received religious instruction. However, Wesley was disappointed at her ignorance of the rudiments of the Christian faith. His Anglican upbringing continued to impact his thinking about conversion to the Christian faith.

Wesley made a second trip to Charleston in April of 1737, but as he prepared to return to Georgia he decided, because of rough seas, to borrow a horse and travel over land. This proved fortuitous, for as he passed through the rich low country of South Carolina he visited many of the most prominent white families in the area, some of whom had a marked interest in the religious instruction of slaves. Planters such as Colonel William Bull, William Bellinger, and Hugh Bryan extended a warm welcome to Wesley and gave him permission to minister to their slaves. One of his first successes was with a slave woman from Barbados who belonged to a Mr. Thompson, the minister of St. Bartholomew's Church near Ponpon. Wesley was pleased to learn that she regularly attended church with her mistress and was impressed by her zeal. But he was saddened that no attempt had been made by her master to teach her the basic tenets of the faith, a situation he promptly attempted to rectify.[10] A few days later, while visiting the slaves on the Bellinger plantation, he encountered an elderly African who told him of her insatiable hunger for the gospel: "When I lived at Ashley Ferry I could go to church every Sunday, but here we are buried in the woods.

Though if there was any church within five or six miles I am so lame I cannot walk but I would crawl thither."[11] Another of Bellinger's slaves whom Wesley met was "a Negro lad who guided him through the woods to Purrysburg" (a town purported to be the birthplace of chattel slavery in Georgia). Wesley did not miss the opportunity to teach the lad to sing and pray. After his departure the lad left Wesley with the impression that he was "very desirous and capable of instruction."[12]

One of the prominent South Carolina landowners whom Wesley visited on this trip, Hugh Bryan, is of particular interest for our story. Wesley's diary says that he had a "useful, religious talk with Bryan" although it does not indicate whether he spoke to Bryan's slaves.[13] We do know from other sources, however, that Bryan had such a sincere interest in the spiritual welfare of his slaves that he later encouraged the Society for the Propagation of the Gospel to supply them with Bibles and Psalters. Another time as Bryan was preparing to receive the sacrament of the Lord's Supper, he had a mystical experience and thereafter began to make "sundry enthusiastic prophecies of the Destruction of Charles Town and the Deliverance of Negroes from servitude." Thus did his embrace of "heart religion" lead him directly to radical social and political views. This, however, aroused the opposition of other white landowners, who feared that a widespread spiritual awakening might lead to slave revolts! The prophesied general deliverance did not take place, but at least there was a rather dramatic revival among his own slaves.[14] Eventually this group of fervent souls would help to found the independent Black Church movement.[15]

When John Wesley departed from Georgia and returned to Britain in December 1737, his evangelistic work among slaves was one of his few notable missionary accomplishments. He continued his association with the Moravians, and it was largely thanks to them that he eventually underwent his famous "heart-warming" Aldersgate Experience of May 28, 1738. This radically changed his life and ministry, and Methodism as we now know it dates from that time. The work of later Methodist evangelists in America therefore has no direct connection with the abortive Georgia mission. But there is an *indirect* connection, insofar as Wesley's published *Journal* from his Georgia years established him as one who had a heart for ministry with blacks. And in later works he expressed his loathing for American chattel slavery, which he had observed firsthand.[16] When his followers first took the Methodist message to the New World in the 1760s, they had Wesley's own demonstrated concern for the spiritual and physical welfare of people of color, and especially those held in bondage, firmly in mind. Moreover, they were steeped in the "heart religion" that Wesley preached after Aldersgate, a form of piety that, as we shall see, proved extremely popular among African Americans. Thus we can say that although John Wesley himself founded no congregations in America—white or black— that endured, he may still be credited for much of Methodism's attractiveness to African Americans.

One of the first Methodists to plant Wesleyan "heart religion" in the New World was the Irish preacher Robert Strawbridge. Strawbridge visited Antigua in the 1760s and did evangelistic work on the plantation of Nathaniel Gilbert, a prominent landowner and political leader of the island. Gilbert himself was a Christian and seems to have felt a sincere (if rather typically condescending) concern for the spiritual welfare of his slaves, judging from his remark that they were "in a state of inconceivable darkness and diabolical superstition."[17] And because the treatment of slaves in the Caribbean and in Hispanic America was typically less draconian than in the thirteen British colonies, slaves were better able to retain their ancestral religious customs. Hence, it is not surprising that Gilbert welcomed Strawbridge to work among them. Moreover, Gilbert's household had already had some contact with Methodism. In 1758, when Gilbert was on a journey back to England, he took three of his house servants with him, and two of them, both females, heard John Wesley himself preach at the Gilbert family estate in Wandsworth. Wesley took note of them, too. He recorded in his *Journal* on January 17, 1758, that "two Negro servants of [Gilbert's, one of them possibly Sophia Campbell] and a Mulatto [possibly Mary Alley] appear[ed] to be much awakened."[18] Some months later, Wesley noted, "I rode to Wandsworth, baptized two Negroes belonging to Mr. Gilbert . . . ; one of them is deeply convinced of sin, the other rejoices in God her savior."[19]

Another early Methodist evangelist to work among blacks in the New World was Joseph Pilmore. In his diary, he records a time when he was preaching in the area of Portsmouth, Virginia: "Two poor slaves came to me and begged I would instruct them in the way of salvation, so I gave them a short and plain account of the plan of the Gospel, and showed them how sinners may come to God and be saved. We then joined in singing and prayer, and they expressed great thankfulness for what they had heard and seemed determined to be Christians." Three days later, when Pilmore preached again, guards had to be posted at the door of the meeting house "to keep Negroes out till the White people were got in."[20] Wesleyan "heart religion" thus generated a common ground, a common interest, a common loyalty, a common cause, and a common need among members of both races. Regrettably, it did not lead to an equitable sharing of power in the congregations. There, as elsewhere, blacks were often segregated and placed in subordinate roles, a fact which ultimately led to a schism along racial lines.

Another significant feature of the warm-hearted Methodist faith was a willingness to give women a greater role in the leadership of the church. The common early Methodist practice of holding revival meetings in local homes naturally encouraged active participation by women and children in the movement. This, in turn, fostered populist informality and the free expression of religious emotion in Methodist worship and the frequent crossing of racial barriers. As Sylvia R. Frey and Betty Wood have noted, "white women demonstrated religious zeal equal to that of black women who were already skilled in ecstatic religious behavior such as visions, trances, prophecies and spirit possessions."[21] Revivalism engulfed quarterly conferences, which women of both races attended. The quarterly meeting was an important event in Methodist polity, for it was there that preachers were licensed and their salaries set and church property was sold or acquired. During the 1770s quarterly conferences were usually held on Sundays to allow a larger attendance on the part of both blacks and whites. These meetings sometimes attracted as many as two or three thousand people of both races from many miles around. Blacks and whites were seated separately, but the common worship experience—which included prayer, testimony, hymn singing, and the love feast—transcended race and gender. Many times the spiritual fervor of these conferences was initiated by the African Americans' participation.[22] The early African American Methodist preachers received their local preacher's license to exhort in these quarterly meetings.

In the early years of American Methodism, any gathering, whether it was a church conference, a quarterly conference, or an annual conference, might experience a powerful outpouring of the Spirit. For example, Thomas Rankin was holding a quarterly meeting on the Baltimore and Kent Circuit in 1774 when, near the end of the meeting, he asked those assembled to look in the rear, where the blacks were stretching out their hands, hearts, and minds to God, who was the joy of their salvation. In his memoirs, Rankin recorded a moving and vivid description of the experience: "It seemed as if the very house shook with the might, power and glory of Sinai's God. Many of the people were so overcome, that they were ready to faint and die under his mighty hand."[23] These African Americans were living testimonies to Paul's affirmation, "For to me to live is Christ and to die is gain" (Phil. 1:21).

The Emergence of the Visible Institution

As we move from the last half of the eighteenth century to the first half of the nineteenth, we find two issues coming to dominate American public life: race and religion. Abolitionism and revivalism were both on the rise throughout the country during this period, and these issues, though distinct, influenced one another in various ways. Some people favored both; some opposed both; some favored one for the sake of the other. Representatives of these conflicting views could be found in every Protestant denomination, but the debates within Methodism were particularly bitter.

Methodism was, on the one hand, not associated with any one state or region (as, say, Anglicanism was in Virginia and Congregationalism in New England), but was growing rapidly everywhere, especially in the Mid-west and South. This was precisely because of its embrace of revivalism. Moreover, its effective system of governance—with policy set by quadrennial general conferences that were attended by delegates from every corner of the country, and with the day-to-day management of the church firmly in the hands of itinerant bishops, who went everywhere and saw everything—was designed to make it a truly national church. On the other hand, because of increasing tensions over slavery, regionalism was also on the rise, and its impact was keenly felt in the bitter controversies that broke out in the general conferences of the 1840s and 1850s. Many Methodists, especially in the North, felt that racial equality, both in the church and in society as a whole, was both a divine imperative and a political necessity. They pointed to the fact that African Americans had fought and died in the Revolution for a freedom they themselves did not enjoy. They pointed also to the strong tradition of interracial ministry that had already developed within the denomination. Most of all, they pointed to the Wesleyan message that God is no respecter of persons and makes salvation freely available for all, a message that implies that people of every race and nation should be on an equal footing. Yet not all of these concluded that abolitionism as such was the proper solution to the slavery issue. Some, particularly in the Mid-west and the border states, were gradualists, who believed that converting slaveholders to Christ (e.g., at revivals) would induce them to free their chattel voluntarily, and that converting slaves would make them patient and brave until the day of their manumission.[24] And Methodists in the South generally opposed the abolition of slavery, or at least the efforts of Northern Methodists to subject clergy and lay members who held slaves to disciplinary measures. Fearing the socially leveling effect that interracial revivals often had, but still believing it to be their gospel duty to carry out evangelistic and catechetical work among slaves, white Southern Methodists devised a system of what were called "plantation missions." In themselves, these missions had little enduring effect, but their very failure led blacks to devise their own clandestine system for cultivating "heart religion." This, in turn, paved the way for the development of the independent Black Church after the Civil War. Let us examine the reciprocal influences of race and religion, first in the revivals that swept the nation generally, and then in the plantation missions and "bush harbor" gatherings in the Slave States.

The Second Great Awakening (1800–1840) was extremely beneficial both for the growth of American Methodism and for the spiritual freedom of African Americans. Revivals and camp meetings featured frenzied preaching and demonstrative worship that attracted people of both races and both sexes. Thousands of people were led to embrace a deeply personal and highly emotional brand of Christian faith.[25] Initially, African American participation in white camp meetings was probably quite spontaneous, but as time went on it became a regular and accepted thing and provided opportunities for intense interaction between blacks and whites. Many people welcomed this, and where they did, revivalism became a means for African Americans to gain access to the churches and other institutions supported by evangelical Christians, whose religious ethos was generally compatible with black culture and temperament. But the interracial character of the revivals was feared by others, and when they were unable to prevent it altogether, they sought to erect barriers against too much interracial fraternizing. The Methodist Episcopal Church, South, for example, enacted a law stating "that slaves be allowed to participate in prayer meetings back of the pulpit led by one or more of the regular preachers with the aid of colored leaders when available."[26]

Insulting as such segregation was, it must also be said that African Americans have often felt most comfortable with their own preachers and have generally accorded those in their communities who have a call to preach great respect. Since the seating arrangements at the camp meetings were segregated, it was not uncommon for African Americans to seek out a preacher from among themselves and wander into the thickets to have their own service. For example, at a camp meeting held on Virginia's Greenville Circuit in 1789, the white minister preached to the white people inside the church, but on the outside of the church was a huge crowd of blacks. When the white minister came outside to minister to the Africans, he was surprised to find that a slave exhorter was already preaching to them with phenomenal success. African Americans would often have their own service at the close of a camp meeting. In one Georgia camp meeting, as the meeting closed, slaves gradually dispersed and carried on individual penance in their tent by pounding their chests and dancing the "holy dance."[27] The special effectiveness of black preachers has always lain in their ability to use the human voice to evoke powerful religious emotions and to create a sense of community among their audiences by articulating the common needs, experiences, and convictions of the people.

Preaching, of course, has always been central to Protestant worship. Similarly, storytelling and other forms of oral communication have been central to the cultures of West Africa. It is no surprise, therefore, that American slaves, most of whom came originally from West Africa, would soon be attracted to Protestantism and would eventually develop their own distinctive preaching style. This style is marked by rhythmic and repetitious speech, is rich in illustrations and anecdotes, and is enlivened by demonstrative gestures and "whooping." Such methods were reminiscent of the emotional expressiveness and the close intimacy between speaker and audience that characterized the oral traditions of their ancestral homeland. George White, who was licensed by the Methodist Church as a "colored preacher" in 1807, reported that during the meeting where he was preaching, "a numerous body of people . . . fell prostrate under the divine power . . . at which my own heart glowed with unexpressible joy, and renewed resolution to proceed in obedience to my Master's command; exhorting to repentance all it met with."[28]

According to the eminent black scholar W. E. B. DuBois, dynamic preaching, along with soulful music and frenzied emotion, is the centerpiece of the African American religious tradition. Ministers have the longest tenure of leadership in the black community, and the black preacher has been described as "the most unique personality developed by the Negro on American soil."[29] James Weldon Johnson, who feared the threat of the extinction of colorful, charismatic, highly charged old-time preachers, sought to preserve their legacy by documenting seven of their sermons in God's Trombones. As Johnson noted, "it was through [the black preacher] that the people of diverse languages and customs who were brought from diverse parts of Africa and thrown into slavery were given their first sense of unity and solidarity."[30] With the advent of the black preacher, African Americans ceased being a mission people, and congregations and churches sprang up wherever their masters would permit it. The recognition of the authority of the spirit that emerged from the "heart religion" of the Second Great Awakening combined with individuals' personal gifts and graces to give black preachers a position of dominance in the black community. "In pursuit of his calling the black preacher was frequently without degrees but never without the dignity of his office. He was often without honor but never without integrity. He was often without a visible church but never without an invisible spirit. He was often stymied but never completely stifled."[31]

The spiritual fervor of the Second Awakening spread from Canada to Georgia and from East Coast to West. It touched urban and rural areas, tidewater flats, and back country settlements. It transformed rich people and poor people, the lettered and the unlettered, black and white. The theological objective of the spiritual revivals was to seek balance between religion of head and religion of heart. The focus was on the whole person, where reason and emotions operated simultaneously to nurture spiritual growth. The key to a healthy religion is the balance between the religion of the head and heart.[32] An old preacher echoed this holistic approach to religion when he remarked, "If your religion don't make you feel somethin', think somethin', and do somethin', then you can be sure you ain't got nothin'."[33] One notable example of an African American from this period whose oratorical skills brought him to national prominence was Harry Rosier, a member of the evangelistic team of Francis Asbury, Thomas Coke, and Freeborn Garrettson. "Black Harry" was known for his very dark skin, his keen eyes, and his thunderous voice. Although illiterate, he became one of the most popular preachers in America. Dr. Benjamin Rush, who heard him preach, labeled him the greatest orator in America. On one occasion, Rosier accompanied Asbury to Wilmington, Delaware, where a large crowd had gathered expecting to hear the great bishop. The auditorium could not accommodate all the people, but the overflow could still hear the sermon even though they were unable to see the preacher. At the conclusion, a person on the outside remarked, "If all Methodist Preachers can preach like the Bishop, we should like to be a constant hearer." Someone replied, "That was not the Bishop, but the Bishop's servant that you heard." So that inquirer concluded, "If such be the servant, what must the master be?"[34]

Another illustrious offspring of the Second Great Awakening was Richard Allen. He was born a slave in Maryland, and he and his household were sold to another slaveholder who resided near Dover, Delaware. Not uncommon in that day, was the fact that those slaveholders who demonstrated the most compassion to their slaves did not profess Christianity. So it was with Allen's new master: He was not a church-goer, but he was good to his slaves and provided religious training for them. Allen was converted at the age of 17 under the enthusiastic and dynamic preaching of Freeborn Garrettson. In Allen's autobiography he recorded his emotional conversion experience:

> Now my confidence was strengthened that the Lord, for Christ's sake, had heard my prayers and pardoned all my sins. I was constrained to go from house to house, exhorting my old companions, and telling to all around what a dear Savior I had found. I joined the Methodist Society and met in class at Benjamin Wells', in the forest, Delaware State. John Gray was the class leader. I met in his class for several years.[35]

After Allen's conversion, he secured permission from Garrettson to preach on his master's plantation. Like Wesley, Asbury, and other early Methodist preachers, Garrettson opposed the institution of slavery, and after the sermon Allen's master began to view slaveholding as immoral. He offered Allen and his brother their freedom for $2,000. In five years the industrious Allen had accumulated enough money to purchase his freedom. After receiving his freedom, he moved to Philadelphia, where he discovered that the temporal welfare of free blacks was often as deplorable as it was under slavery. Richard Allen and Absalom Jones organized the Free African Society to address the social and economic plight, as well as the spiritual welfare, of the free blacks of Philadelphia.

Allen's dramatic conversion experience to Methodism was a decisive moment that he never forgot. In Philadelphia, Allen joined the St. George's Church, and he received his license to preach in 1782. The St. George's Church was a mixed congregation, and the white pastor, immediately recognizing Allen's innate gifts, appointed him class leader, exhorter, and teacher to the nearly 50 black members in the congregation. Occasionally the African American congregants would gather at the church at 5:00 A.M. and Allen would preach to them. Unfortunately, the congregation grew increasingly uncomfortable with the large number of blacks who were attending and began subjecting them to disgraceful indignities. In 1787, Allen felt obliged to lead an exodus of his people from St. George's church, and by 1816 he had founded a new denomination, the African Methodist Episcopal Church.

Nevertheless, Allen remained faithful to Wesleyanism. He believed its brand of piety was best suited for the temperament of African Americans and felt a sense of personal indebtedness to the Methodist revivalism for his heart-warming conversion experience. His new organization provided him with a more adequate base from which to enunciate his religious and racial views. He was by no means opposed to the reconciliation of the races, but he felt the need for a place where black Christians could worship in dignity. Yet as necessary as it was for the spiritual freedom of Black Methodists to have their own denomination, the fact that whites would not accept them as equal members of the Body of Christ is a moral tragedy. As a modern United Methodist bishop, Jonathan D. Keaton has written: "For this simple reason, we lost him. He had the leadership skills to grow the Black church and the denomination. We made no room for him."[36] We now turn our attention to the South, where the socially leveling effects of revivalism were feared by many whites, who remained anxious to keep the profitable system of human bondage intact. One means devised by evangelically minded slaveholders to save the souls of African Americans without doing anything that might alter their social status was the system of "plantation missions." Whites furnished their slaves with "praise houses" and sponsored Sunday services for them. But the worship experiences were generally staid, unemotional, and always laden with promises of the eternal salvation that awaited those who made no effort to improve their earthly circumstances. The slaves went through the motions of attending these—how could they not?—but most despised them. Meanwhile, whenever possible, they were beating paths to remote swamps and thickets, where they could worship freely away from the "big house" and the prying eyes of their overseers. This was the genesis of what has been called "the invisible institution," the clandestine network of Christian congregations founded and organized exclusively by and for slaves.

The style of worship typical of these bush harbor meetings contrasted with that of the services sponsored for them by their masters. At these meetings slaves could vent their pent-up feelings of pain, sorrow, and supernatural joy in a Spirit-filled manner. Fiery preaching, fervent prayers, and soulful singing were the joyful alternative to the restrained worship permitted by the slaveholders. Yet the "invisible institution" existed not merely to provide emotional catharsis. It was an authentic expression of hope in and commitment to the God who breaks the chains of the oppressed. And after the Civil War, when freedom had come, those who had been leaders in the bush harbors became the first leaders of the independent Black Church movement.

Bush harbor worship stressed extemporaneous preaching, immediate conversion, and the call to ministry. None of these depended on educational attainments on the part of preacher or hearer (although the Black Church movement that sprang up later strongly advocated Christian and secular education). Preaching without written notes was encouraged because it indicated that the message came from the heart rather than the paper. In the African American tradition, the call to preach is taken very seriously. At the 1870 organizing General Conference of the Colored Methodist Episcopal Church (now the Christian Methodist Episcopal Church), one of the most heated debates was over the educational requirements of its ministers, who were only five years removed from slavery. The most colorful opposition to literacy requirements came from a delegate from Alabama, who said, "It ain't for us, brethren, to measure out a man by a book, and say who God shall call and whom he shan't. My father, sir, didn't know A from B, and yet by his preaching hundreds—yes thousands—was converted. Scores of 'em in heaven, now, white as well as black."[37] In short, he was arguing that knowing how to read the Bible was not a prerequisite to knowing its author.

The emotionalism of evangelical Christianity among slaves was especially well represented in the Negro spirituals. The spirituals were folk songs that were born out of the oral tradition of the collective trials and tribulations of a disinherited and dispossessed people. The Negro spiritual is one of the few musical traditions with an American origin. The spirituals were the unrehearsed spontaneous creations of the slave community. They were unique and different from hymns and psalms. William B. McClain has characterized the spirituals as "songs which speak of life and death, suffering and sorrow, love and judgement, grace and love, justice and mercy, redemption and conciliation."[38]

Many of the spirituals originated as spin-offs from extemporaneous preaching. The preacher said something that captured the imagination of the congregation and they gave it a tune. Black sermons and prayers were delivered in a kind of singing declamation that evoked a musical response. Humming, mourning, and singing created a communal web of support for praying and preaching in the black tradition. When the spirit falls afresh on a black congregation, it has a ripple effect on every aspect of the worship experience. Thus, preaching, singing, and praying were, and still are, corporate activities in African American worship, activities in which all participate and from which communal identity is established and fostered.

Thus, in the North, where black Methodists were politically free, even if socially stigmatized and economically impoverished, the consequence of the wave of revivalism in the first half of the nineteenth century was the relatively early foundation of two independent denominations: the African Methodist Episcopal Church in 1816, and the African Methodist Episcopal Zion Church in 1827. In the South, the founding of independent churches had to await emancipation. Yet, it was precisely the racial segregation that was enforced in camp meetings in the South, as well as the ineffectiveness of the plantation missions, that led blacks under slavery to establish for themselves a network of secret religious gatherings and to develop styles of preaching and sacred music suitable to their own needs; this set the stage for the later founding of independent black churches, including the Colored (Christian) Methodist Church in 1870. The "invisible institution" was thus the incubator of what later became the most visible and powerful institution in the African American community.

Since their founding, all three black Methodist denominations have experienced phenomenal growth. Their popularity, like that of all independent black churches, is due in part to the fact that they are completely owned and controlled by African Americans, and to the fact that they have a proud heritage of providing people who have been generally excluded from the social, political, and economic life of this country with opportunities for free self-expression, recognition, empowerment, leadership development, and family nurturing.

Paradigm Shifts in African American Methodism

Yet the end of the Civil War brought new problems for black churches in general, and for the African American Methodist denominations in particular. For one thing, slavery left many African Americans with a feeling of shame, just as it left many white Americans with a feeling of guilt. Where people felt a sincere desire to "integrate" the races, there was pressure on black churches to eschew the demonstrative and enthusiastic style of worship that originally characterized them. In order to shake the stigma of slavery, African American worshipers often felt obliged to behave like whites in black skin. Moreover, with the end of Reconstruction in 1877, African Americans were recipients of the displaced aggression of the defeated white Southerners, who replaced slavery with segregation, Jim Crow laws, lynching, and disenfranchisement. As the nineteenth century came to a close, there were a series of crop failures and natural disasters, which prompted large numbers of black tenant farmers and sharecroppers on southern plantations to move north to find jobs in factories and to distance themselves from the blatant racism in the south. This doubled and sometimes tripled the membership rolls of some black churches in the north. But the more restrained and formal worship style of northern African American Methodists made their congregations less appealing to the new arrivals. Consequently, many of the migrants shunned the black Methodist churches for freer and less formal denominations, such as Baptists and Pentecostals.[39]

Since the turn of the twentieth century, therefore, African American Christianity in general, and African American Methodism in particular, has been in search of an authentic identity,[40] at once true to its African and African American heritage and to Wesleyan theology. Probably no one has ever stated the African American identity problem as sharply and poignantly as W. E. B. DuBois:

> One ever feels his twoness—an American, a Negro; two souls, two thoughts, two unreconciled strivings; two waning ideals in one dark body, whose dogged strength alone keeps it from being torn asunder. The history of the American Negro is the history of this strife—this longing to attain self-conscious manhood, to merge his double self into a better and truer self. In this merging he wishes neither of the older selves to be lost. . . . He simply wishes to make it possible for a man to be both a Negro and an American, without being cursed and spit upon by his fellows, without having the doors of opportunity closed roughly on his face.[41]

African Americans were discouraged from affirming their Africanism and denied the freedom and opportunity to become Americans. They were told they had no history worth remembering, no ancestors worth honoring, and no religious beliefs worth practicing.

The result of forever hearing such a degrading (as well as patently erroneous) account of African and African American history, culture, and religion has been that black churches have often preferred being anything but themselves. This self-demeaning undervaluation has made some "Negro" churches more "white" in their ritual behavior and social attitudes than many of the white churches they have sought to emulate. The effort to exclude from worship every vestige of emotionalism has at times illustrated the uncertainty of African American Methodism about its identity, origin, function, and purpose.[42] The myth and misconception of the African American past has had a chilling and schismatic effect on the African American Methodist tradition. For example, during the second half of the nineteenth century Bishop Daniel Payne of the AME Church worked ardently to eliminate all forms of religious enthusiasm from worship. He excoriated it as the religion of the "ignorant masses."[43]

Yet as we have seen, it has been precisely the effort by these "ignorant masses" to preserve such practices from their African heritage as ecstatic behavior, shouting, dancing, spirit possession, trances, visions, and prophecies that had enabled them to maintain some sense of human dignity in the face of terrible oppression. The question that faced the black church after emancipation and Reconstruction was whether such practices *still* had a legitimate role in the life of the autonomous black church. Some, like Bishop Payne, thought not, and believed that the way forward was to conform to the religious patterns of the white American church.

Many other black Methodists, however, saw continuing spiritual value in their ancestral customs.[44] They understood that these practices produced a collective emotional catharsis for people who, though now legally free, were everywhere treated as second-class citizens and sometimes subjected to lynch mobs and Ku Klux Klan activities. Yet they also understood that the style of worship developed in the bush harbors was much more than a method of psychic cleansing or a compensatory mechanism for an oppressed people. It had theological legitimacy in its own right. The traditional African belief in a Supreme God who reigns and a lesser God who rules in their everyday activities had obvious parallels with the Christian belief in a God who is at once transcendent and immanent, a God who is "high and lifted up" and yet closer to believers than their own breath. Spirit possession, a feature of ancient African religion, could, in light of John 13–17, easily be reinterpreted in Christian terms; those brands of Christianity, such as Methodism, that emphasized the role of the Holy Spirit in the Christian life are particularly appealing to blacks. Thus, many African Americans felt that the preservation of ancestral religious customs and the reinterpretation and adaptation of these customs in light of Christian Scripture helped to protect their identity and dignity as a people and, furthermore, establish the Black Church as a distinct and theologically authentic tradition within the wider Body of Christ.[45] Let us look at one notable example of a turn-of-the-century African American Methodist leader who drew deeply from black experience and culture in communicating the Wesleyan gospel and who, in doing so, exerted considerable influence on white American Christianity as well: Charles Albert Tindley.

Tindley (1851–1933) was born on Maryland's Eastern Shore. In colonial times, this region had been a haven for revivalists of both races and of various denominational affiliations. Tindley, who was reared Methodist, imbibed this enthusiastic style of preaching and worship from his youth and brought it with him to Philadelphia, where it proved intensely popular. He built one of the greatest congregations in all of Methodism. Its building had a seating capacity of 3,500 worshipers, but so great were the weekly crowds that often as many as 1,500 more had to stand throughout the services. Some who came—all too aware, perhaps, of how widely the views of those like Bishop Payne had taken root—were surprised to find such fervor in a northern African American Methodist church.[46] Bernice Johnson Reagon, for example, said of her first visit to Tindley Temple, "Because it was a Black Methodist Church, I expected a middle-class, staid, reserved elderly congregation. After the testimony service, I went outside and looked to be sure it was not a Pentecostal Church."[47]

Yet Tindley's approach to worship was eclectic. He made good use of a variety of liturgical and cultural forms, and his services sometimes corporated "high church" elements as well, such as classical hymnody, local anthems, set prayers, and creeds. The congregation would respond as enthusiastically to Handel's *Messiah* as they would to Tindley's own gospel song, "We'll Understand It Better By and By." The same folks who could enjoy Rossini's "Inflammatus" on a Sunday morning would return later for an all-night tarrying and healing service. It is understandable, therefore, that Tindley Temple has been described as "high church with soul."

Or perhaps it would be better to say that Tindley's approach to worship was *balanced*. It attended to both the transcendence and the immanence of God, to both the objective message of the gospel and the subjective responses of the worshipers. Tindley insisted on using hymns that praised the greatness of God, such as Charles Wesley's "O, for a Thousand Tongues to Sing," and insisted just as strongly on using those that expressed the spiritual needs and aspirations of the congregation, such as "I Need Thee Every Hour" by Annie Hawks. His people would shout "Holy!" after "Inflammatus," as well as "Amen!" after "Precious Lord, Take My Hand."[48]

Still another manifestation of Tindley's characteristically Wesleyan sense of balance was his insistence that the quest for personal salvation must never be divorced from the work of social transformation. Tindley refused to confine his ministry within the safe walls of his church and was frequently seen walking up and down the streets of the neighborhood in which it was located, meeting and greeting the people on their level, talking and preaching to people of all classes and conditions. Methodist preachers are, of course, ordained as "traveling elders." They are trained to regard the entire community as their congregation, the entire world as their parish. Rev. Henry Nichols once said that what impressed him about Tindley was how "He made his church a sort of vessel into which people were welcome to bring all their traditions. He believed that the spiritual needs of the community could not be addressed without taking into consideration the practical and material needs for food, housing, and clothing."[49] He was known and loved by his congregation as much for his willingness to help them find employment or raise the money for a down payment on a house as for his masterful preaching and skillful orchestration of Sunday worship.

Tindley's sense of balance and proportion is characteristic of the Methodist gospel and marked other great leaders in the tradition, such as Richard Allen and John Wesley himself. Africans were attracted to Methodism because of its way of combining the "warm heart with the consecrated mind,"[50] its attempts to keep Christian doctrine, Christian praxis, and Christian experience in dynamic tension. Thus the official *beliefs* of Methodism as summarized in Wesley's *Twenty-Five Articles of Religion,* the standard *practices* of Methodism as spelled out in the *General Rules,* and the characteristically warm-hearted *piety* of Methodism as expressed in Wesleyan hymnody are seen as complementary and equally necessary elements of a fully orbed faith. This instinct for balance is discernible, too, in the Methodist approach to the Bible, which grants that the Scriptures are inspired but refuses to make extravagant (and potentially idolatrous) claims about the text's inerrancy, and which draws theological insight from the whole of the biblical message rather than fixating on a few selected passages. Again, the balance of Methodism is seen in its understanding of the Christian life: On the one hand, it emphasizes the significance of life-changing conversion experiences. On the other hand, it recognizes the need for steady, lifelong Christian education and spiritual nurture. Traditionally, older black preachers have encouraged and inspired young ministers to balance their burning with learning, to be open to the Spirit, who works in surprising ways, and at the same time to cultivate a fondness for education.

Perhaps nothing summarizes and expresses Tindley's brand of heart religion better than the following story: He was sitting in his backyard one day, writing, when a gust of wind came up. It blew a piece of trash onto his paper, just where he was about to apply his pen. As he reached down to move the bit of trash out of the way, he thought to himself, "Now that's what sin does, come between a person and God." Thus inspired, he promptly penned what was to become one of his best-known hymns, "Nothing Between."

> Nothing between my soul and my savior,
> So that his blessed face may be seen,
> Nothing preventing the least of his favor,
> Keep the way clear, let nothing between.[51]

That is what Tindley's ministry was all about: reconciling enemies, making connections, giving every aspect of life its proper due, holding the contrary elements in creative tension and dynamic equipoise, seeing and making things whole.

Another significant paradigm shift in the African American religious experience took place in the 1960s, when there were large-scale innovations and changes in the community. Blacks became impatient with living as second-class citizens and tolerating the crumbs that fell from the master's table. Black churches, which were the strongest institutions in the African American community, provided the leadership and became the meeting place for the Civil Rights movement. Martin Luther King, Jr. marshaled a mass movement under the banner of nonviolence to end legal segregation and discrimination based on skin color.

Other members of the African American community, however, took a more radical position, maintaining that the race problem could not be resolved by integration, since that idea seemed to imply the loss of ethnic and cultural identity. Hence Stokely Carmichael's call for "Black Power" represented a shift in the thinking of many blacks toward the theme of racial liberation. This theme was articulated in theological terms by such notables as James H. Cone and Joseph A. Johnson, Jr. Cone was a member of the AME Church and the late Bishop Johnson was a member of the CME Church. These two black Methodist scholars were key figures in crafting a black theology to complement Black Power. Cone and Johnson fashioned a theology emanating from the black experience to address the quest for black identity and explored biblical themes that focused on "Jesus and the disinherited" and "the God of the oppressed." In short, black theology was to free the black mind from white images and beliefs that frustrated the thrust for black liberation.

It is important to note that many who embraced black liberation theology regarded the characteristic emotionalism of African American Christianity very favorably, not only as a token of ethnic identity but also because it was evidently compatible with their own theological agenda. Hence Black Power and liberation theology helped to fuel the wave of neo-Pentecostalism in the black Methodist churches of the 1980s and 1990s. These churches were about breaking the bonds of tradition and renouncing a racist theology that systematically denied blacks their African beliefs and heritage. Many (though of course not all) black churches in the mainline Methodist denominations have rekindled the holy fire of Pentecost by incorporating such gifts as speaking in tongues, Spirit possession, shouting, dancing, and the laying on of hands.

Today in urban areas across America, the Pentecostal and early Methodist styles of worship, once popular mainly in the rural south, have moved into college-educated, middle-class churches. The emotionalism that has traditionally been associated with anti-intellectualism is becoming more and more fashionable. African American youth and young adults in particular have become more comfortable with their Africanism and are no longer striving for—because they are no longer impressed with—whatever it means to be white.

The piety of African American Methodism, however, goes much deeper than protesting the cultural dominance of whites. It is the celebration of the free gift of grace to sinners. Black Methodists identify with John Wesley at Aldersgate, where he said: "I felt my heart strangely warmed. I felt I did trust in Christ, Christ alone, for my salvation: and an assurance was given me, that he had taken away my sins, even mine, and saved me from the law of sin and death."[52] In fact, neo-Pentecostalism is not new but a return to the roots of Wesleyan Methodism, where deliverance from personal and corporate sins elicits a response of praise. One of the prophets said, "Let him who glories glory in this, that he understands and knows God" (Jer. 9:24).

Neo-Pentecostal worship takes a page from Charles Albert Tindley's style of worship, as it attempts to meet the spiritual needs of all the congregants in worship. The music and liturgy are diverse in order to be appealing to the masses and classes, traditionalists and nontraditionalists, youth and adults, lettered and unlettered. Today most of the ministers and some of the laity in these neo-Pentecostal churches are college and seminary trained. For example, the pastor of the prominent Saint Matthew's CME Church in Milwaukee, Wisconsin, Dr. Daniel Fitten, is both a major figure in the neo-Pentecostal Movement and a recognized biblical scholar. The proponents of this dynamic approach to worship maintain that the inclusion of the heart and head, the intellect and emotions in worship, is a corrective to the spiritual holocaust that attempted to kill the emotional side of worship and thus prompted the exodus of many youth and young adults from black Methodist denominations. The African traditions of call and response between the pulpit and pew, vocal praise, and spirit possession are very evident in these demonstrative worship experiences. From beginning to end, the ministers and the laity are caught up in the most intense and enthusiastic worship style. Drums, tambourines, cymbals, and electric keyboards are fully incorporated into the liturgy. These neo-Pentecostals have the potential of redefining black Methodism. Let us look briefly at three congregations, belonging to different Methodist denominations, that have adopted this style of ministry and, in consequence, are experiencing a spiritual awakening and phenomenal numerical growth: the Ben Hill United Methodist Church in Atlanta, Georgia; the Saint Paul Christian Methodist Episcopal Church in Savannah, Georgia; and the Bethel African Methodist Episcopal Church in Baltimore, Maryland.

The Ben Hill Church, formerly pastored by the Rev. Cornelius Henderson before he was elected bishop in 1996, has emerged as one of the largest and fastest-growing congregations in United Methodism. It has revised many long-standing African American Methodist traditions to be more compatible with contemporary tastes. For instance, the devotional prayer service, which, in many small rural churches, used to be conducted by the stewards as a "warm-up" to the formal Sunday worship service, has been revamped to incorporate a modern praise team. The members of the praise team, dressed in casual attire and equipped with modern musical instruments, line up across the front of the chancel and open the worship service by leading vibrant congregational singing and exhorting the audience to exhibit overt praise to God.

Unchanged from the earlier period in African American Methodism, however, is Ben Hill's way of connecting the scriptural story of God's redeeming and liberating work with the lives of the worshipers. I attended a first Sunday communion service during the summer of 1999 at Ben Hill. The senior pastor, Rev. McAllister Hollings, preached a soul-stirring sermon and conducted the Lord's Supper in a way that evoked enthusiastic praise and thanksgiving from the overflowing congregation. This approach to worship is true to the African American Methodist heritage, where Word and sacrament alike have attested to God's desire to deliver people from physical and spiritual bondage: The story of the Exodus has been seen as a paradigm of black liberation, and the story of Jesus' suffering, death, and resurrection as the good news of God's identification with and salvation of all who are weary and heavy laden.

Another contemporary neo-Pentecostal Church is the Saint Paul CME Church in Savannah. Before the arrival of the Rev. Henry Delaney as pastor in 1989, it was a struggling, mainline, inner-city church with fewer than 300 members. Under Delaney's dynamic, charismatic, and visionary leadership, Saint Paul is now one of the largest and fastest-growing churches in the denomination. In addition to the Bible-based, Holy Ghost-filled and fire-baptized worship experience, Saint Paul has been addressing the inner city problems of drugs, violence, school dropouts, homelessness, and cultural deprivation with innovative urban ministries. In 1993, the church opened an academy for black males to counter the dismal, oft-quoted statistic that there are "more African American males in jail than in college." Some of the 28 faith-in-action ministries at Saint Paul include a community cultural center, the Kids' Café, an after-school feeding program, the Hallelujah House for men recovering from substance abuse, the Heavenly Dee-Lite Ice Cream Parlor, a foster care program for children, and a jail ministry.

A third example of the neo-Pentecostal movement in contemporary African American Methodism is the Bethel AME Church in Baltimore. Led by the Rev. Dr. John Bryant, Jr., until his election to the episcopacy in 1988, this congregation illustrates why liberation theology and neo-Pentecostalism go hand in hand in contemporary African American Methodism. Bethel skillfully blends the traditional AME involvement in progressive politics with newer forms of dynamic worship.[53] Bethel ministers to the practical as well as the devotional needs of its members with equal effectiveness.

These three "mega-churches," and others like them, provide a variety of ministries especially geared to the needs and interests of the African American community. They are like spiritual shopping malls, offering scholarships, schools, programs for community economic development, books, libraries, and computer labs. The holistic ministry that these churches provide, however, is not new to the African American religious experience. Historically, the black church has been the cultural womb of the African American community. For example, the black church gave birth to the first schools, banks, insurance companies, literary clubs, orphanages, drama clubs, and publishing companies. In short, applying God's word to contemporary problems, whether they be spiritual or temporal, is inherent in the African American Methodist tradition.

Conclusion

African Americans were separated from Africa and excluded from the mainstream, cultural, and religious life in America, but through the African American religious tradition, they have carved out an ecclesiastical home in a strange land.[54] It is a place where they can reestablish their African spiritual roots after more than three centuries of cultural separation. Religion is a spiritual domicile where African Americans can sing and pray in the old-time way. Through it all—slavery, segregation, discrimination, and today's self-destruction—the Black Church continues to be a way out of no way for a disinherited people. It has provided a context for answering the age-old question, "How shall we sing the Lord's song in a foreign land?" (Ps.137:4).

Notes

1. It was upon the recommendation of Dr. C. Eric Lincoln that the author first wrote this essay, originally published in Richard B. Steele, *"Heart Religion" in the Methodist Tradition and Related Movements.* (Lantham, MD: Scarecrow Press, Inc., 2001). Used by permission.

2. Jon Butler, *Awash in A Sea of Faith: Christianizing the American People* (Cambridge, MA: Harvard University Press, 1990), p. 158.

3. Melville J. Herskovits, *The Myth of the Negro Past* (Boston: Beacon Press, 1958), p. 2.

4. Ibid., pp. 158–59. E. Franklin Frazier, who represented the extreme viewpoint about the lack of African retentions, wrote: "Probably never before in history has a people been so nearly completely stripped of its social heritage as the Negroes who were brought to America. Other conquered races have continued to worship their household gods within the intimate circle of their kinsmen. Through force of circumstances, they had to acquire a new language, adopt new habits of labor, and take over, however imperfectly, the folkways of the American environment. Their children's children have often recalled with skepticism the fragments of stories concerning Africa which have been preserved in their families. But, of the habits and customs as well as the hopes and fears that characterized the life of their forebears in Africa, nothing remains." (E. Franklin Frazier, *The Negro Family in the United States* (Chicago: University of Chicago Press, 1939), p. 21.

5. W. E. B. DuBois, *The Negro Church* (Atlanta: Atlanta University Press, 1903), p. 1.

6. John Wesley, *The Journals of the Rev. John Wesley, A. M.: Sometime Fellow of Lincoln College,* Nehemiah Curnock, ed., (London, Epworth Press, 1938) January 25, 1735; John Wesley, *The Works of John Wesley* (1872: Hendrickson Press, 1984), 18:142ff.

7. Sylvia R. Frey and Betty Wood, *Come Shouting to Zion: African American Protestantism in the American South and British Caribbean to 1830* (Chapel Hill: University of North Carolina Press, 1998), p. 84.

8. Ibid., p. 85. Even today, the Bible is the most respected and probably the most widely read book in the African American community. The fastest-growing churches in the black community are the so-called "word churches," whose pastors apply the message of scripture to the daily challenges faced by their members at work, at home, and at school.

9. Wesley, *Journal* (July 31, 1736), Wesley, *Works,* 18:169.

10. Wesley, *Journal* (April 23, 1737), Wesley, *Works,* 18:179.

11. Wesley, *Journal* (April 27, 1737), Wesley, *Works,* 18:181.

12. Ibid.

13. Wesley, *Journal* (April 26, 1737), *Works,* 18:503.

14. This revival drew the attention of the local Anglican clergyman, Lewis Jones, who, in a report written to the Society for the Propagation of the Gospel in 1743, complained: "The great bodies of Negroes assembled together on Pretense of Religious Worship are taught rather Enthusiasm than religion and [they] pretend to see visions, and receive revelation from heaven and to be converted by an Instantaneous Impulse of the Spirit." Allan Gallay, *The Formation of a Planter Elite: Jonathan Bryan and the Southern Colonial Frontier* (Athens: University of Georgia Press, 1989), 45. Jones was forced to acknowledge, however, that "the Anglican Church did not offer a religious experience suitable to the temperament of the African." Alfoyd Butler, *The Blacks' Contribution of Elements of African Religion to Christianity in America: A Case Study of the Great Awakening in South Carolina* (Ph.D. diss., Northwestern University, 1975), p. 162.

15. Gallay, *The Formation of a Planter Elite,* p. 45.

16. See, for instance, "Thoughts upon Slavery," in Wesley, *Works,* 11:59–79.

17. Ann Gilbert to Reverend Richard Patterson, *English Harbor* (Antigua, June 1, 1984, folder 1803–4, box m, 1803–13, MMS, West Indies).

18. Wesley, *Journal* (January 17, 1758), Wesley, *Works,* 21:134.

19. Wesley, *Journal* (November 29, 1758), Wesley, *Works,* 21:172.

20. Frederick E. Maser and Howard T. Maag, eds., *The Journal of Joseph Pilmore, Methodist Itinerant, for the Years August 1, 1769 to January 2, 1774* (Philadelphia: Message Publishing Co., for the Historical Society of the Philadelphia Annual Conference of the United Methodist Church, 1969), 149. Quoted by Frey and Wood, *Come Shouting to Zion,* p. 107.

21. Frey and Wood, *Come Shouting to Zion,* p. 109. For more literature on the subject of spirit possession see John Beattie and John Middleton, eds., *Spirit Mediumship and Society in Africa* (New York: African Publishing Carp., 1969), and Bennetta Jules-Rosette, "Privilege Without Power," in

Women in Africa and the African Diaspora, ed. Rosalyn Terborg-Penn, Sharon Harley, and Andrea Benton Rushing (Washington, D.C.: Howard University Press, 1987).

22. Frey and Wood, *Come Shouting to Zion*, p. 110.
23. Ibid.
24. See, for example, Peter Cartwright, *Autobiography* (1856; Nashville: Abingdon, 1984), chs. 11, 27–28.
25. Frey and Wood, *Come Shouting to Zion,* p. 120.
26. *Journals of the General Conference of the Methodist Episcopal Church South* (Richmond, 1846) 1: 66.
27. Charles A Johnson, *The Frontier Camp Meeting: Religion's Harvest Time* (Dallas, TX: Southern Methodist University Press, 1955), p. 115.
28. George White, "A Brief Account of the Life, Experience, Travels and Gospel Labours of George White, an African," in *Black Itinerants of the Gospel: Narrative of John Wesley and George White,* ed. Graham Russell Hodge (Madison, WI: University of Wisconsin Press, 1993), p. 61.
29. See W. E. B. DuBois, *The Souls of Black Folk* (Greenwich, CT: Fawcett Publications, 1961), p. 211.
30. James Weldon Johnson, *God's Trombones: Seven Negro Sermons in Verse* (New York: Viking, 1969), p. 2.
31. Joseph A Johnson, Jr., *The Soul of the Black Preacher* (Philadelphia: Pilgrim Press, 1971), p. 12.
32. Winthrop S. Hudson and John Corrigan, *Religion in America,* 5th ed. (New York: Macmillan, 1992), p. 124.
33. I heard this story from a participant in a stewardship workshop when I was the senior minister of the Russell Memorial Christian Methodist Episcopal Church, Durham, NC.
34. Carter G. Woodson, *The History of the Negro Church* (Washington, D.C.: Associate Publishers, 1921), p. 57.
35. Richard Allen, *The Life Experience and Gospel Labors of the Rt. Reverend Richard Allen, to Which is Annexed the Rise and Progress of the African Methodist Episcopal Church in the United States of America* (New York: Abingdon, 1960), p. 15ff.
36. Jonathan D. Keaton, "Strengthen the Black Church," *CircuitRider* 232, no. 2 (March/April l999): 4.
37. Cited in Othal H. Lakey, *The History of the Christian Methodist Episcopal Church* (Memphis, TN: C.M.E. Publishing House; Nashville: Parthenon, 1985), p. 207.
38. Quoted in C. Eric Lincoln and Lawrence H. Mamiya, *The Black Church in the African American Experience* (Durham: Duke University Press, 1990), p. 350.
39. See William Seraile, *Fire in His Heart* (Knoxville: University of Tennessee Press, 1998), p. 181.
40. On the acute identity crisis in the African American experience, see esp. Charles E. Silberman, *Crisis in Black and White* (New York, Random. House, 1964), pp. 68–122.

41. Quoted by Elliott Rudwick, "W. E. B. DuBois: Protagonist of the Afro-American Protest," in *Black Leaders of the Twentieth Century,* ed. John Hope Franklin and August Meier (Chicago: University of Illinois Press, 1982), p. 64.

42. C. Eric Lincoln, *The Black Church Since Frazier* (New York: Schocken, 1974), p. 113. For the most comprehensive study of the African American religious experience, see Lincoln and Mamiya, *The Black Church in the African American Experience.*

43. Daniel Alexander Payne, *Recollections of Seventy Years* (1888; New York: Arno Press, 1968), pp. 253–55.

44. The deep division within the African American Methodist community on this question may be illustrated by the following anecdote: In 1892, when Bishop Benjamin Tucker Tanner appointed the Reverend Dr. William H. Butler to the Bridge Street AME Church in Brooklyn, New York, it split the congregation because some of the members did not like his "scholarly sermons." The young and more literate members embraced Butler's dignified style of delivery while the older and less educated wanted someone who would stir up their feelings and allow them to shout, "Amen, glory be to God." See Seraile, *Fire in His Heart,* p. 132.

45. Of course, this does not imply that white American Christians always *approve* of the emotionalism and demonstrativeness of Black Church worship, particularly when the buildings in which it takes place are in close geographical proximity to white communities. For example, on November 30, 1909, in the town of Rome, Georgia, a lawsuit was brought against the pastor and trustees of the Metropolitan Methodist Church for building a new edifice on Broad Street, the town's main thoroughfare. The suit was filed by whites who complained that the church was a nuisance to the neighborhood because of the "loud preaching, singing, shouting, shrieking, or crying out" that marked its worship services. After several postponements in the case, Judge Moses Wright eventually ruled in favor of the church, which was allowed to continue the construction of its building. However, the judge's decision did "prohibit any ringing of the bell or holding of meetings at unseemly hours, and any unusual noises." *Rome Tribune-Herald,* 30 November 1909, p. 1.

46. According to Mack B. Stokes, *Major Methodist Beliefs* (Nashville: Methodist Publishing House, 1967), p. 11. African American Methodist worship of this period was generally assumed to be rather staid and dignified, and was not punctuated with too many "amens."

47. Bernice Johnson Reagon, ed., *We'll Understand It Better By and By: Pioneering African American Gospel Composers* (Washington, D.C.: Smithsonian Institute Press, 1992), p. 38. It is not uncommon for African American Methodist preachers who preach with zeal and conviction to be charged with infringing upon the Baptist or Pentecostal traditions. To take another example, Methodist preacher Charles Webster, upon preaching a soul-stirring sermon at a revival attended in Atlanta, was accosted by one of the elderly matriarchs of church, who remarked, "Boy, I believe you got a little Baptist in you." Ibid., 37.

48. Reagon, *We'll Understand It Better By and By,* p. 39.

49. Ibid.
50. Ibid., 40
51. Ibid.
52. Wesley, *Journal* (May 24, 1738), in Wesley, *Works*, 18:250.
53. Lincoln and Mamiya, *Black Church in the African American Experience*, pp. 385–88.
54. Cheryl J. Sanders, *Saints in Exile: The Holiness-Pentecostal Experience in African American Religion and Culture* (New York: Oxford University Press, 1996), pp. 143–51.

16

Stalking George Washington Williams

John Hope Franklin

It was more than a half-century ago when I had the experience, but I remember it as distinctly as if it were yesterday. In the spring of 1945 I was just beginning the work on a book that was to be called *From Slavery to Freedom: A History of Negro Americans*. A good way to begin, I thought, was to read the shelves in the library of North Carolina College where I was teaching to see what, if anything, had been written, aside from Carter G. Woodson's *The Negro in Our History*, published in 1922. To my astonishment, my eyes fell on a two-volume work called *A History of the Negro Race in America from 1619 to 1880: Negros, as Slaves, as Soldiers, and as Citizens*, by George Washington Williams. Upon examination, I discovered that it had been published in 1882 by the reputable publisher G.P. Putnam's Sons. The work was about 1,000 pages long and covered African civilization and virtually every aspect of the African American experience in the New World. It was carefully researched, logically organized, and well written. Williams had been the author of still another work, *A History of Negro Troops in the War of the Rebellion*, published in 1887 by Harper and Brothers.

Although I had never had a course in African American history, I reproached myself for not having heard of this man, and I wondered why this historian of Africans in America had dropped into complete obscurity in *my* time. I knew enough about his time to know that his obscurity was at least in part the result of the function of social forces at work in this country at the end of the nineteenth century. These forces indicated quite clearly that African Americans were not to be remembered for their constructive ministrations to society, their contributions to the literary heritage of the country, or their revelations, such as

Williams had made. If he was unknown in the two generations that separated me from him since his death in 1891, I was determined to do what I could to repair the situation. The following is an account of my effort to do so.

Fortunately, there had been a sketch of Williams in the recently published *Dictionary of American Biography*,[1] and I devoured it immediately, not knowing then that it was replete with factual errors. Shortly thereafter, I was in Washington and called on Dr. Carter G. Woodson, the founder and executive director of the Association for the Study of Negro Life and History (recently renamed the Association for the Study of African American Life and History). I asked Dr. Woodson about George Washington Williams, and to my pleasant surprise he said he knew something of him but not much. He also said that if I wrote a paper on Williams he would invite me to read it at the fall meeting of the association. He believed Mrs. Williams was still living and was there in Washington. I could hardly accept that anyone whose husband had died in 1891 would still be living in 1945. Shortly after I returned to Durham, Dr. Woodson wrote me that Mrs. Williams was indeed living and gave me her address, whereupon I wrote her immediately.

Within a few weeks I heard from one Henry P. Slaughter, who told me that Mrs. Williams had just died (at 92 years of age) and that he had what letters and materials of George Washington Williams that the wife possessed. He indicated to me that he would be pleased to have me examine the materials whenever I wished to do so. Since I had accepted Dr. Woodson's challenge to write a paper on Williams, I did not have much time. As soon as I could arrange it, I went to Washington and was received graciously by Henry P. Slaughter, who brought out the small bundle of letters and three notebooks containing the diary that Williams kept while in Africa.

Slaughter himself was a remarkable man. As a minor civil servant in the federal government, he spent much of his spare time and most of his resources collecting materials—manuscripts, books, pamphlets, newspapers—by and about African Americans. In 1945, his collection was, perhaps, the finest of its kind still in private hands. His three-story townhouse had been converted into a library, with book shelves running the length of the house on every floor. It was cluttered, and at his advanced age, late seventies, he had difficulty keeping things in order. His wife had left him because there simply was no place for her in that house. He graciously permitted me to read the score of letters from Williams to his wife, from which I took notes. He showed me the diary and offered it to me to take back to North Carolina and use, but I declined, a decision that I will always regret.

In the autumn of 1945, I read a paper before the Association for the Study of Negro Life and History entitled "George Washington Williams, Historian." The following January it was published in the *Journal of Negro History*.[2] Except for the brief sketch in the *Dictionary of American Biography (DAB)*, this was the first piece on Williams to appear since his death. It added something to what the author of the article in the *DAB* wrote, but when I read it now, I am depressed by the number of factual errors I made and by the things I did not then know about Williams.

Williams was born in Bedford Springs, Pennsylvania, October 16, 1849, the son of a free Negro father from Virginia and a mother who was the offspring of African American and Pennsylvania Dutch parents. He had almost no formal education until he was grown. As a child he drifted with his family from one Pennsylvania town to another as his father looked for work. He was about 14 years old when President Lincoln permitted blacks to enlist in the Union army in 1863. He took an assumed name, set his age forward, and volunteered in the United States Colored Troops. He saw action in numerous engagements in Virginia, and at the end of the war was transferred to border patrol duty in Brownsville, Texas. He was mustered out in Brownsville but enlisted almost immediately in the army in Mexico that was attempting to overthrow the Emperor Maximilian. Having helped to accomplish that feat, Williams headed back to the United States, where he enlisted in the Tenth Cavalry, one of the four newly organized black units in the regular army. After receiving a gunshot wound through the left lung under questionable circumstances in 1868, Williams received an honorable discharge and headed out of the Indian Territory toward home.

En route, Williams learned that a new university primarily for blacks, Howard University, had been founded in Washington. Since his "heart was burning," as he put it, to receive an education in order to serve humankind, he wrote to General Oliver O. Howard and pleaded to be admitted. He was granted admission and enrolled for a portion of the academic year, 1869–1870. By this time, Williams wanted to become a Baptist minister, and he left Howard and sought admission to the Newton Theological Institution in Massachusetts. In September 1870, Williams appeared before the faculty and requested admission. It was clear that he was not prepared to meet the requirements of the theological department. He was therefore admitted to the "English course," which must have been a remedial program. Within two years

Williams had completed the English course, and was then admitted to the theology department, completing the four-year course in two years. At this time a very articulate, thoughtful theologian, Williams was selected as one of the speakers at the commencement exercises in 1874. He chose as his subject, "Early Christian Missions in Africa."

Upon graduation and ordination, Williams became a pastor of the largest and most important black church in New England, the Twelfth Baptist Church of Boston. He and his bride of a few months, Sarah Sterett of Chicago, were royally entertained by a congregation looking forward to a long period of ministry from Williams. At this point, however, Williams showed a kind of restlessness that would take him many places within the next few years, and he resigned before the end of the year to go to Washington to establish a newspaper. His stay there was of short duration, and in 1876 he accepted the pastorate of the Union Baptist Church in Cincinnati. Soon Williams was engaged in a number of secular activities, including writing a column for the *Cincinnati Commercial,* taking a leading part in civic affairs, studying law in the office of Judge Alphonso Taft, and becoming politically active. In 1879, in a second run, he was elected to the state legislature, the first black to sit in that body. In 1876, Williams had delivered a centennial oration on the American Negro, after which he became so interested in the history of his people that he resolved to write a complete history of them.

Upon the publication of his *History of the Negro Race,* Williams became well known in the United States and Europe. Never before had an African American written such a work of its length and of such consistently high scholarship. The work was reviewed widely and, on the whole, favorably. He gave up the ministry and politics, devoting himself to the practice of law and lecturing. In 1885, President Chester Arthur appointed him United States Minister to Haiti, an appointment that led to an unhappy period in his life since he was not permitted to serve. He then turned to the task of completing his book on the *Negro in the Civil War* and began a serious study of Africa. Soon, he was writing articles on the Congo, and on one of his several trips to Europe he met Leopold, King of the Belgians, whose personal control of the Congo was to be the subject of considerable controversy in the future.

Williams proposed to the king that what was needed in the Congo was for him (Williams) to take a group of well-trained African Americans there to perform some of the much-needed tasks and to provide an example for the Congolese. Leopold seemed quite impressed with the general proposal, but when Williams expressed an interest in making a survey of conditions in the Congo in order to be able to inform young black Americans of conditions there, the king objected. After some extensive exchange of heated words, Williams left Brussels, went to England, and made his own plans to go to the Congo. At the end of January 1890 he embarked for the Congo from Liverpool. He spent several months there, traveling more than 3,000 miles, seeing everything it was possible to see.

Upon leaving the Congo, he wrote a lengthy open letter to the king, excoriating him for his merciless, barbaric rule, for the manner in which he took advantage of the people and their land, and the cruelties to which he subjected them. He called on the civilized world to join him in condemning Leopold's rules. His call fell on deaf ears. Not until a full decade later did the civilized world become aware of conditions in the Congo about which Williams had earlier tried to inform.

Meanwhile, Williams visited much of Africa, Angola, South Africa, Zanzibar, British East Africa, and Egypt. From Egypt he sailed in the spring of 1891 for England, where he planned to write a full-scale book on Leopold's rule in the Congo. He worked in the Public Records Office in the late spring and early summer of 1891. In July, his health began to fail, and since it was obviously a respiratory ailment, a British lady friend and her mother decided to take him to Blackpool, on the west coast, where he could enjoy the sea air. He did well for a few weeks, but suddenly he took a turn for the worse, and died there on August 2, 1891, at the age of 41. There were accounts of his death in such papers as the *London Times,* the *New York Times,* the *Cincinnati Commercial,* the *Huntsville Gazette,* and the *Indianapolis Freeman.* The last named paper had taken a poll of its readers in 1890 asking them to name the ten greatest Negroes who ever lived. George Washington Williams was selected as one of the ten. Within a decade after his death almost no one knew who he was.

Nearly all of what I have said thus far was discovered in the course of my research. Virtually all of the details regarding the activities of Williams had to be dredged up by painstaking efforts to *reconstruct* his life. There were no Williams papers except for the few letters and the African diaries held by Henry P. Slaughter. And after the initial examination of the letters, I had the misfortune not to be able to look at any of that material again. Each time I visited Washington, I would call on Mr. Slaughter and ask to see the Williams diary and he would deny me the privilege. In addition to being a remarkable, even cunning bibliophile, he was something of a bon vivant. On one occasion when I asked to see the diary, he informed me that he had some very good cognac and he wanted to open it and share it with me. No Williams diary was produced on that visit. On another occasion he told me of an absolutely wonderful restaurant where he wanted to take me for dinner. Again, no Williams diary on that visit. On a third visit he shocked me by declaring that he was planning to do a biography of Williams himself and preferred not to let me see the materials again. I was not worried about competition from Slaughter, for one does not usually begin a writing career at age 79. But I did wonder why he did not want me to examine the material.

Shortly thereafter, Mr. Slaughter sold his collection to Atlanta University, whereupon I rushed to Atlanta and requested to see the Williams diary that presumably had come down with the collection. I was informed that there was no Williams material at all in the collection that came down from Washington. I was crushed, for by this time the desire to see the Williams diary had almost become an obsession; and I wondered if I, or anyone else, could write a biography of Williams without seeing this diary. The one consolation I had came from my tentative conclusions about what had happened to the Williams manu-script. Slaughter's house was cluttered beyond belief, as I have indi-cated. At that time he was older, forgetful, and easily distracted. There were piles and piles of papers from which he planned to take clippings but never did. I suspect—just suspect—that one day, when some of that clutter was hauled away as trash, the Williams materials also went out. Slaughter could not find them, and I believe that he had too much pride to tell me. My conclusions have been confined by 50 years of fruitless searching for them. If they do exist, I really do not need them now, as you will see.

I knew almost nothing of the early life of Williams until one day, at Howard University, I discovered the letter he wrote in March 1869, to General Howard seeking admission to that university. It was a long letter, barely literate to be sure, telling the general about his early life, his drifting from one town to another with his parents, his service in the army during the Civil War, and his burning desire to secure an education and be of service to his people. This letter opened up new leads to his life with his parents and siblings at Bedford Springs, his army career, and his training for the ministry. As a fund-raising project during his pastorate in Boston, Williams wrote a history of the Twelfth Baptist Church. I was successful in securing a printed copy of the history and learned a great deal not only about the history and importance of that church but also about the Boston years of Williams as a student and as a pastor. The history contained accounts of the service at which

Williams was installed and of the lavish reception tendered Williams and his bride, Sarah.

It was almost impossible to learn anything about the year that Williams spent in Washington after he left Boston in 1875. It was an important year not only because Williams went there to found a paper, *The Commoner*, successor to the one published by Frederick Douglass that had folded during the panic of 1873, but also because this occurred in the *midst* of the Reconstruction era, where the fate of blacks was literally being decided in Washington. There was nothing about Williams in the Douglass papers and very little in the daily press. I searched everywhere for copies of the newspaper that Williams allegedly edited, but there were none at the Library of Congress and other likely places, and it was not listed in the *Union List of Newspapers*. That period in his life remained a blank until one day my research assistant told me that he had seen a reference to a newspaper, *Commoner*, that was in the library of the American Antiquarian Society in Worcester, Massachusetts. I would not allow myself to believe that this was the same *Commoner* edited by Williams. I wrote to the society, almost casually, expressing an interest in the paper and inquired about the editor and its contents. I was shocked and delighted to receive a reply saying that the paper had been edited by the Reverend George Washington Williams, that they owned what they thought to be the full run of the paper—about six months—and they would send it to me on microfilm if I cared to examine it. This was a veritable treasure trove of the writings of Williams, for he was the editor, publisher, columnist, reporter, and just about everything else. In it I learned much about his interests, values, views on numerous subjects from religion to reconstruction, and his relationships with others.

Even in *The Commoner*, one sensed the burning ambition as well as the restlessness of Williams. He was constantly on the go, promoting the paper, but also lecturing and politicking. In a note to his readers just before Christmas, 1875, Williams said that there would be no Christmas issue of the paper because he intended to spend the holidays in Chicago with his family. That was the very last issue of the paper, but there was no hint of this in that issue. Within a few weeks Williams had accepted the pastorate of the Union Baptist Church in Cincinnati, Ohio. It seems that with every passing day he became more visible, and the material from these Ohio years is in abundance. Shortly after his arrival in Cincinnati, he became acquainted with Murat Halstead, editor of the *Cincinnati Commercial*, who invited him to write a column for the paper. For several years, Williams was not too busy with his ministerial duties to write a column under the pen name "Aristides." Many of his columns were autobiographical and through them one got to know more about Williams, especially his years in the army and his service with the republican forces in Mexico.

Nor was Williams too busy to engage in partisan political activities. He arrived in Ohio just before the beginning of the presidential sweepstakes in 1876, and he could not resist the opportunities afforded an articulate, able young man to wade into the political waters. As a Republican he supported the local ticket, and as an Ohioan, he supported the candidacy of Rutherford B. Hayes. Even after the election he supported the so-called Hayes southern policy, much to the consternation of some other blacks, who thought Hayes too soft on the South. Soon, Williams himself was a candidate for public office. As a columnist and pastor, he was one of the best-known blacks in the city; and he decided to capitalize on that fact by running for the legislature. Losing in 1877, he was successful in 1879, but not before he had received the strictures of several of his rivals, who accused him of conducting a campaign that did not meet the highest standards.

By 1879, Williams had added to the string of adjectives by which he was known still another, that of being a "controversial" figure. While in the legislature he was denied service in a Columbus restaurant, and he threatened to have the owner's license revoked. The daily press criticized Williams, not the restaurant owner, despite the fact that the Civil Rights Act was already on the statute books. When the general assembly voted to relocate the black cemetery in Cincinnati, Williams was accused by Cincinnati blacks of having engineered the deal at the request of white businessmen who wanted the cemetery property for their own use. Despite the controversies he stirred up, he managed to become a member of several important committees, including one on colleges and universities; another on libraries, of which he was chairman; and a special committee on railroad terminal facilities. Even so, some of his constituents began to wonder if he could be reelected. He declined to run again but by this time he had made his indelible mark on Ohio and its history.

It did not matter, however, for Williams had decided to devote his full time to writing his *History of the Negro Race in America*. Indeed, he had already begun while he was a member of the state legislature. One of the benefits that one derives from working on a problem as long as I had been working on researching Williams is that eventually most people learned about it; and if they heard anything that might have been of value they told me about it. One day, at a meeting of the board of the

Chicago Public Library, one of the staff members who had done her doctoral work in Ohio libraries asked me if I would like to have a list of the books that Williams borrowed while in the legislature. I said that I did not mind if I did. She had come across it in the state library in Columbus. The list is filled with works on general history, histories of the United States, military history, and books out of which he could have pieced together some information about blacks. It was clear that he was a serious student of history. Since he indicated in the preface to the history his indebtedness to librarians in many parts of the country, I decided to inquire of those libraries whether there was a record of his having done research there. In each case—the American Antiquarian Society, the Boston Athanaeum, the Massachusetts Historical Society, etc.—there were records of his having done research there, of having used manuscripts, of having requested services from time to time. There were also records of his having paid for all of the copying of manuscripts he engaged clerks at the libraries to do for him.

Once Williams had gained considerable attention through the publication of his first major work, he was not at all satisfied. He had left Cincinnati and settled in Boston, where he was admitted to the bar and began to practice law. After a few months in this activity, he was off to Washington, presumably to begin his research on a history of reconstruction. He had not cut his ties with politics, however, and through the recommendation of Senators John Sherman of Ohio and George F. Hoar of Massachusetts, President Chester Arthur appointed Williams United States Minister to Haiti. Although the Senate had confirmed him before the president left office on March 4, 1885, the new secretary of state would not issue his commission of office. I knew of his appointment, but I was unable to understand some of the reasons for holding up his commission until I discovered that there was a complete file on the matter in the department of state papers in the national archives. President Arthur appointed Williams to this high post on the day before he left office, creating an unlikely prospect that the new Democratic administration would permit Williams to take up his duties. The new secretary of state had ample reason, besides the political one, for withholding commission. From the African American community came various protests regarding his appointment. Ambitious black politicians, working full-time, had hoped to secure this political plum, one of the very few that blacks could hope to secure. They vehemently protested his appointment. There were petitions from Ohio, moreover, claiming that he was unfit to represent his country abroad. One, signed by a large number of citizens from Middletown, declared that his conduct in their town had not been exemplary, in view of the fact that although a married man with a child, he had wooed and won the hand of one of the fairest young ladies of the town. Leaving with a solemn promise that he would return as soon as he had arranged his business affairs and marry her, he was not heard from again.

When the secretary of state would not issue a commission to Williams, he sued the U.S. government in the court of claims for salary and expenses. After a long period of litigation, the court decided against Williams on the ground that he had never qualified for office since he had not posted the required bond and the secretary had not sent him on his mission. Once more, he was the center of controversy and once again he had become the brunt of severe criticism by his own people. Jealousy certainly accounted for a part of the difficulty, but indiscretion on the part of Williams was certainly a factor. In the following year, he sued for a divorce on the ground of desertion, but when his wife filed a counter-suit, detailing the unfaithfulness of her estranged spouse, he withdrew his suit.

In many ways the African phase of Williams's career is the most interesting, and it was, by far, the most difficult to reconstruct. There was almost nothing to go on. I knew that he went to the Congo early in 1890 and, in due course, I was able to locate the open letter that he wrote to the King of the Belgians as well as a report to the president of the United States and another on the problem of building a railroad through the Congo. These three documents told me much, but not nearly enough. How did Williams get to the Congo? He was certainly not a man of wealth, despite his sartorial splendor and his pretensions when living in the best hotels and dining in the finest restaurants. Whom did he see in Africa and what did they think of his venture? Did anyone in Britain know him and have any connection with his African venture? These and many other questions plagued me for years. Gradually, I began to acquire the information that led to the answers to some of these questions. I worked at the libraries of Belgium and secured considerable information about the role of the king and some offhand remarks about the "imposter and blackmailer" George Washington Williams. In England, I worked at the public records office and other libraries and learned a great deal about Williams. For example, the Baptist Missionary Society maintained missions in the Congo in the early 1890s, and the missionaries sent full reports that are still in the London office about problems they encountered, accounts of Leopold's policies that affected the missionaries as well as the Congolese, and information about visitors. One of those visitors was Williams, who spent a good deal of time with the missionaries; and before he wrote his open letter to King Leopold, the Baptist Missionary Society in London knew what Williams thought of the king and his policies through the reports of missionaries, which I read. The society also knew that the views of Williams coincided with those of the missionaries, although the missionaries were unable to speak as freely as Williams.

The criticism of King Leopold by Williams was the first ever leveled against the Belgian monarch. The open letter created quite a stir in Brussels, and a special session of the Parliament was called for the purpose of praising Leopold's policies and, by indirection, criticizing Williams for his temerity in speaking ill of the king. I also discovered that the best vantage point from which to watch developments in Brussels was not in the Belgian capital, not in Washington (for the U.S. minister to Brussels took almost no notice of the matter), but in London, where the British minister to Belgium watched events very closely and sent a report. For example, he gave a lengthy account of the proceedings in Parliament and concluded by saying, "Williams is denounced as an imposter and blackmailer, and I do not know if the accusations are accurate. But when Williams denounces the king for his inhuman and cruel policies in the Congo, I am afraid that he is right."

I still did not know how Williams got to the Congo, who financed the trip, what his day-to-day experiences were, and why he wrote a report on the Congo railway. For years I fretted over these questions. Then, one day the only sentence that I could remember from the ill-fated diary stood out in my mind, and it went something like this: "Today, I wrote Mr. Huntington." Perhaps this was *the* Collis P. Huntington, president of the Southern Pacific Railroad, who just might possibly have had an interest in a railroad in the Congo. I knew that Huntington was a trustee of Hampton Institute and had expressed an interest in Africa. I inquired of the Huntington Papers at the Huntington Library, Stanford University, the Museum at Norfolk, and Syracuse University. There was no encouragement from any of these places, but Syracuse's discouragement was a kind of encouragement since they simply said that the collection there was so large that they did not know what they had and it would be years before they could get around to organizing and cataloging the manuscripts.

A few years later, I was in the vicinity of Syracuse and decided to visit the Arents Research Library there. They were cordial but reminded me of what they had written to me. I asked if they had the letters arranged by year, and they answered in the affirmative. I asked for just a few boxes of letters, beginning with January 1890. I went through more than a few boxes. There must have been a half dozen boxes of letters sent to Collis P. Huntington the first three days of the year 1890 from all sorts of persons asking for railroad passes or for a renewal of the passes they already possessed. Then, although these were *incoming* letters, I came across a letter written *by* Huntington dated January 7, 1890, to George Washington Williams, who was in Brussels. In two or three sentences the letter told me all that I wanted to know. It read, "I enclose herewith my check on London and Westminster Bank . . . for £100 . . . I hope all will go well with you in your new field of work, and shall await with interest your first letter giving impressions of the Congo Country." Huntington did not have to wait until Williams reached the Congo to receive reports. Williams began writing from the Canary Islands, and from that point on until Williams sailed from Egypt for England almost a year later, his letters to Huntington constitute a true diary, for he shares with Huntington, his benefactor, all of the experiences that he had. It was at this point that I began to feel that I no longer needed the diary that Slaughter presumably lost.

Since Williams died outside of the United States without any relatives at his bedside, I regard this as his last great favor to posterity. That is because the U.S. consul from Liverpool went up to Blackpool and took charge of everything. He made an inventory of Williams's personal effects, arranged for the funeral and the interment. He also made daily reports to the secretary of state; and it is in these reports that we learn, for example, that Williams was engaged to an English lady whom he had met en route from Egypt to England in the spring of 1891. It was this lady and her mother who took him to Blackpool for the sea air, and it was she who was at his side when he died in the Palatine Hotel on August 2, 1891. The consul arranged for an auction of the artifacts that Williams brought from Africa in order to pay his medical and funeral expenses. He also sent to Mrs. Williams, in Washington, certain personal effects, including three notebooks containing the African diary of George Washington Williams.

Some five years ago, my wife and I were visiting in England and decided to go to Blackpool to see what we could learn about Williams's last days and hours. On my first morning there I went to the town hall and encountered the director of the Blackpool tourist bureau. Since I had no one else to talk to, I told him the story of Williams and how he came to die in Blackpool. The director of the tourist bureau expressed great interest in the story but was not charmed by the fact that Williams died in Blackpool, since it was a place which people were supposed to visit to have fun and really live it up. Even so, he volunteered to help in every way that he could. He called the local newspaper, which sent over a reporter who wished to interview me as well and to escort me to the newspaper office where I could read the newspapers for August 1891. I wondered aloud if Williams was buried in the vicinity, and the man from the tourist bureau said that he would ask his secretary to look into it. In less than five minutes she returned with the following bits of information: The funeral of Williams was held in the local Baptist church, just across the square, on August 5, 1891, and the services were conducted by Reverend Samuel Pelling. Williams was buried in the Layton Cemetery, section F, grave 23. The reporter asked me if I was going to the grave. I indicated that this was the thirtieth anniversary of my "stalking" George Washington Williams and now that I had caught up with him, I was surely going. He asked to go and said that he wished to bring along a photographer. When I said that I did not mind, my wife remarked that this was becoming quite a happening, and she thought we should get some flowers.

That afternoon at 2:30 P.M., two reporters and a photographer, the warden of the cemetery, my wife, and I formed a procession down to section F, grave 23 at the Layton Cemetery. I laid a wreath on the unmarked grave of the man whose career I had followed for so long. The grave is no longer unmarked. Now he sleeps beneath a black granite slab on which are engraved these words: George Washington Williams, Afro-American Historian, 1849–1891. Even in death Williams continued to stir curiosity and controversy. You see, his death certificate, duly filed in St. Catherine's House in London, said that he died of tuberculosis, brought on by his constant exposure during his participation in the Egyptian Wars. Williams had been in Egypt less than two weeks; and all that he was fighting for was his health, which was rapidly deteriorating as he lay in a Cairo hotel.

This adventure—stalking George Washington Williams—has been worth every minute that I have spent on it. This is so not merely because of the pure joy of the sleuthing involved, though as a delightful diversion that alone would certainly have been worth it. It was also because this genius of a man had made enormous contributions to his own people, to his own country, and to the well being of the peoples of the world. In 41 short years he had fought in two wars—the Civil War and the Mexican Revolution—had become a distinguished member of the clergy, had been an editor, lawyer, legislator, historian (the first serious one of his race), diplomat, world traveler, and the first critic of King Leopold's policies in the Congo. Along the way he had been erratic, restless, controversial, overly ambitious, faithless, and capable of some misrepresentation if not prevarication. As such he was human. Whether he was one of the ten greatest African Americans who ever lived can be debated. As one of the small heroes of this world, it is well that we should not try to make more of him than he was. One of the abiding defects of our culture is that we attempt to make little gods out of our heroes. George Washington Williams would never qualify, and it is to his credit that with all his gifts he still comes through to us not as a god or even a demi-god but as a human being.

Notes

This speech was first presented at The C. Eric Lincoln Lectureship Series, Clark Atlanta University, Atlanta, GA, 1992.

1. American Council of Learned Societies, *Dictionary of American Biography* (New York: Charles Scribner's Sons, 1944).
2. John Hope Franklin, "George Washington, Williams, Historian," *The Journal of Negro History* 2, no. 31 (January 1946): 60–90.

17

The Social Responsibility of the Modern University

John R. Silber

It is always an honor to give a lecture named for an eminent scholar; it is always enjoyable when that eminent scholar is alive and present; it is most enjoyable when he is also a good friend of many years' standing. When Eric and I first met, he was a trustee of Boston University, and the university and I were considering whether we wanted to live together. Eric's presence on the board, I suspect, contributed substantially to the outcome.

In the years that followed I came to know Eric in a number of contexts and my admiration for him, as a scholar and as a man, which had always been high, increased. Familiarity bred respect. And so today I feel great honor in delivering the C. Eric Lincoln lecture, and great pleasure in being with my old friend.

My topic is the social responsibility of the university. Few terms are as widely used and as ill-defined as "social responsibility." The concept is now almost universally defined in an artificially narrow and hence misleading manner as "the obligation toward a particular political agenda." Thus we now have "socially responsible" mutual funds. Most of these respond to the agendas of the Left, but we are beginning to see such funds attuned to the agendas of the Right. Using the term "social responsibility" in this sense begs the question of what is socially responsible.

The social responsibility of the university cannot be understood in this narrow sense. To do so would politicize the university at its very core. The university's true social responsibilities are at once more varied and more demanding than simply responding to politics, Left or Right.

The first, greatest, and quintessential social responsibility of the university, the one for which it was created and which, in itself and alone, justifies its existence, is the search for, and dissemination of, truth. Because the search for truth is a gradual process of approximation in which progress is difficult to achieve and fulfillment is never complete, the search for truth extends from the first appearance of the human race to the present. Each achievement must be recorded and preserved for subsequent testing, revision, dismissal, or retention. The search for truth can often lead one into the promulgation of error until subsequent generations, through further testing, reflection, and examination, recognize mistakes and discover a new truth or recover an earlier truth. Just as surely as time makes ancient truths uncouth, an uncouth age may mistakenly displace an ancient truth.

The search for truth extends to all aspects of human concern, from mathematics to what we now include in the field of science, to medicine, to the humanities, ethics, morals, law, and the arts. And thus, the responsibility of the university is to continue not only the search for truth but also the preservation and transmission of our cultural heritage.

Simply put, the university is the memory of civilization, and unless it shares that memory, each generation will be condemned to repeat the first halting steps toward a fully developed humanity and then to bequeath the same Sisyphean task to its successor.

There is no anomaly in the university's birth as an offshoot of monasticism. To carry out its principal tasks, it required isolation from the turbulence of the chaotic transitional age that followed the fall of Rome. In our time, it has become fashionable to disparage the notion of the ivory tower, but rightly understood, the ivory tower defines the neutral space in which men and women can think and debate constrained by no forces other than logic, shared experience, and moral and intellectual integrity. The provision of that neutral space, or intellectual agora, is the university's most important social responsibility, for it is essential to meeting all the others.

Next in importance is the responsibility to make this privileged neutral space available to all those qualified to use it. This was a responsibility clearly understood by the founders of my own university. In their charter of 1869, the founders of Boston University required it to admit students and appoint faculty without regard to race, sex, or religious opinion. Although the university, founded by Methodists, was given the right to consider religious opinion in selecting faculty for the school of theology, it used the exemption rarely if at all, and by the turn of the century, it was defending its theologians from heresy charges made by the Church.

Boston University opened as the first university to admit women to every program.

In the same year, making his inaugural address, President Eliot of Harvard announced that Harvard would not admit women. He states this reason: "The difficulties involved in a common residence of young men and women of immature character and marriageable age are very grave." Dr. Eliot wanted to make it perfectly clear that he was not proceeding out of what he called "crude notions about the innate capacities of women." Indeed, he said, "the world knows next to nothing about the natural mental capacities of the female sex." Given this ignorance, he concluded, caution was the watchword.

At Boston University, President Warren made the case for the education of women along with men in language that is not likely ever to be bettered:

> Artificially to restrict the benefits of such an institution to one-half of the community, by a discrimination based solely on a birth distinction, is worse than un-American. It is an injury to society as a whole, a loss to the favored class, a wrong to the unfavored.

These words explain why a university that discriminates in admissions against students on the basis of any irrelevant category fails in its social responsibility. It may bear the name university, but it lacks the full substance.

At the same time, if it fails to uphold the highest standards by restricting admission to those fully qualified in terms of native ability, intellectual curiosity, prerequisite knowledge, and the self-discipline needed for hard work, it fails in a crucial social responsibility. And if it fails in this, it cannot succeed in any other.

Today all such notions are condemned as "elitist." But they are in fact as American as apple pie.

"That all men are born to equal rights is true," said John Adams. "Every being has a right to his own, as clear, as moral, as sacred as any other being has. . . . But to teach that all men are born with equal powers and faculties . . . is as gross a fraud as glaring an imposition on the credulity of people as ever was practiced by monks, by Druids [or] by Brahmins."

Jefferson identified "a natural aristocracy among men. The grounds of this are virtue and talents." To which Jefferson contrasted "an artificial aristocracy, founded on wealth and birth, without either virtue or talents." A natural aristocracy, Jefferson believed, was "the most precious gift of nature." "May we not say," Jefferson continued, "that that form of government is the best which provides most effectively for a pure selection of these natural *aristoi* into the offices of government?"

Democracy freed from a counterfeit and ultimately destructive egalitarianism provides a society in which the wisest, the best, and the most dedicated assume positions of leadership.

Democracy is also counterfeited by the claim that every institution in a democracy ought to be democratic. That the government must be democratic follows from the principle that it derives its authority from the consent of the governed. But it does not follow that every institution within a democracy should be organized democratically. In fact, most institutions ought to be run on an elitist basis—that is, decisions within them ought to be made by those most qualified to make them.

Elitism, like aristocracy, has its proper and mistaken forms. Elitism is mistaken only when it creates an elite whose qualifications are nonexistent or irrelevant. Among the irrelevant qualifications still all-too-often imposed are those of sex and race. Whenever an unqualified man or woman is given a job merely because *he* is male or *she* is white, the principle being followed is not elitism, but it is counterfeit. The elite thus created is artificial rather than natural. That this is not now an elitist society is shown clearly by the existence of serious discrimination against members of minorities. In a society that was genuinely and efficiently elitist, the proportion of African American physicians, professors, and corporation executives would be 13 percent. That is what genuine elitism would mean for this country; we fall short of it through the continuing scandal of our denial of equal opportunity in education and employment.

Those who are excluded and deserve to be included have everything to gain from true elitism: It is notable that one rarely finds African American educators and students arguing against high education standards; rather, they ask for a fair chance to meet the standards required of everyone else. By and large, the opposition to higher standards within higher education comes from that group that has the most to lose from a genuine elitism—middle-class whites.

Rightly understood, there is nothing wrong with elitism; it is a principle essential to the quality of life. Indeed, life itself may depend upon it. All would agree that the practice of surgery should be restricted to those with the requisite knowledge and skill. No one would give consent to surgery if procedures were chosen by polling all those present in the operating room. We recognize that the surgeon's opinion should prevail without plebiscite because with extraordinarily rare exceptions that prove the rule, the surgeon's is better than the opinion of the intern, the nurse, the medical student, or the patient.

A university that strives for the commonplace and is content with mediocrity would be roughly comparable to a Supreme Court on which seats were reserved for mediocrity. Similarly, a professional sports team that reserved positions for the mediocre would shortly lose not merely games but spectators. And a racing stable that conducted its breeding on other than elitist principles could not race its plugs even at county fairs and would rightly attract the interest of the IRS as an obvious money-laundering operation. Thus handicapped, none of these institutions could fulfill their missions in society.

It is the social responsibility of the university to practice genuine elitism in the admission and retention of students and in the recruitment, retention, and promotion of faculty. This is a challenging task, because it cannot be accomplished through the mindless numerology by which test scores become not merely an important but the only criterion for admission.

As president of Boston University, I had the authority to admit students to the Law School and the Medical School. I did not intervene often, but when I was convinced that a student's capabilities were not accurately gauged by the LSAT or the MCAT, I did so. The students I admitted, all of whom had worse LSAT or MCAT scores than the students admitted through the standard process, all graduated. Many graduated in the top half of their class, and some law students made the Law Review. The conclusion I draw from this is that although the LSAT and the MCAT are useful as a measure of the capacity to be a lawyer or doctor, they are not infallible guides.

Similarly, when we base undergraduate admissions on the SAT, we engage in numerology. We ignore the context of the students' earlier preparation. For many students, black and white, low SATs reflect the lamentable quality of the schools in which they have been educated or the lack of educational support in their homes. The lower scores attained on the SATs by African Americans as a group are an extremely important index of the educational discrimination from which they still suffer. But they suffer this discrimination as *individuals*. The scores of an African American senior educated in the wretched public schools of Chicago will doubtless reflect devastating educational discrimination. An African American senior educated at New Trier High School, by contrast, has not been discriminated against, but, like all New Trier students, has been positively advantaged. That there are many more of the former than of the latter should not keep us from considering discrimination in individual rather than group terms.

It is, after all, a refusal to consider African Americans as *individuals* that got us into our national dilemma in the first place, and it is this mistake that has placed the future of affirmative action in jeopardy. If affirmative action evaluates applicants on the basis of their personal history rather than their membership in racial or ethnic groups, affirmative action will be immune from constitutional challenge. It will also survive referenda such as California's Proposition 209, for it will be seen accurately by citizens as no less and no more than fair play.

In the fulfillment of its social responsibility, the university must be concerned to preserve and, to the fullest extent possible, to enhance the quality of primary and secondary schools. There are two principal reasons. First, universities and colleges cannot insist on their own high standards of admission unless highly qualified students are graduated from the secondary schools. Second, the teachers, principals, and superintendents of the primary and secondary schools cannot withstand local parental pressure for social promotion unless their commitment to high standards is strengthened by universities and colleges that refuse to admit students who have failed to meet these standards.

Far too many colleges and universities compete for students whose principal qualification is a body temperature approximating 98.6°F. Unless all colleges and universities, both in state and the independent sectors, insist on reasonable standards of admission, it will be difficult, if not impossible, for principals and teachers in the secondary schools to raise standards. And if they can't raise standards, it will be difficult to raise them in the primary schools. As long as deficient high school seniors continue to be admitted to colleges, public school administrators who try to raise their standards are opposed by complacent parents who say, "Don't argue with success. Since my child has been accepted by the university, how dare you tell me that my child can't have a high school diploma?"

Universities, by lowering standards, are therefore in major part responsible for the accelerating failure of our public schools. This is a profound failure to meet our social obligations.

The chief victims of that failure are those students who never go to college and who, through an inability to read, write, and do simple mathematics, drop out and are largely unemployable. Corporations like IBM and Motorola do not expect that the schools will train students to work for them. Like most major corporations, they have massive and highly effective educational programs designed not merely to prepare employees for entry-level jobs but to provide continuing education in a field where today's training may be obsolete tomorrow. What IBM and Motorola do expect, and resent not getting, are well-educated students who have basic competence in reading, writing, and mathematics. To teach these subjects is not their job. But in self-defense they must spend massive sums of money on programs of remedial education to finish the job left undone by the most expensive public schools in the world.

The task of preserving high standards in the public schools and in the universities has been considerably undermined by those, including President Clinton, who propose to make it possible for every American child to go to college. We should recognize that not all children should go on to college. Those who should are of both sexes, all colors, and all ethnicities. But we must also recognize the importance and the dignity of those who do not *choose* to go to college, either for the lack of ability or for the lack of interest. There must be a dignified place for them to work and a sense of personal fulfillment for them, even though college is not their route. Orville and Wilbur Wright, Thomas Edison, Bill Gates, Louis Armstrong, and Satchel Paige are not lesser beings because they never went to college. To the contrary, their talents led them in other directions.

If every American child were to be awarded a high school diploma, sending them all to college would degrade standards even further. When open admission leads to open retention and open graduation, all justification for higher education is lost. The City College of New York was once one of the greatest colleges in the United States. Open admission quickly destroyed not only its reputation but the educational achievements that lay behind its reputation.

Of course, no qualified student should be denied a college education because of sex, race, religion, or economic status. But when every high school graduate can and does go on to college, higher education will no longer be higher than anything, and the term "postsecondary education" will finally become indispensable.

The university must do whatever it can to end the scandal of the public schools. To this end our responsibility is to ensure that our schools of education admit highly qualified students and prepare them to be excellent teachers.

We are a long way from meeting this responsibility, for we now tolerate mediocrity and worse in schools and departments of education. In 1996, the average combined verbal and math score on the SAT for all students taking it was 998. But the average for students intending to major in education was 948, 50 points below average. This is a sobering statistic: The teaching profession attracts not students of better-than-average ability, but students of worse-than-average ability. An optimist might hope that the schools and colleges themselves would impose higher standards by limiting admission to their education programs to the best students in the pool. The evidence provides no support for such hope. In 1995, for example (the most recent year available), at the Massachusetts state colleges, the average combined SATs of students preparing to be teachers was 959. The lowest average score in the state, however, was posted by a college in the independent sector: the average combined SAT of all students entering the education program was 740, 258 points below the national average. And this is the good news. At one institution, a student was admitted with a score of 598. The student did not score 598 verbal or 598 math: The student's combined score was 598. And one can score 400 merely by showing up and signing one's name.

You may fairly ask me whether Boston University is guilty along with the rest, and I'm very glad you asked that question: At Boston University's School of Education, the average combined score is 1245, 247 points higher than the national average, but, by the way, still the lowest score of any student at Boston University.

Boston University did not achieve its high scores simply by attracting more gifted students. It did it by deliberately imposing higher standards and accepting the smaller classes and lower tuition income that resulted. Between 1970 and 1996 the freshman class of our School of Education dropped from 489 to 98. During that period, the SAT scores rose from 1146 to 1245. But it cost us $35 million in tuition. That was a heavy price to pay for a university with a small endowment, but a small price to pay for academic integrity and for an education school of which we can be proud, a school which is part of the solution rather than part of the problem. It is a shocking fact that few institutions, independent or taxpayer supported, are willing to follow our example.

But so long as education schools enjoy a virtual monopoly on the supply of teachers and typically graduate persons below average in competence, we cannot sustain present standards, much less regain the very high standards we once enjoyed when schools of education admitted students with superior qualifications and graduated excellent teachers.

If all universities insisted that their schools of education require high standards of admission, a rigorous liberal arts curriculum, and demanding exit examinations, that reform alone would eventually fulfill the university's social responsibility for public education.

It is important for us to remember that, while universities should treasure their status as ivory towers, they do not exist in a vacuum but are in fact highly dependent on the community and the nation in which they exist. And that dependency imposes a major responsibility on the university to support the community and the nation on which it depends.

In the late 1960s and early seventies, many students and faculty challenged the idea that the university should in any way support the nation. This demand of students all over the country developed a social pressure many universities acquiesced to but that responsible universities had to resist. To the extent that the freedom of the university depends upon the freedom and security of the United States, the university has an obligation to contribute to the nation's security.

There are many ways in which this obligation can be met. ROTC units provide officers for the armed services and provide the officer corps with a leaven of officers who are not graduates of the service academies but of civilian institutions. The quality of officers produced by ROTC is measured in their achievements. In 1989, an ROTC graduate was appointed to the nation's highest military rank: chairman of the joint chiefs of staff. His name was Colin Powell.

Some universities also serve the nation through defense-related research. Most will perform basic research that will be of use at least indirectly to military programs. No university need be intimidated from serving the national defense by the bizarre doctrine that the national defense is an immoral activity from which the academy ought fastidiously to abstain.

Just as the university has an obligation to national security, it has also an obligation to contribute to the nation's economic strength.

In the 1960s, left-wing critics of the university commonly complained that the university had sold out corporations by preparing workers for business and industry. These critics must have assumed that the ideal economic state was high employment combined with an acute labor shortage.

A university whose graduates were useless in business and industry would be largely a failure. This does not mean that universities should be vocational. But it does mean that university graduates should have at minimum the qualities of intellect and character that will fit them to earn their livings and fulfill their obligations as parents and citizens. As graduates of the university, they should have a thorough command of the English language and be thoroughly at home in the use of mathematics and computers. Beyond the undergraduate program the university remains, as it was in its founding, the principal locus for professional training. And as business and industry become increasingly complex and technologized, so do the social responsibilities of the university in this area.

It has long been recognized that part of the university's social obligation to seek the truth is the obligation to engage in basic research. But it has a further social obligation to develop the technologies that our basic research makes possible. Europe and Japan are far ahead of us in integrating the work of the universities and industry to serve this end.

This country's one major attempt to combine basic research with technological transfer ended in fiasco: Our aborted attempt to build the Superconducting Super Collider (SSC). This was not a failure of technology but of character in the government itself. The SSC provided an opportunity for scientific breakthroughs on the fundamental nature of the universe. It would have created particle collisions that stimulate the state of nature a millisecond after the Big Bang. It would have allowed us to see whether the four forces now known in nature were once a single force.

All of that scientific discovery aside, however, our country would have profited technologically and economically by the discoveries required simply to *build* the SSC. These discoveries would have put the United States ahead technologically and ensured our growing prosperity well into the twenty-first century. Building the SSC would have transformed the tunneling industry. There would have been similar advances in computers, elevators, magnetic technology, lasers, and air-conditioning technology.

Three hundred companies in Massachusetts alone were working on the SSC when it was canceled. It was canceled partially out of political expediency. Jim Wright, of Texas, was no longer Speaker of the House, and the SSC had lost its best friend. When Texans had the indiscretion to elect a Republican senator, the Democratic congress punished Texas by canceling the SSC. I have no doubt that a Republican majority would have done the same to a state whose voters were similarly indiscreet.

There were other forces working against the SSC. Scientists working in their laboratories on relatively small programs feared that the SSC would be a competitor for their National Science Foundation money. Dogs in the manger, they failed to consider the hundreds of young physicists put to work on thousands of small projects *because* of the SSC. They were left without work, their talents wasted by the cancellation of the SSC. The corporations who were building it, led by executives who had no vision or concern beyond their next quarterly report, joyfully took cancellation payments totaling $800 million and cried all the way to the bank.

Here, both the short-term interests of the nation and its long-term goals were forfeited. The fruits of Yankee ingenuity were cast aside for pretty short-term, penny-ante financial gains. We lost innumerable jobs for our people and immeasurable financial returns for a half-century to come while furthering the technological transfer of American ideas to foreign businesses overseas.

Fortunately, the picture appears brighter in photonics, a field analogous to electronics: The photon, or particle of light, is, in photonics, what the electron is in electronics—the basic particle. The best-known photonic device is the laser, which makes possible CDs, fiber optics, and bar codes. At Boston University we have just opened a major center to encourage photonic development.

We have also formed the Boston University Production Technology Collaboration in association with the Fraunhofer Institute of Germany, establishing a state-of-the-art manufacturing laboratory where entrepreneurs can consult with scientists and engineers from the university and industry and see and use the latest in high-technology manufacturing techniques and machinery. Through the marriage of photonic processes and plastics, in a few weeks a prototype of a product can be made that would once have required many months and many dollars.

By making use of our photonics faculty, our photonics laboratories, and the Fraunhofer center, a start-up company can save perhaps $1.5 to $2 million and a year and a half in developing a basic idea into a commercial product. This boost to technology transfer also reduces capital requirements of start-up companies by shortening the time to an initial public offering. The Massachusetts Institute of Technology, the California Institute of Technology, the University of Texas, and many other universities have similar programs.

The United States has been a textbook case of the folly by which brilliant innovations conceived in our country have been brought to market not here but in other countries. The VCR is an American invention, but it is a Japanese commodity. Magnetic-levitation trains were invented in this country, and this country, with its vast and empty distances, is ideally suited to maglev technology. But that technology is being developed in Germany and Japan, where a maglev train has just broken the world speed record by traveling 250 miles an hour. Its design speed is 350 miles an hour, erasing the distinction between trains and aircraft. In August, China announced its intention to license Japanese magnetic levitation technology.

At Boston University, through such initiatives as the Photonics Center and the Fraunhofer center, we are determined to minimize such dreadful examples in the future.

To the university, much has been given. Society subsidizes us through government scholarships and grants, corporation and foundation gifts and grants, and private philanthropy. It has made us the gatekeeper to the professions and, increasingly, to all work more demanding intellectually than serving fast foods. It has also given us high prestige. It is not so clear, however, that from the university much is expected, because our failures do not seem to attract a great deal of attention. With pervasive complacency we describe American higher education as the best in the world. But we in the university ought to be aware of our mistakes and failures and understand that from those to whom much is given, is much required.

The English jurist Lord Moulton spoke tellingly of the domain of the unenforceable, that is, the area between the domain of law and the domain of personal preference. The university's social responsibilities are, it appears to me, largely in the domain of the unenforceable: neither enforceable by law on the one hand, nor matters of mere institutional preference on the other.

Anyone who has any experience with the state and federal regulation of higher education may find this a foolish saying. But very little of the regulatory artillery is trained on our social responsibilities. The government may be concerned with Title IX enforcement or EPA violations that pollute the environment. But it largely ignores the pollution of the academic agora. No agency of government has challenged lapses of academic standards, the introduction of curricula full of trendy nonsense but devoid of meaning, the endorsement of nihilism and relativism, or the abandonment of the university's historic responsibilities as custodian of our cultural heritage.

These standards may not, and perhaps should not, be enforceable. In any case they are certainly unenforced, and as we increasingly fail in our social responsibility in these areas we contribute to a growing deficit in public trust. It is up to us in the university—not the government or its regulatory agencies—to understand our social responsibilities and to meet them.

In considering our responsibilities, we would do well to hold before us the example of a single individual—the life and work of C. Eric Lincoln, whose scholarly excellence and committed life exemplify the best that the university can bring to bear as it tries to meet its social responsibilities.

This speech was first presented at The C. Eric Lincoln Lectureship Series, Clark Atlanta University, Atlanta, GA, 1997.

Epilogue

The C. Eric Lincoln Lectures

Ralph Ellis and Lillian Ashcraft-Eason

The original title of the lecture series in honor of C. Eric Lincoln, which was later shortened, was "The C. Eric Lincoln Lectureship in Social Ethics." The idea was to encourage scholarly dialogue on social and ethical issues in a context larger than the relatively exclusive study of religion and philosophy in academic courses, and to do so in a way that would reach across disciplines and be of value to the entire university community, indeed to the larger community beyond the university. In fact, the initial reason for honoring C. Eric Lincoln as the focal figure of the lectureship was that he especially personified the spirit of relevant social and ethical discourse that the initial planners sought to foster.

Over the years, the Lincoln tradition of creative and engaged intellectual work has been purveyed not only through the invited lecturers—who, as the original planners envisioned, must be selected according to the standard that their ideas have scholarly rigor and ethical importance, yet are communicated in ways relevant to the larger society—but also through the less formal discussions of the "Student-Scholar Forum." The Student-Scholar Forum is usually held in the afternoon after the main lecture. At these discussions, in addition to the main lecturer, other prominent scholars and public figures who are engaged in activities relevant to social ethics are invited, and students are encouraged to ask questions and engage in debate with these intellectuals. Many of the discussions have promoted very useful moral thinking of the kind that is helpful to all persons of conscience who are concerned about social issues.

The Lincoln Lectureship was therefore from the beginning an academic enterprise, but one that was geared toward relevance to the community at large. Intellectual discourse becomes a sterile parlor game when it loses its social relevance or its ability to communicate outside of narrow academic circles. But the rare achievement to which this lectureship aspired, and to a great extent has achieved over the decades, is to say something of significance rather than water down ideas for popular consumption. In the original planning sessions, it was emphasized that three conditions must be met for each lecture: 1) The ideas in it must embody scholarly rigor and respectability; 2) they must be communicated clearly; and 3) they must be relevant to the social concerns of the community.

A cadre of Lincoln's former students remembered his accessibility, and these memories helped inspire them to support a lectureship in his honor. Lincoln took seriously the proposition that a teacher must be accessible and must meet the student halfway. In his early years as a professor of religion and philosophy at Clark College, he lived in a student dormitory and made his room available as a sort of informal lending library for students. This tradition precipitated discussions that lasted for hours and resulted in students for whom the intellectual life was a living reality. Long after Lincoln's departure from Clark, he retained an interest in the welfare of the institution, composing the University's Alma Mater, "Reign Clark Atlanta," and donating his papers to the Special Collections of the Robert W. Woodruff Library in the Atlanta University Center.

During the lectureships, which he attended each year, Lincoln continued to make himself available to a new generation of students. Similarly, informal meetings in connection with the lectureship took place with Clark Atlanta University (CAU) religion and philosophy faculty. A tradition developed in which a small group of involved parties would hear Lincoln speak over dinner the night before the lecture. At one of the last of these dinner meetings, Lincoln revealed his view that the concept of race could quite literally become obsolete during the twenty-first century, as a result of demographic changes and racial intermarriages in America. Most people would no longer consider themselves either "black" or "white" but would traverse the entire range of skin colors and cultural mixtures. Lincoln believed that he could already see the beginning of this movement in the popular culture, where many young people already mix linguistic, artistic, and cultural forms of expression at will. At that point, issues of social ethics will be discussed in economic and social class rather than racial terms, and the most difficult struggle will be in behalf of new immigrants.

The Initial Concept and Purpose of the Lectureship

After Lillian Ashcraft-Eason joined Sylvia Walsh-Perkins and Raymond Boisvert on the CAU faculty in the department of religion and philosophy, the idea of the lectureship originated as a way to support the college's initiative of revitalizing the humanities. After much discussion, the department decided to honor a well-known scholar and dean of religious studies, former member of the department, and professor venerated by Clark College alumni/ae—C. Eric Lincoln. It was further determined that because this esteemed scholar also was a life-long member of the United Methodist Church with which the college is affiliated, there was likely to be strong support for this idea.

The idea was presented to Dr. Elias Blake, the president of the college, who enthusiastically received the idea. The president then proposed that several distinguished alumni/ae whom Lincoln had taught and other faculty be invited to join members of the department in forming a coordinating committee. The Lincoln Lectureship Planning Committee of 12 convened for the first time at the college on February 10, 1983. In addition to the president, faculty from the department of religion and philosophy, and faculty from the college, Lenora Stephens and Alfred Spriggs, there were four graduates of Clark College: Wilmatine Hood Elam, an educator in Nashville, Tennessee; the Reverend Cornelius Henderson, trustee of Clark College and Pastor of the Ben Hill United Methodist Church in Atlanta, Georgia; Prince E. Holliday, Director of Civic Affairs of Blue Cross and Blue Shield of Detroit, Michigan; and William B. McClain, professor of homiletics at Wesley Theological Seminary in Washington, D.C.

The committee elaborated on the qualities and accomplishments of the honoree that should be reflected in the purpose and structure of the lectureship: It would provide a forum within the college setting for a creative interchange of views on moral and ethical issues of contemporary importance. Each year a person of exceptional professional stature and accomplishment would be invited by the college to be the Lincoln Lecturer, and there would be four events: 1) a public lecture where moral and ethical issues would be critically analyzed by the Lincoln Lecturer; 2) a student forum featuring majors in the department who would interface with the Lecturer by asking questions and making comments relevant to the lecture; 3) a creative arts performance; and 4) a worship service. Consistent with Lincoln's career as a college and university professor, the main beneficiaries of the lectureship would be students. The Lincoln Lecture would seek to cultivate among student majors appreciation for the intellectual and artistic functions as opportunities for personal enhancement.

The committee reached consensus on the following points:

1. The C. Eric Lincoln Lectureship will be an ongoing activity at Clark College. It will be held yearly.
2. The lectureship will aim at involving the entire community: Clark College and adjacent schools, as well as the wider Atlanta community.
3. The lecture series will focus on topics that deal with contemporary issues from a perspective of religion and ethics.
4. The lectureship will preferably be a two-day event, which will include a range of activities such as: the formal lecture, class visitations, discussions with the faculty, discussions with the Board of Trustees (if feasible), and informal meetings with students.
5. The original funding goal will be $10,000.
6. The first lecture will tentatively be scheduled for October 19–22, 1983, or February 1984 if the earlier date proves to be impractical.
7. The purpose of the C. Eric Lincoln lecture series is "to address issues associated with the topic of 'living responsibly' in contemporary society. It emphasizes the specifically religious and moral dimensions of the varied activities, whether professional, personal, or social, that comprise an inescapable part of human existence."[1]

President Blake agreed to accept the committee's recommendation that the inauguration of the lectureship be set for October 19, 1983, and that he should notify Lincoln of the inaugural lectureship event being planned in his honor. The chair and faculty of religion and philosophy accepted responsibility for implementing the plans. Several members of the committee, but particularly McClain and Holliday, both former students of Lincoln at Clark College, and Alfred Spriggs, a friend of Lincoln's on the CAU faculty, were fully engaged in the planning process, suggesting sources of funding and the names of Lincoln colleagues, friends, peers, and other associates to invite to the inaugural event.

One of the first people contacted was Alex Haley. When contacted to inquire about his availability for that date and what fee he would charge, he responded in the affirmative and added that he would charge no fee for his participation in a program honoring his long-time friend. Interested in supporting the fundraising he wrote, "As I told Dr. . . . . [Ashcraft-Eason], any way I can do something useful for my old and respected and cherished friend, Dr. Lincoln, I'll count it a privilege! I couldn't have been happier that the date was clear in my book, and in a trice I'd inserted there 'Atlanta, Clark College, for C. Eric.'"[2]

President Blake also requested and received approval from the Board of Trustees to award Lincoln an honorary degree.

The Inauguration Event

The lectureship was inaugurated with three main events that reflected aspects of Lincoln's professional life as academician (the inaugural lecture), literary person (poetry reading and dialogue), and member of the clergy (worship service). The inaugural lecture was on Tuesday evening, October 19, in the Exhibition Room of the Atlanta University Center's Woodruff Library. Speaking before a capacity audience, Dr. Lincoln delivered the inaugural address on "Human Values and Inhuman Systems," after which he was awarded the honorary degree by the academic dean of the college, Dr. Melvin Webb, and President Blake.

The next morning, Lincoln delivered a lecture on "Thinking About Thinking" primarily for the Clark College student body. Again there was standing room only. Many called the poetry and dialogue session that afternoon the main event, because Lincoln was joined by two of his closest friends, Alex Haley and Lawrence Jones, Dean of the Divinity School at Howard University in Washington, D.C. Haley congratulated and cajoled Lincoln, pointing out how upon becoming acquainted with his skills he had tried to get Lincoln to give up his career as an academician and become a professional writer. During his good-humored ribbing, Haley asked Lincoln how many students he had taught. Lincoln replied: "I don't know the answer to that question, but I do know that I have inspired over 50 students to become doctors of philosophy." Lawrence Jones gave a moving reading of Lincoln's poem "This Road Since Freedom." Representing Pope John Paul, II and indicating Lincoln's international stature in religious circles, the Right Moses Anderson of the Archdiocese of Detroit reflected on the meaning of black religious scholarship such as Lincoln's to the life of the Church.

Other Lecturers of the Early Years, 1983–1989

Over the following six years, several persons—among whom were representatives from the corporate, academic, and social services arenas—were selected because of their prominence to be C. Eric Lincoln

Lecturers: John C. McCabe, chair and chief executive officer of Blue Cross and Blue Shield of Michigan; the Reverend Nyika Mutambara of Harare, Zimbabwe; Dr. Patricia Johnson, assistant to the commissioner of the Georgia Department of Human Resources; Dr. Cornel West of Princeton University; Dr. Billie D. Gaines, slavic linguist and president of Horizon Productions in Atlanta; and Dr. Sekazi Kauze Mtingwa, physicist at Argonne National Laboratory in Illinois.

Religion and philosophy majors presided over the afternoon dialogues between scholars, with occasional comments and questions from students. Kevin Houston, who subsequently became a M.A. student in religion at Yale University, was one of the first moderators. In the fourth year (1986) Timberly Whitfield, who later received a masters degree in communications from Columbia University in New York, moderated when Charles Long, Patricia Johnson, Ella Mitchell, and Larry Mamiya interacted with Lincoln and the audience, indicating the vigorous atmosphere in which these afternoon dialogues occurred.

In 1989 there were two Lincoln Lecturers, Drs. Mtwingwa and Asa Hilliard, III. Mtwingwa dazzled students with his scientific alacrity and interest in using science for humanitarian purposes. Hilliard held them spellbound as he presented the idea of Africa as the cradle of *Homo sapiens* and of African origins of aspects of world civilization.

Lecturers from the Second Decade, 1990–2002

The annual lectureship series continued to host persons of exceptional professional stature and accomplishment. Lecturers invited to exchange their views on religious, political, social, and ethical issues of contemporary importance to the academic community included: Dr. Charles H. Long at the University of California-Santa Barbara; Dr. Alton B. Pollard, III, of Wake Forest University; Dr. Gardner C. Taylor, Pastor Emeritus of Concord Baptist Church of Christ in Brooklyn, New York; Jacqueline L. Burton, program director for the Eli Lilly Endowment; Dr. Robert M. Franklin, program officer for the Ford Foundation; Dr. John R. Silber, chancellor of Boston University; Rev. Floyd H. Flake, pastor and former member of the United States House of Representatives; Robert E. Pincham, retired justice and human rights activist; Benjamin L. Hall, city attorney for Houston, Texas; and Dr. James H. Cone of Union Theological Seminary.

To celebrate the tenth anniversary of the distinguished lectureship, internationally acclaimed scholar Dr. John Hope Franklin was invited to be the lecturer. In addition to the lecture, a C. Eric Lincoln Lectureship

Series Endowment banquet was held at the Omni Hotel, CNN Center, to launch a $200,000 endowment campaign. As of this writing the C. Eric Lincoln Endowment Campaign, sponsored by the Department of Religion and Philosophy at CAU, has reached a total of $135,000 toward the endowment of the lectureship. Also the lectureship received substantial financial support from Dr. Thomas W. Cole, the first president of CAU; Dr. Samuel DuBois Cook, president emeritus of Dillard University; and Dr. John R. Silber, chancellor of Boston University. This fundraising endeavor continues so that the future of the lectureship can be secure.

In September of 1994, the lectureship was cited in the Congressional Record as "the oldest" continuing series honoring a living black scholar. Two years later, the lecture theme was the "Empowering of Women in Ministry," with Dr. Delores C. Carpenter, a pastor and professor of the Howard University School of Divinity, as the lecturer. The year 1996 also featured the university's leading female administrator, Provost Yvonne B. Freeman, as the speaker at the Spiritual Renewal Breakfast for faculty and staff. These events, which focused on enhancing the status of women in the church and academy, attracted female clergy and scholars from across the country.

In 1997, a special tribute was paid to the artistic genius of Lincoln, featuring an evening of music and poems composed by the honoree. There was also a special musical presentation by 15-year-old violinist James Thomas Dargan, who began playing the violin at age three in Durham at the Duke University String School. He was accompanied by Joyce Finch Johnson.

At the 2000 C. Eric Lincoln Lecture, in honor of the death of Lincoln, a memorial banquet was held at the historic Paschals Restaurant. The special guest speaker for the affair was Benjamin Chavis Muhammad, a former mentee and student of Lincoln's and a spokesperson for the Nation of Islam. The 2001 lecture continued to represent the diverse religious, cultural, and ethnic interests of Lincoln, collaborating with the Candler School of Theology of Emory University. Candler's Program of Black Church Studies hosted a C. Eric Lincoln forum featuring Drs. Jualynne E. Dodson, Lawrence H. Mamiya, and Mary R. Sawyer, and a public lecture by Minister Ava Muhammad, legal counsel and former national spokesperson for the Nation of Islam.

At the twentieth lectureship, Lynn Walker Huntley, president of the Southern Education Foundation, crafted a fictional letter that Dr. Lincoln would have written to us. In her opening remarks, she recalled that when she worked for the Ford Foundation, she was given a breakfast in her honor by some Black Church grantees that her institution supported. Ms. Walker shared with her audience Lincoln's sense of humor, telling them about remarks he had made at the breakfast, which ended with the following words:

> Hallelujah, Thine the Glory
> Hallelujah, Amen
> Hallelujah, Thine the Glory
> Please fund me again!

C. Eric Lincoln and the Lectureship

Lincoln attended every lectureship, often arriving on the afternoon before the main lecture, where he engaged student majors in a forum format, discussing academic issues, race, religion, practical matters of scholarship, and his life as a scholar. He talked with them about graduate school and the ministry, and he encouraged them to love to learn. Students looked forward to these visits and many majors were inspired to continue on to graduate studies. Most attended theological institutions and many of them became ordained clergy. Some entered the pastorate of various denominations while at least one helped to establish the media center for the Atlanta City Public Schools. Using her skills as a journalist, Timberly Whitfield was for a time an anchor for the children's history program out of the city of New York.

Performing Arts

There were very interesting creative arts programs, ranging from *Jazzman,* a soviet film with English subtitles about a young Russian in the late 1920s who sought to introduce black American jazz to the Russian masses, to a creative performance by the Atlanta School of the Arts, to an evening with "Paul Robeson," with Paul Mabun singing Robeson's songs along with Theolophilus Reed, an accompanist from Chicago. Most of the creative performances were given by Clark College students and faculty: the group Tyehimba (a Shona word meaning "We stand as a nation."), the Clark College Philharmonic Society, and the Gospel Choir. On one evening, Dr. Lincoln read to the assembly from his novel, *The Avenue, Clayton City.* In 1986, there was a tribute to the orishas or deities of Africa—the Oba of Oyotunji African Village of Sheldon, SC and members of that movement danced and sang the songs.[3] The following year featured a tribute to Marcus Garvey.

At the 2000 C. Eric Lincoln Lectureship, in honor of the death of Lincoln, a large painting by Lynda Ellis was unveiled, serving not only as a portrait but as a chronicle of the events, themes, and important people in Lincoln's life. The painting now hangs at CAU as a permanent memorial to the life and work of Lincoln. It is appropriate that Lincoln's lifelong friend Alex Haley, who introduced Lincoln at the inaugural lecture in 1983, finds a prominent place in this painting. Lincoln and Haley were close friends since their early years, when both were aspiring young writers. Later, as Haley explored his African roots, Lincoln was writing "America, my native land. . . . How long this road since freedom."

Notes

1. Summary notes from the C. Eric Lincoln Lectureship Planning Committee Meeting, February 10, 1983, McPheeters Hall Conference Room, Clark College.
2. Alex Haley to Ms. Kathleen Capels, Georgia Endowment for the Humanities, Atlanta, May 8, 1983.
3. Oba is a formal leadership title in traditional Yoruba (Nigeria) society. Oyotunji African Village was founded by African Americans in Beaufort County, South Carolina, in 1970.

Appendix

The C. Eric Lincoln Lectureship Series

Clark Atlanta University

1983	C. Eric Lincoln, Sr.
1984	John C. McCabe
1985	Alex Haley
1986	Patricia Johnson
1987	Cornel West
1988	Billie D. Gaines
1989	Sckazi Mtingwa
	Asa G. Hilliard
1990	Charles H. Long
1991	Alton B. Pollard, III
1992	John Hope Franklin
1993	Gardner C. Taylor
1994	Jacqueline L. Burton
1995	Robert M. Franklin
1996	Delores C. Carpenter
1997	John R. Silber
1998	Floyd H. Flake
1999	R. Eugene Pincham
2000	Benjamin L. Hall
2001	James H. Cone
2002	Lynn Walker Huntley
2003	William C. Turner

The C. Eric Lincoln Forum

Candler School of Theology, Emory University

2001	Jualynne E. Dodson
	Mary R. Sawyer
	Lawrence H. Mamiya
	Ava Muhammad

About the Contributors

Editors

Alton B. Pollard, III, is Director of Black Church Studies and Associate Professor of Religion and Culture at Emory University's Candler School of Theology. He is the author of *Mysticism and Social Change: The Social Witness of Howard Thurman* and associate editor of the journal *Black Sacred Music*.

Love Henry Whelchel, Jr., is Chairperson of the Department of Religion and Philosophy and Professor of Religion at Clark Atlanta University. He is the convener of the C. Eric Lincoln Lectures and author of *Hell Without Fire: Conversion in Slave Religion and the Founding of the C.M.E. Church.*

Contributors

Lillian Ashcraft-Eason is Associate Professor of History and Director of Africana Studies at Bowling Green State University. She is the author of *About My Father's Business: The Life of Elder Lightfoot Solomon Michaux* and co-editor of *Inside Ethnic America: An Ethnic Studies Reader.*

Delores C. Carpenter is Professor of Religious Education at Howard University School of Divinity and Senior Pastor of Michigan Park Christian Church in Washington, D.C. She is the author of *A Time for Honor: A Portrait of African American Clergywomen* and general editor of the *African American Heritage Hymnal.*

James H. Cone is the Charles A. Briggs Distinguished Professor of Systematic Theology at Union Theological Seminary. He is the author of such publications as *Black Theology and Black Power, A Black Theology of Liberation, God of the Oppressed, The Spirituals and the Blues, Malcolm and Martin and America*, and *Risks of Faith*.

Jualynne E. Dodson is Professor of Religious Studies and African American and African Graduate Studies at Michigan State University. She is the author of *Engendering Church: Women, Power and African Methodism*.

Ralph Ellis is Professor of Philosophy at Clark Atlanta University. He is the author of *An Ontology of Consciousness* and *The Craft of Thinking*, among other works. In addition, he is editor of the journal *Consciousness and Emotion*.

Floyd H. Flake is a former United States Representative and Senior Pastor of the 11,000-member Allen African Methodist Episcopal Church in Queens, New York. He is the author of *The Way of the Bootstrapper: Nine Action Steps for Achieving Your Dreams*.

John Hope Franklin is the James B. Duke Professor Emeritus of History, and former Professor of Legal History in the Law School at Duke University. His numerous publications include *The Emancipation Proclamation, The Free Negro in North Carolina, From Slavery to Freedom: A History of African-Americans, Race and History: Selected Essays, 1938–1988*, and *The Color Line: Legacy for the Twenty-first Century*.

Cheryl Townsend Gilkes is the John D. and Catherine T. MacArthur Professor of Sociology and African American Studies at Colby College in Waterville, Maine. She is a contributor to numerous publications and the author of *If It Wasn't for the Women: Black Women's Experience and Womanist Culture in Church and Community*.

Asa G. Hilliard, III, is the Fuller E. Callaway Professor of Urban Education at Georgia State University. He is the author of *The Maroon Within Us: Selected Essays on African American Community Socialization, The Teachings of Ptahhotep, The Reawakening of the African Mind*, and other publications.

C. Eric Lincoln was the William Rand Kenan, Jr., Professor of Religion and Culture at Duke University. He is the author of such publications as (with Lawrence Mamiya) *The Black Church in the African American*

Experience, The Black Muslims in America, The Black Church Since Frazier, Coming Through the Fire, Race, Religion, and the Continuing American Dilemma, a novel, *The Avenue, Clayton City;* and a collection of poems, *This Road Since Freedom.*

Charles H. Long was the Director of the Research Center for Black Studies and Professor of History of Religions at the University of California-Santa Barbara. Now retired, he is the author of *Alpha: The Myths of Creation* and *Significations: Signs, Symbols, and Images in the Study of Religion.*

Lawrence H. Mamiya is Professor of Sociology and African American Studies at Vassar College. He is the author (with C. Eric Lincoln) of *The Black Church in the African American Experience.*

William B. McClain is the Mary Elizabeth McGehee Joyce Professor of Homiletics and Liturgy at Wesley Theological Seminary. He is the author of *Come Sunday: The Liturgy of Zion* and *Black People in the Methodist Church.*

Ava Muhammad has served as legal counsel and is a National Spokesperson for the Nation of Islam. Also the first woman to lead a mosque, Minister Muhammad is the author of *The Force and Power of Being, A New Way of Life* and other books on African American spiritual life.

Mary R. Sawyer is Chairperson of the Department of Philosophy and Religion and Associate Professor of Religion at Iowa State University. She is the author of *The Church on the Margins: Living Christian Community* and *Black Ecumenism.*

John R. Silber is the Chancellor of Boston University. Previously, he served as the university's president, a position he held for more than 25 years. He is the author of *Straight Shooting: What's Wrong with America and How to Fix It* and numerous other works.

Jon Michael Spencer is Professor of Religious Studies at the University of South Carolina. He is the author of such works as *Sing a New Song, The Rhythms of Black Folk, Protest and Praise, The Tribes of Benjamin,* and editor of the journal *Black Sacred Music.*

Gardner C. Taylor is Pastor Emeritus of the Concord Baptist Church in Brooklyn, New York. Named 1 of the 15 greatest preachers in America by Ebony magazine, he is the author of such books as *Lectures, Essays, and Interviews: The Words of Gardner Taylor, We Have This Ministry,* and *How Shall They Preach,* among others.

Index